# THE ILLUSTRATED HISTORY
# OF THE COUNTRYSIDE

# THE ILLUSTRATED
# HISTORY OF THE
# COUNTRYSIDE

## OLIVER RACKHAM

*with commissioned photographs by Tom Mackie*

PHOENIX ILLUSTRATED

To Susan Ranson and the late Colin Ranson,
my trusty friends and helpers in the original
*History of the Countryside*

First published in 1994 by George Weidenfeld & Nicolson Ltd
This paperback edition first published in 1997 by Phoenix Illustrated
Orion Publishing Group, Orion House
5, Upper St. Martin's Lane
London WC2H 9EA

British Library Cataloguing-in-Publication Data
A catalogue record for this book is available from
the British Library

ISBN 1-85799-953-3

A DPB book, created and designed by
Duncan Baird Publishers
Highlight House
57 Margaret Street
London W1N 7FG

Designer: Paul Reid
Editors: Simon Ryder, Clifford Bishop
Picture Research: Brigitte Arora
Editorial Assistant: Judy Dean
Design Assistant: Sue Bush
Line artwork for OS maps and aerial photographs: John Laing
Illustrated maps and diagrams: David Atkinson
Type formatted by Sheena Leng

Typeset in Sabon
Colour reproduction: Bright Arts, Hong Kong

# CONTENTS

# INTRODUCTION

This is a re-working of my book *The History of the Countryside*, first published in 1986. The text has been abridged, omitting many of the diagrams and maps and nearly all the references. The two versions are complementary: anyone who wants more detail, or who seeks the source of a statement, is referred to the earlier book.

In my south Norfolk childhood I wondered why roads had bends, why lanes were sunk into the ground, what dogwood and spindle were doing in hedges, why fields were of odd shapes, and why elms stopped abruptly just north of Bungay. These are difficult questions, and their roots go deep into the past. The object of this book is to discover some of the meanings of landscape.

Historical ecology sometimes involves the set-piece methods of scientific research: problems defined in advance and information collected wherewith to solve them. But in many areas this will not work because the facts are too thinly scattered to justify a deliberate search. Much of the material for this book came my way in the course of other researches: facts turned up and were filed away until enough was hoarded to suggest questions and answers. Insights also came at random from travels made or documents read, for some quite different purpose. I went to Texas to discuss Cretan archaeology, and what I saw made me revise my views on hedges.

The ordinary landscape of Britain and Ireland has been made by the natural world and by human activities, interacting with each other over 140 centuries. This is an idea that is not easy to grasp. In the last century, people (that is, writers) often thought of the country as the world of Nature, in contrast to the town. The opposite exaggeration now prevails – that the rural landscape, no less than Trafalgar Square, is merely the result of human design and ambition. The popular version of this belief, the 'Enclosure-Act Myth' – the notion that the countryside is not merely an artefact but a very recent one – exerted its defeatist influence against conservation as recently as 1986.

In reality the countryside records human default as well as design, and much of it has a life of its own, independent of human activity. Trees are not just things that people plant, like gateposts. A friend of mine cut a good crop of ash trees which arose as a result of his predecessor planting pines. The landscape ranges from the almost wholly artificial, like the middle of a barley field, to the almost wholly natural, like the moors of Caithness. Most of this book is about the 'semi-natural' areas that are neither virgin vegetation nor planted crops. With many features such as ponds and hedges it is still not possible to say where Nature stops and human activity begins.

I am concerned with the history of the landscape since the last Ice Age. I am not primarily concerned with longer-term geological events, nor with the history of country folk, nor with the history of what people have said about the landscape, nor with the history of land use, nor with buildings, settlements and recognized archaeological 'sites', all of which are dealt with in other books.

Plants and animals do not enter into the story merely as part of the environment, as scenery in the theatre of landscape. They are actors in the play; each has its own character, which needs to be understood. Horses behave differently from eels, and ash trees play a role different from that of pines. (Cutting down a pine kills it, but an ash sprouts and thrives.) A sad little mark of the 1980s was the 'area set aside as a haven for wildlife' attached to any large development – as though there was something called wildlife which would come when summoned, and would do what its masters told it.

Landscape history enters into conservation in three ways. History is part of the understanding of how landscapes work and how to maintain them. For example, what it means that Hatfield was a (Royal) Forest, and what type of Forest it was, are questions that bear directly on the management of Hatfield Forest today. History helps to isolate the unconservable: to separate features that are inherently shortlived and the result of some passing land-use fashion (like poplar plantations) from those with more stability and permanent value.

A historical dimension is needed for the most critical and least recognized aspect of conservation: how to identify the abnormal. The present is a time of abnormally little woodcutting, abnormally much tree-planting, and abnormally abundant deer. Service tree and pasque-flower are both rare; service has always been rare and its scarcity is not abnormal and is no cause for concern, but pasque-flower has greatly declined through the destruction of its habitat and needs protection in its remaining habitats. Savants make pronouncements about acid rain on the basis that it is a new and unprecedented development. The acid-rain campaign of the late 1980s, based on its supposed effects on trees, largely ignored the campaign of the 1970s, which was based on its well-established effects on lichens. In reality, there have been complaints of acid rain for nearly 400 years, and anyone who believes it kills trees has to explain why there are any old trees left in, for example, the east of London, once far more polluted than it is now.

The present ought to be a golden age for the science and teaching of ecology. But in practice it remains too often a matter of fashion (acid rain one year, global warming the next), of vague generalizations rather than identifiable detail, and of the study of distant and glamorous parts of the world rather than of what is familiar at home. (It is easy to be deluded by television into thinking one can understand another country without going there.) These islands have much to give the world in terms of understanding how human activities can enter into a stable and harmonious relation with landscape.

Oliver Rackham
Cambridge, April 1994

# RURAL DETECTION

Do you know, Watson ... I must look at everything with reference to my own special subject. You look at these scattered houses, and you are impressed by their beauty. I look at them, and the only subject which comes to me is a feeling of their isolation, and of the impunity with which crime may be committed there.

A. Conan Doyle, *The Copper Beeches*

Why is Herefordshire more like rural Essex than either is like Cambridgeshire? Herefordshire and Essex are lands of hamlets, of medieval farms in hollows of the hills, of lonely moats in the claylands, of immense mileages of little roads and holloways, of intricate footpaths, of irregularly-shaped groves and thick hedges colourful with maple, dogwood and spindle, of pollards and ancient trees. Cambridgeshire is a land of big villages, wide views, brick farmhouses in exposed positions, flimsy hawthorn hedges, ivied clumps of trees in corners of fields, few, busy roads, and above all of straight lines.

The difference is not just the effect of natural variation in hills, soils and rainfall. A simple explanation is that in Cambridgeshire, as in most of the English Midlands, hedged fields are derived from the Enclosure Acts of the eighteenth and nineteenth centuries, before which the land had been farmed in great open prairie-farming fields. The landscape, laid out hurriedly in a drawing-office at the enclosure of each parish, has a mass-produced quality of regular fields and straight roads. It may have medieval woods, Anglo-Saxon hedges and ancient trees, but only as isolated antiquities which the enclosure commissioners failed to destroy. This is *Planned*

*Right: Haverdale in Swaledale, Yorkshire. A complex highland landscape with a succession of layers: grassland, hay-barns, straight field-walls and lead-mining remains on moorland (mainly nineteenth century); pollard trees, ridge-and-furrow, crooked field-walls, lanes and scattered farms; hummocks of Roman or Iron age settlements; all superimposed on rows of shake-holes (a geological feature). (TM, February 1994)*

0          1 mile

0          2 km

*Scale: top map*

0          1 mile

0          2 km

*Scale: bottom map*

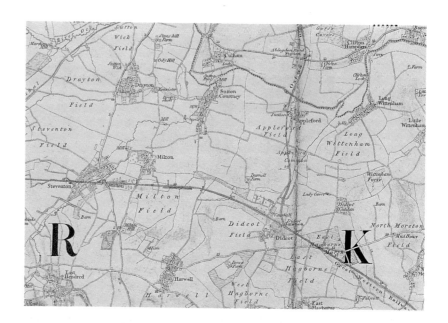

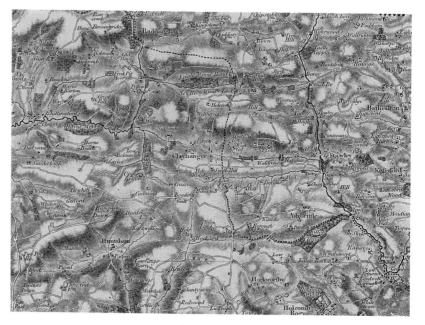

## Ancient *versus* Planned Countryside

This distinction has been recognized for centuries (p. 80). F.W. Maitland put it thus in 1897:

> We are not entitled to make for ourselves any one typical picture of the English vill ... we must keep at least two types before our minds. On the one hand, there is what we might call the true village. ... In the purest form of this type there is one and only one cluster of houses. It is a fairly large cluster; it stands in the midst of its fields, of its territory, and until lately a considerable part of its territory will probably have consisted of spacious 'common fields'... the parish boundaries seem almost to draw themselves. On the other hand, we may easily find a country in which there are few villages of this character. The houses ... are scattered about in small clusters; here two or three, there three or four. These clusters often have names of their own, and it seems a mere chance that the name borne by one of them should be also the name of the whole parish ... We see no traces of very large fields. On the face of the map there is no reason why a particular group of cottages should be reckoned to belong to this parish rather than to the next ...
>
> Two little fragments of 'the original one-inch ordnance map' will be more eloquent than would be many paragraphs of written discourse. The one pictures a district on the border between Oxfordshire and Berkshire cut by the Thames and the main line of the Great Western Railway; the other a district on the border between Devon and Somerset, north of Collumpton and south of Wiveliscombe.
>
> *Domesday Book and Beyond, 1897*

The two maps which he had in mind are reproduced here (Ordnance Survey, 1830 and 1809, with railways added later). Maitland realized that the difference was more than a thousand years old: he conjectured that it was a matter of Celt *versus* Saxon, although this is unlikely to be the true explanation.

*Countryside.* The other half of England, *Ancient Countryside*, has a hedged and walled landscape dating from any of forty centuries between the Bronze Age and Queen Anne. The fields sometimes bear traces of much earlier phases of planning, but in general they have the irregularity resulting from centuries of 'do-it-yourself' enclosure and piecemeal alteration.

The distinction, however, cuts much deeper in human affairs. It is found all over Europe, from France (*champagne* versus *bocage*) to Crete. Human endeavour has made different landscapes out of similar natural environments, or the same landscape out of different environments. We ask how the villages and the prairie-fields arose, and why they did not arise everywhere.

There are other regional differences. The *Highland Zone* of England runs discontinuously from Cornwall to Northumberland and on into the Southern Uplands of Scotland. This is a land of moors, dales, ancient oakwoods, and a mountain way of life. It too is a land of hamlets and scattered farms. The *Highland Line* is a sharp division of Scotland. It is sharper than the gradual rising of the mountains. In one mile we are in a neat land of wide hedged fields, thickly scattered farmsteads, conifer plantations, and Anglo-Danish place-names. The next mile we are in a wild country of moors, ancient pinewoods, small farms set precariously among bogs, and Gaelic place-names. This frontier cuts deep in Scottish history: the Highlands differ more from the rest of Scotland than the latter does from England. I also separate the strange arctic landscape of the far north beyond the natural limit of continuous woodland.

### Early Evidence

The landscape historian has to combine all the kinds of evidence. A story based on one form of evidence is never so complete or secure as one that is corroborated from some different direction. The nature of evidence varies. Pollen analysis and archaeology are all that we have for prehistory and down to the early Anglo-Saxon period in England. In historic times they complement the written word. In the Highlands of Scotland, usable written documents do not begin until nearly a thousand years later than in England. Archaeology does not lose its importance as time goes on, for verbal evidence is rarely complete or fully trustworthy. A story that an oakwood was felled in World War II needs to be confirmed – or disproved – by looking for the stumps.

Historical evidence lies in the *pollen grains* of trees and other plants, preserved in vast numbers in peat-bogs, lake muds, etc. In a peat-bog or lake a stratified deposit has been laid down year by year. The pollen analyst takes a core, identifies the pollen grains centimetre by centimetre through the deposit, and reconstructs the vegetation that produced the pollen in the centuries while the deposit was building up.

*Landscape archaeology* is the study of features visible on the surface: for example, soil-marks and crop-marks, woodbanks and hedgebanks, ridge-and-furrow. This and other kinds of archaeology, especially walking fields to map scatters of potsherds, have revolutionized the understanding of landscape in the last forty years: the land was filled with habitation and agriculture thousands of years earlier than had been thought possible. Knowledge of ancient trees has come from the study of timber and wood, preserved in standing buildings or excavated from waterlogged ground.

The earliest written records of extensive value are *place-names* – names of rivers, towns, villages, hamlets, woods, roads, and prehistoric earthworks. In England many of these go back well before the Norman Conquest. Being in dead languages – Old English or Anglo-Saxon, Old Norse, Cornish – they can be roughly dated on linguistic grounds. Celtic place-names in Wales, Scotland and Ireland are often ancient but difficult to date. Many place-names tell us something by their mere

■ *Far North*

■ *Highlands of Scotland*

■ *Lowlands of Scotland*

■ *Southern Uplands*

■ *Highland Zone of England (including Cornwall)*

■ *Ancient Countryside* } *Lowland Zone of England (and Wales)*
□ *Planned Countryside*

■ *Highland Zone (Wales)*

■ *Ireland*

**Regions of the British Isles**

**Pitfalls of Pollen Analysis**
Pollen analysis tells us nearly all we know about wildwood – the natural vegetation of early prehistory – and about the impact of prehistoric men. It has limitations: one can (just) identify the two species of lime tree, but the two oaks produce indistinguishable pollens; among grasses all that can be done is to separate the pollens of reed and of cereals from the others. Many plants, especially those pollinated by insects, shed little pollen and are difficult to detect. Early agriculture is recognized more from the pollen of weeds (for example, plantains) than of crops. Pollen analysts have recently begun to allow for the fact that the pollen of some trees is shed more abundantly, or scattered more widely, than that of others.

*The original manuscript of the Traboe and Trethewey perambulations, which Walk V (pp. 210-13) follows on the ground. The marked words are place-names and features (in Old Cornish) named in the account of that walk. (By kind permission of the Dean of Exeter.)*

**Pitfalls of Place-names**

Most place-name research deals with meanings. Place-names have developed independently of the rest of the language, often in ways that suggest false derivations, as when Furze Wood is corrupted into Firs Wood. Place-name scholars have a tradition of clutching at straws and reading into place-names more than they say. Allusions to trees, for example Elmham, have wrongly been taken to imply woodland. Scholars assume that 'cat' in place-names means wildcat and compound this error by assuming that wildcats imply woodland.

A single place-name is weak evidence. Even a thousand-year-old spelling may already be corrupted. Places may be named after unusual, rather than commonplace, features: 'Birch Wood' may have been a hornbeam wood with just one conspicuous birch tree. Place-names are more difficult to date than used to be thought.

existence: a wood which has an Old Norse wood-name must go back to Viking times.

A particular treasure of England (and southeast Wales) are the many hundreds of charter *perambulations* which tell us what specific pieces of country looked like at some date between about AD700 and 1080. An Anglo-Saxon charter is the legal conveyance of a piece of land, defined by walking round the boundaries and noting features point by point. The charters conduct us through a familiar world of rivers, millstreams, ditches, hedges and hedgerow trees, roads, lanes, paths, bridges, heaths, thorns, small named woods, stumps, pits and old posts. It was already a world of antiquity, with hillforts, 'heathen burials', 'ancient cities' and Roman roads. Only rarely do the charters mention something, such as wayside crucifix or a dragon's hoard, which has disappeared from the modern scene. Surprisingly often, a thousand years later, one can still find the same woods, roads, hedges, heathen burials, and even ditches, pits and stones.

## Medieval and Later Records

Domesday Book, the great survey of 1086, was commissioned and used as a record of land tenure, the work of William the Conqueror wanting to know who owned what in his new kingdom. It does not record minor features like hedges, trees and roads; it is poor at recording transport and industry. It fails to record the far north of England.

Within its limitations, Domesday is surprisingly accurate. It records an England that was about 35 per cent arable land, 30 per cent pasture, 15 per cent woodland and wood-pasture, and 1 per cent meadow. The remaining one-fifth of England was taken up with mountains, heaths, moorland and fen (where not recorded as pasture), houses and gardens, and lands wasted by the Conqueror's wrath.

Among later documents, *surveys*, beginning with the *Ely Coucher Book* commissioned by Bishop Hugo de Northwold in 1251, are detailed verbal descriptions of landed estates, listing the types of land, names of fields, woods and meadows, and duties of manorial tenants. *Accounts* give the year-by-year income and expenditure of an estate, including sales and transport of produce, purchase of materials and hire of craftsmen. *Court rolls* deal mainly with banalities such as petty assault and inheritance, but reward the searcher with occasional pearls of information about highways, hedges, pits and watercourses. The king's correspondence, enrolled in the *Close Patent*, and *Liberate Rolls*, tells us about Forests, feasts, royal gifts, and materials and transport for the king's building works.

Ireland and Scotland are poorly documented for early centuries. Ireland, however, has the *Civil Survey*, a greater and more detailed Domesday Book, for the 1650s. Scotland has the *Statistical Accounts* of 1791-9 and 1845, more detailed than anything in England.

## Boundaries

England and Wales are traditionally divided into parishes, anciently called *townships*, *towns*, or *vills*; these are grouped into *hundreds* or *wapentakes* and these into counties. Large townships sometimes have subdivisions. Irish parishes are regularly divided into *townlands*, and grouped into *baronies* and these into counties.

The English system was already old by Domesday Book. Boundaries are very conservative and were preserved by memorable customs: at Great Gransden (Huntingdonshire), when 'cessioning' the bounds, they used to dig a hole at a certain spot and hold the Vicar's head in it. Many a parish boundary on the modern map exactly corresponds to an Anglo-Saxon perambulation.

Parishes are full of curiosities. There are huge ones like Writtle (Essex), 13,568 acres, and tiny ones like its neighbours Shellow Bowells, 469 acres, and Chignall Smealy, 476 acres. There are parishes with two or more villages, and villages divided among two or more parishes. Sometimes we suspect deliberate planning in blocks of long narrow parishes, set out at right angles to some natural feature (especially a chalk scarp), as if designed to give each community a share in all the types of land.

Where possible, boundaries usually follow streams, roads, hedges, woodbanks, and so on. Zigzags are clear evidence that the land had already long been parcelled into fields or furlongs. In Planned Countryside, parish boundaries are likely places for ancient hedges. Boundaries may follow the ghosts of forgotten Roman roads or of tidied-up rivers.

There are some pitfalls. Especially in woodland, boundaries are occasionally forgotten, and even Tithe Maps may disagree. It has long

### Sample Entries From Domesday

Harold held Hadfeld in the time of King Edward for 1 manor and for 20 hides. Then 51 villeins, now 60. Then 19 bordars, now 30. Then 20 slaves, now 22. Then 9 ploughs in demesne, now 8, & 3 rounceys [ponies?] & 40 animals & 195 swine & 192 sheep. Then 40 men's ploughs, now 31½ – this loss was in the time of all the sheriffs and through the death of the beasts. Wood for 800 swine, 120 acres of meadow. Pasture whose rent is 19 wethers in the manor & 41 acres of ploughing.
*Hatfield Broad-oak, Essex*
[a cluster of hamlets]

This more detailed record, including the lord of the manor's livestock and his 'demesne' ploughs, is typical of Norfolk, Suffolk and Essex.

Gratedene is assessed for 5 hides. There is land for 9 ploughs. In demesne 2½ hides. & there is 1 plough and 2 could be made. There 8 villeins & 3 bordars with 6 ploughs. There 4 slaves. Meadow for 3 ploughs. Pasture for the cattle of the settlement. Wood for 60 swine & 2 shillings from the custom of the wood. In all it is worth in value 8 pounds. When received 9 pounds. In the time of King Edward 15 pounds. This manor lies & has always lain in the possession of the church of Ely.
*Little Gransden, Cambridgeshire*
[a village with open fields]

Domesday notes changes since before the Conquest: 'in the time of King Edward'.

[Richard] holds THERSENT. Alwin held it in the time of King Edward & paid geld for 1 hide. But there are 2 hides there. There is land for 12 ploughs. In demesne are 2 ploughs & 6 slaves & 5 villeins & 11 bordars with 5 ploughs. There is pasture 3 leagues long & 2 leagues wide. Wood 1 league long and ½ league wide.
*Trezance, that is Cardinham, Cornwall*
[a scatter of farms]

Note the measurements of woodland. Woods are recorded in eastern and southeastern counties in terms of swine. This was probably an archaism, abandoned in counties surveyed later, such as Cornwall, when it was found that people no longer thought of woods in this way.

## Maps and Mapmaking

Maps run in cycles of technical perfection and decline. Accurate mapmaking appears suddenly in about 1580. Some of the earliest large-scale maps show every hedge, hedgerow tree, pond, and even identifiable buildings. In the seventeenth and eighteenth centuries large-scale maps, though more numerous, are not necessarily more accurate.

For about half the parishes in England there is an *Enclosure Act* of the eighteenth or nineteenth century; its accompanying map usually covers the whole parish, though in less detail than some earlier maps.

Accurate small-scale mapmaking (at 1 or 2 inches to the mile) comes later. Most English counties have a late-eighteenth-century map, such as Chapman and André's Essex surveyed in 1772-4. These are of varying quality, for instance good for Forests (and common-land generally) and poor for woods; they can include fictitious information (such as conventionalized field boundaries).

Large-scale mapmaking was revived in the nineteenth century with the published Ordnance Survey of Ireland at 6 inches to the mile (1834-44). At the same time a manuscript *Tithe Award Map* was made for most English and Welsh townships that had not had an Enclosure Act.

From 1853 to 1893 all England and Wales was surveyed by the Ordnance Survey at 6 inches and 25 inches to the mile. The beautiful maps of the 1860s and 1870s, which attempt to record every hut and hedgerow tree, are the zenith of rural mapmaking in Britain and perhaps the world.

been the custom of officialdom to while away idle hours by tinkering with boundaries and removing enclaves, meanders, and so on.

## Plants

Plants furnish primary information. Annual rings of trees are a dated record not only of the age of the tree but of the circumstances in which it grew when young, and of pollarding, Elm Disease, drainage, and other things that have affected its growth. Many trees, such as the pollards of deserted villages and the giant coppice stools of ancient woods, are historical monuments themselves. Some plants, such as fairy-ring fungi and lichens on stones and walls, go on growing in ever-widening circles at a rate which can be measured.

It is also observed that areas of vegetation of recent origin differ from those of the same kind which are ancient. One does not find oxlip in a wood, spindle in a hedge, or pasque-flower in grassland that is less than a century old. These differences can also provide a record of management such as grazing.

## History and Pseudo-history: the Triumph of Unreason

> The sort of 'History' that was taught in Narnia under Miraz's rule was duller than the truest history you ever read and less true than the most exciting adventure story.
>
> C.S. Lewis, *Prince Caspian*

A fascinating aspect of landscape history is that there is an opposing version. I do not refer to conflicts of evidence and scholarly debate. The reader will doubtless be 'aware' that woods were destroyed by people felling trees to build houses and ships, that medieval England was still very wooded, that forests were strictly preserved for hunting by severe laws and barbarous penalties, that there was a 'timber famine' in the Tudor period, that iron was smelted with coke because there was no wood left, and that the last remnants of the old woodland perished when cut down in World War I (or was it II?). All this forms a consistent, logical, widely accepted story, which cannot, however, be sustained from the records of actual woods or Forests. It is a pseudo-history, unconnected with the real world.

Pseudo-history is made up of *factoids*. A factoid looks like a fact, is respected as a fact, and has all the properties of a fact except that it is not true. An example is the belief that the hedged and walled landscape of England is (with unimportant exceptions) no more than 250 years old. Anyone can disprove this within an hour by looking at pre-1700 maps or landscape pictures; yet the fallacy was still repeated as recently as 1987.

Pseudo-history is not killed by publishing real history. This does not lead to a controversy in which one or the other version wins. In practice, either the old version is re-told as if nothing had happened, or authors try to combine the two versions as if both could be true at once. Pseudo-history wins ground at the expense of real history. Seventy years ago, the natural change of farmland or heath into woodland was a hot theme of ecology, on which research was done, books written, and students examined. It is now all but forgotten. How many recent proposals for converting redundant farmland to woodland so much as mention natural succession?

What is it that makes the landscape so productive of factoids? Authors confuse the history of the countryside with the history of country *folk* or the history of what people have *said* about the countryside. These are very different things. Landscape changes through natural causes and human default as well as through human action. People notice some things, such as felling trees, but fail to notice others, such as trees springing up on an abandoned heath. Historians forget that plants and animals are living things, with their own agendas in life independent of man. A huge argument has been built on the belief that trees die when cut down – flatly denying the whole basis of woodmanship of the last 5,000 years.

Many historians stick to documents and are reluctant to put on their boots and ask questions of the land and the things that grow on it. Documents are wonderful things: one misses them when working in the Scottish Highlands. But they have their limitations. The most often overlooked is that to rely on documents cuts one off from ever knowing what was going on at times when people were not writing. It over-emphasizes the economic and legal aspects of the landscape, for accountants and lawyers wrote many of the surviving archives. It exaggerates the achievements of people who had much to say for themselves. The belief that the Fens were first drained and farmed by Dutch engineers and their English patrons in the seventeenth century is a factoid created by those men themselves, who deliberately played down the activities of their inarticulate predecessors.

This is how to write pseudo-history:

1. Stick to the documents and do no fieldwork.
2. Rely on contemporary documents of a generalized kind – the things that learned writers said about the landscape – instead of the year-to-year records of individual fields, woods and rivers.
3. Take the documents at face value: for example, interpret medieval laws as if they were intended to stop people from doing things.
4. Copy what other scholars have said, rather than going back to the original evidence.
5. Treat animals and plants as 'environment'; as scenery in the theatre rather than as actors in the play.
6. Generalize: blame every deserted settlement in the Scottish Highlands on the infamous Highland Clearances.
7. Have an answer for everything, and never admit you don't know.

Let us not suppose that sifting out the factoids we shall be left with a grey, banal, workaday residue. On the contrary, the true history is much more colourful and complex, more entertaining in human accomplishment and folly and the nemesis of Nature, than anything pseudo-historians have invented. The real history of the countryside is more romantic than the romance.

### Evidence from the Air

Aerial photography reveals traces of earthworks and buildings, and also natural features such as pingos (p. 168). Slight 'humps and bumps' cast shadows early and late in the day. Differences in vegetation show up especially on infra-red false-colour film. Ploughed-out features may produce *soil-marks*, patterns of different soil colour. Buried foundations and ditches often create *crop-marks*, differences in the height, colour or ripening of crops growing over them.

Air photographs are also historical documents themselves. There exists a large mosaic of the district around Cambridge, assembled from hundreds of exposures taken in 1922. A great survey of much of Britain, especially the east and south, was flown by courageous German pilots during the Battle of Britain. These magnificent photographs, which record almost every tree, hedge, bush, pingo and pond in several counties, were captured by the Americans and are now in the National Archives in Washington, D.C. The fortunes of war have preserved a convincing record of what was still, in many places, a medieval landscape.

### Testimony and Tradition

G.E. Evans has reminded us that folk who actually did things, or whose grandfathers did them, can tell us details which were never thought worth writing down. This is useful for familiar activities, such as anything to do with horses. It is more difficult to find out about specialized crafts such as woodmanship: once the crafts have died the traditions soon disappear. In Britain (unlike Africa or Polynesia) testimony should seldom be used on its own or for more than three generations back. Aged countrymen, like the rest of us, enjoy telling and embroidering a good story; they do not always separate what they have read from what they have seen; and are tempted to guess at explanations of what they do not know.

With testimonies written down in earlier centuries there is often the difficulty of not knowing the status of the story. Tales told as fiction are re-told as if they were fact. Tap-room gossip achieves semi-respectability as 'tradition', passes into print, and acquires a date from which even the *circa* is dropped in reprinting.

# ANIMALS
# AND PLANTS

What is wildlife? Animals and plants do not just happen, but are affected by human activities. If mankind had originated in South America, Britain would still have elephants and lions, but no rabbits, no rats or mice, no sycamore trees and almost no conifers.

There is usually a hard-and-fast distinction between wildlife and cultivated plants or domesticated animals. Dogs, sheep, tame pigs, wheat, sugar-beet, Corsican pine and planted oak trees all exist because somebody has put them there and tends them. Most have either been imported from overseas or have been invented by breeders, farmers and gardeners. Those which have not, such as the oaks of plantations, are often genetically different from wild individuals of the same species. It is cultivation, not exploitation nor the original introduction, that makes animals and plants domestic.

Some species of wildlife, such as the oak tree and fox, are *native*; they arrived here by natural processes in prehistoric times. Other plants and animals were originally introduced by human agency from overseas, but now maintain themselves without further intervention. These are *naturalized*, in contrast to *exotic* species which are dependent on domestication. Rabbit, pheasant, sweet-chestnut and Oxford ragwort are naturalized; guinea-pig, peafowl, walnut, horse-chestnut and *Cannabis*, although introduced centuries ago, remain exotics and have not become wildlife. The distinction does not depend on lapse of time, nor has it anything to do with political correctness.

Right: *Is the red squirrel native or not? Red squirrels were fairly well recorded in the Middle Ages, partly in the form of fur. In the eighteenth and nineteenth centuries they were re-introduced to Scotland and Ireland, where they were thought to have become extinct. Later in the nineteenth century red squirrels multiplied all over the British Isles and for a time became a pest. It looks as though the introduced animal displaced the native one. This might explain why the modern red squirrel favours conifer plantations, which did not exist before the seventeenth century. (GL/BCL)*

*The coat-of-arms of Bury St Edmunds (Suffolk). The crest is a wolf guarding the head of King Edmund, martyred in 869. Was it a wolf of this world or the next? (Borough of St Edmundsbury/PS)*

**Wolves and Metaphorical Wolves**

Wolves could be fabulous beasts like lions or dragons. It can be difficult to distinguish records of zoological wolves from symbolic, spiritual, or two-legged wolves. In Anglo-Saxon times, unpersons and men on the run were declared to be 'wolf's-head' and if caught ended on a wolf's-head-tree. There are wolf-springs, wolf-hedges, wolf-leaps etc. in Anglo-Saxon charters: who knows which of them refer to metaphorical wolves and which to the actual animal? Woolpit (Suffolk) is named after a 'wolf-pit', identified in the twelfth century with certain 'very ancient ditches'. If this is evidence for wolves in Suffolk, is the place 'Giant's Grave' evidence for giants?

## EXTINCT AND DIMINISHED ANIMALS

In prehistoric times Britain was full of great beasts: lion, leopard, hyena, woolly rhinoceros, cave bear, sabre-toothed cat. They died out probably through the greed and new technology of Palaeolithic men.

Destruction of habitat followed in later prehistory, continuing into historic times. This affected large woodland mammals – bear, wild swine, and the like – and big fenland or heathland birds such as crane and bustard. The British Isles, densely populated and little-wooded for millennia, lost nearly all their large and middle-sized mammals.

### Wolf, Aurochs, Bear, Beaver

Wolves are not specifically woodland animals; their demise was caused by extermination campaigns. Records in medieval England are mostly confined to the Welsh Border and the north. In 1281 Peter Corbet, commissioned by Edward I, apparently made an end of them.

In Scotland there are unsubstantiated 'legends' of woods being burnt to deny cover to two-legged and four-legged wolves. The last certain record is of a huge bounty paid for a wolf in Sutherland in 1621. Less definite stories of 'last wolves' follow up to 1682. In Ireland the last wolf was killed in c.1709. After this, history slides into fiction. Writers repeat, as if it were fact, the slaying of the last wolf in Scotland in 1743 near Tomatin south of Inverness. The story is a fine bloody Homeric narration, but does not state that the victim was a wolf; this 'fact' was alleged in a re-telling nearly a century later. Whether its author originally meant it as history we shall never know.

The aurochs, wild ancestor of European domestic cattle, was probably always a woodland animal. Destruction of wildwood would have reduced its habitat to a point at which the survivors could easily be caught.

The bear in Britain is a shadowy beast who died out probably before the Roman period and left no mark on the landscape.

The beaver, once widespread throughout Europe including Britain

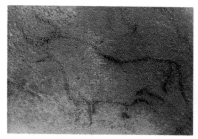

*A Palaeolithic picture of an aurochs in the cave of Pech-Merle, Lot, France. This animal lingered in Eastern Europe into the seventeenth century. (AA&A)*

and Ireland, survived in a few places into Anglo-Saxon times; Beverley is named after him. He is last heard of in the twelfth century. The beaver is a strictly woodland animal of commercial value – for fur and testicles – who draws attention to himself by building lodges. He survived surprisingly long in a land with no surviving flood-plain wildwood.

## Wild Swine: Pig-sticking and Feasting

The wild pig still flourishes as a beast of the chase in many parts of Europe. It was very different from the tame porker; medieval writers never confused them.

By the thirteenth century English wild pig were confined to the Forests of Pickering (Yorkshire) and Dean. They were official beasts of the king's Forest; he placed orders with his hunters to supply the table royal. The last known free-living wild swine were killed in Dean in about 1260.

The wild pig was a very noble and romantic beast, and some of the most exalted families liked to be thought of as swine. Englishmen knew the courtly science of pig-sticking from visits to France, and represented its weapons and ceremonial in art and literature. The boar-hunt in *Sir Gawain and the Green Knight*, written in the fourteenth century, is set in a chivalrous England of long before. The animals continued to be kept in semi-captivity in a few grand parks. The De Veres, Earls of Oxford, made Chalkney Wood (Earl's Colne, Essex) into a park for wild boar, and imagined their family name to come from Latin *verres*, a swine. Escaped animals probably gave rise to stories of the killing of

*A feast in the medieval tradition, though simplified: no medieval ruler would have been so mean as to serve only one boar's head. Henry III of England ate hundreds of wild sows and boars at feasts in the 1250s. Tudor and Stuart monarchs liked to be given 'wild-boar pye' from animals kept in parks. Note also that the peacock was thought to be edible. (Musée de Nancy/Edimedia)*

*A pig-sticking scene on the Norman doorway of Little Langford church, Wiltshire. It is probably conventionalized, although the boar-spear with its crosspiece is authentic. (OR, 1975)*

'the last wild boar in England' down to the seventeenth century.

Countries which still have wild swine have at least 20 per cent of woodland, more than England had in late Anglo-Saxon times. The Forest of Dean, where they last lingered, was one of the largest wooded areas. Henry III exterminated them, not so much by the excesses of his table (which a large French Forest could support even now), as by industrializing Dean and destroying their solitude.

## Crane

The crane is a great bird which breeds in the fens of Northern Europe and migrates to Africa. Medieval cranes were on feasting menus along with teal, snipe, curlews, fieldfares, hoopoes, bitterns and coots. In 1534 edible birds were protected by statute, but a penalty of 20d. per egg taken failed to save the crane from extinction in Britain. This is usually blamed on fen drainage, although the sixteenth century was not a time of advancing drainage. (Cranes have recently returned.)

## Deer and Super-deer

There have been four native deer in Britain. Reindeer died out soon after the last glaciation. The elk, resembling the North American moose, was the second most important food animal at the Mesolithic site of Star Carr (northeast Yorkshire), but disappeared soon after.

Red deer were almost ubiquitous in woodland, moorland and tundra. They provided meat, skins and antlers and bones for tools. They were the most important mammals at Star Carr. Neolithic flint-miners of Grime's Graves (Norfolk) used over 50,000 antlers as picks.

As farmland advanced deer declined. By the Middle Ages red deer were widespread but seldom common. The coming of parks and Forests gave them the status of semi-domestic animals, although they were outnumbered by the introduced fallow deer. By the thirteenth century the largest numbers were in the moorland Forests of the Pennines, and in the Scottish Highlands. With the decline of the Forest system red deer almost died out in England except in parks.

Roe deer were another major food in prehistory. By the Middle Ages they were rare and unsuitable for systematic management; they were recorded in woodland, fens and probably moorland. By 1800 roe were supposed nearly to have died out in England and Wales.

Red and roe deer have recovered in the last hundred years, partly through reintroduction. They are now more abundant in Great Britain than they were in the heyday of the Forests.

A mysterious survivor are the fierce, shy white cattle of a few very grand parks such as Chillingham (Northumberland). Since the twelfth century 'wild bulls' have been distinguished from domestic oxen. About 20 park herds are known to have existed. Wild cattle were regarded as super-deer, eaten at feasts and maybe the objects of specially thrilling hunts. The Archbishop of York ate six 'wylde bulls' at his enthronement in 1466.

Evidence for wild cattle outside parks is fragmentary. Writers from the twelfth to the sixteenth century mention shy white cattle in

## Garefowl

This arctic sea-bird was incapable of flying and similar (though unrelated) to the penguins of the southern hemisphere which are named after it. It was much eaten in Palaeolithic times. By the historic period garefowl were reduced to about six huge breeding colonies on very remote Atlantic islets. One by one these succumbed to raids for eggs, meat and feathers. The last garefowl were killed in Scotland in 1840 (on St Kilda, for being suspected of Satanism) and in Iceland in 1844.

The garefowl illustrated here was drawn by John Bewick in 1804. The pose is characteristic of this bird when stuffed, as it always is.

England and Scotland, though not in places where park herds were later prevalent. There is no evidence that park herds were derived from free-living cattle or vice versa.

White cattle are still mysterious and controversial. They illustrate the conservation in semi-captivity, as a status symbol, of an otherwise extinct subspecies. A study of the Chillingham cattle shows that their anatomy resembles that of domestic cattle, rebutting the oft-repeated theory that they are more directly related to the aurochs.

## Victims of the Age of Gamekeeping

The polecat, marten and wildcat used to be relatively familiar animals. Although they had been persecuted – marten for fur, polecat as 'vermin' – they did not decline seriously until the nineteenth century. The three declines were not identical: polecat survived in mid-Wales and the Lake District, marten in Snowdon, the Lake District, north-west Scotland and Ireland, wildcat in the Scottish Highlands. In this century they have slowly recovered.

The decline and partial recovery of middle-sized beasts of prey (and of birds of prey such as buzzard, kite and eagles) were closely linked to professional gamekeeping. Gamekeepers, armed with breech-loading shotguns, were very efficient predators. The recovery began when gamekeeping declined during the World Wars and was restored in a somewhat less predatory form afterwards.

**Puttock or Kite**

'... Our monuments
Shall be the maws of kites' *(Macbeth)*

In Shakespeare's time the red kite was familiar in London; it proverbially ate up fallen warriors, although its normal food was probably rubbish and mice. It give rise to *puttock* place-names. In the nineteenth century, being the least shy bird of prey, it was easily exterminated by the modern weaponry of gamekeepers. It survives (and is increasing) in Wales under the most strenuous protection. *(JS/NHPA)*

*The clean, brown appearance of severely polluted bark, scoured by acid rain of every living thing except a few algae. (DW, Denbigh, Clwyd, January 1992)*

**Lichens and Acid Rain**

'The genuine bark of an oak is of an ash colour, though it is difficult to distinguish any part of it from the mosses that overspread it; for no oak, I suppose, was ever without a greater or lesser proportion of these picturesque appendages.'

So Gilpin wrote in 1791, when acid rain, though significant, was mainly in cities. (By 'mosses' he probably meant lichens as well.) Acid rain then began to spread to rural areas, reaching its worst in the mid-twentieth century. For the last twenty years rain has been getting less acid, and lichens have been returning even to central London. But there are disturbing and mysterious reports of increasing damage to sensitive lichens in areas which have hitherto escaped.

*Unpolluted bark with the very sensitive* Lobaria pulmonaria, *which once occurred even in Epping Forest but is now confined to the least polluted parts of Britain, where it is still declining. (LC/NHPA, Morvern Peninsula, Argyllshire, April 1991)*

# EXTINCT AND DECLINING PLANTS

Plants have fared better than large mammals. We shall never see the elephants and rhinoceroses of prehistoric Britain, but we still have one-ten-thousandth of the limewoods which were their habitat.

Destruction of habitat affects certain groups of plants. Fritillary and pasque-flower are destroyed by even a single ploughing of old grassland; they do not return or colonize new grassland. The mania for drainage has drastically reduced many species of fens and bogs. Other declines can be traced to neglect of management. Neglected heathland and increasing fires account for the decline in juniper and clubmosses. Allowing heath, grassland or fen to become overgrown with trees does more damage than burning. Many woodland plants are affected by declining woodland management.

Picking flowers and gathering plants for food has usually done little harm, but during the collecting mania of the nineteenth century people dug up ferns, orchids and other rare plants. It is often asserted that digging up roots for sale has locally exterminated even such a relatively common plant as the primrose, but this is uncertain. Collecting may mask the ill-effects of a change in habitat, such as increasing shade owing to lack of woodcutting. Collecting still threatens rarities such as lady's-slipper orchid; but it is unfortunate that preventing it should be so much emphasized in legislation. The Wildlife and Countryside Act (1981) protects some rare plants against depredation by collectors and scientists, but not against the mass destruction which so often results from 'good agricultural and forestry practice'.

Many declines and extinctions are inexplicable. Nobody knows why the seaside plants *Otanthus maritimus*, *Euphorbia peplis* and *Matthiola sinuata* have become very rare; there is plenty of habitat left.

## Lichens

Extinctions have been more severe among lichens and mosses. Anyone returning from the Middle Ages would immediately comment on the appearance of tree-trunks. Trunks used to be clothed, and still are in remote areas, with a patchwork of grey, brown, white, green and yellow lichens and mosses. But most tree-trunks today are grey-green with at most a thin layer of a single lichen, *Lecanora conizaeoides*.

Nearly all lichens except *Lecanora conizaeoides*, and some mosses, are very sensitive to air and rain pollution, especially sulphur dioxide. Coppice rods, preserved in the wattle-and-daub of buildings in Suffolk, still have their original bark with medieval lichens. Young trees in fifteenth-century Suffolk were as fully covered with lichens as they are now in the clean rain of Devon.

It is probably a myth, as far as Britain is concerned, that acid rain affects trees themselves. There are plenty of other reasons, from drought to honey-fungus, why trees (especially planted trees) should be in less than perfect health. Acid rain has been worse in the past: already by 1620 it had dissolved so much of old St Paul's Cathedral that James I launched an appeal for repairs.

## NATURALIZED ANIMALS

Some foreign animals came in prehistory. The common mouse goes back to the Iron Age. Domesticated livestock went wild – for example, the wild sheep of St Kilda and the wild goats of North Wales.

### Norman Introductions: Rabbit, Fallow Deer, Pheasant

The rabbit, a delicious and commercial animal from the Mediterranean, is first heard of in England about 1100. By the thirteenth century commercial warrens were widely established, especially by monks. They give rise to *Warren* place-names, and also to *Conygre*, *Conyfare* and *Conifer* Wood from *coney*, the old word for rabbit. The medieval rabbit needed cherishing in this climate. Earthworks ('pillow-mounds') were made to encourage burrowing. (Walk III, pp. 106-111).

Rabbit meat and fur, originally articles of luxury, gradually became cheaper. From the mid-eighteenth century onwards a more narrow-minded attitude developed. Rabbits, a staple food of 'people who did not matter', conflicted with the ploughing-up of heaths and commons, and became regarded as a pest. Landowners who still kept them were attacked in anti-rabbit propaganda. By World War II rabbits had almost ceased to be commercial animals.

In 1953 an ill-wisher introduced the South American myxomatosis virus, and promptly killed at least 99 per cent of the rabbits in Britain. The resulting lack of grazing brought disaster to grasslands and heaths.

The rabbit was a successful farming innovation; its decline is part of the modern fashion for concentrating on only a few crops. Its history illustrates Darwinian evolution. The change from the tender,

**'Confounded Rats'**

Rats used to be a mystery. There is an apocryphal story that they were brought by Crusaders from the Holy Land. But if their coming was as late as this, why did no chronicler notice it? Why did no moralist denounce this monstrous new mouse as a divine judgement, as on the sinful Philistines in the days of Samuel?

The matter is resolved by excavation, which shows that the 'black' rat, *Rattus rattus*, originally from India, was present in several English towns from the third century AD onwards. Its coming was one of the momentous events which historians ignore because nobody was writing at the time.

This most terrible of beasts carries bubonic plague, which may well have caused the disruption of Europe in the sixth century. The plague hypothesis covers the known facts of the Dark Ages. It allows us to accept that country life and the landscape should have been less disrupted than town life.

The modern rat of Britain is the 'brown' rat, *R. norvegicus*, which came from eastern Europe and displaced the black rat. Robert Smith, ratcatcher to Princess Amelia, first noticed the difference between the two species in 1768.

*(The illustration dates from c.1830. MEPL)*

*A fourteenth-century picture of rabbits. The king is meant to be John: the real King John hawked rather than hunted. (BL/ET)*

expensive animal of the twelfth century (which at first could not dig its own burrow) to the multiplying, self-reliant rabbit of the eighteenth and the pest of the nineteenth century are almost certainly due to genetic adaptation to the climate. Since 1953, the terrible selection imposed by disease has produced a tough, unsociable rabbit which lives on the surface and so does not infect its colleagues.

Fallow deer are oriental beasts, introduced *c*.1100 by the Normans who could have got them from the Normans in Sicily. They did not roam the countryside but were enclosed in parks or protected in Forests, where they outnumbered native deer. As the Forest system disintegrated their numbers declined.

Since the 1920s there has been a remarkable change. Fallow deer escaped from parks and established themselves in the countryside at large. So did muntjac and Chinese water deer, both introduced from China about 1900. Deer, native and introduced, are now more numerous and more easily seen than for a thousand years. The most likely explanation is that they can now avoid human contact. Before 1920 every field was visited by somebody – usually armed – at least once a week, which is no longer so. Most farmers now tolerate deer, their only natural predator is the motor-car, and numbers are limited by starvation and poaching.

The pheasant, thought to be native in Central Asia, apparently came to Britain along with the rabbit and fallow deer. Pheasants were frequently cited in medieval poaching cases or appeared at feasts. They were very delicate and expensive birds indeed, like swans.

Serious gamekeeping of pheasants dates from the late eighteenth century. Carried to excess, it warred on creatures thought to be carnivorous, corrupted country life and produced ill-feeling between landowners and other folk. Nevertheless, pheasant-keeping maintained the fabric of the countryside: by providing a rival crop it limited the excesses of prairie-farming.

### Squirrels

Much later there was a whimsical fashion for releasing exotic beasts and birds to 'enrich' a supposedly unsatisfactory native fauna. People learnt the hard way that foreign species displace the native fauna (instead of enriching it) and can menace the native plant life. The grey squirrel, from North America, was let loose at least 31 times between 1876 and 1929. It has spread throughout most of Britain and much of Ireland.

Red and grey squirrels cannot live together: the red disappears soon after the arrival of the grey. Apparently they compete for food, and the grey squirrel wins because (though introduced) it is better adapted to British native trees than the red. (The red squirrel is itself partly an introduction: see caption to photograph, p. 16.)

Grey squirrels damage the bark of trees, especially beech and sycamore, and take eggs and young birds. The most drastic ecological effect is probably on hazel. Grey squirrels remove the entire crop of hazel-nuts before they are ripe. Hazel, which has shaped our civilization from prehistoric times, is the most threatened British tree.

# NATURALIZED AND NEWLY-CREATED PLANTS

Whether a plant is native may not be an easy thing to establish. Pollen analysis proves that many plants have been here since before civilization, but the converse is more difficult to prove. Plants producing little pollen or growing in dry places are unlikely to have a pollen record even if present.

## Naturalized Trees: Chestnut and Sycamore

The sweet-chestnut, *Castanea sativa*, is an anciently-introduced tree, native in the Balkans, Italy and probably Spain. The nuts are an important foodstuff, especially in Italy. Chestnut was one of many plants brought to Britain by the Romans. The others, such as walnut, either died out in the Dark Ages or were maintained only in gardens. Chestnut survived, acquired an Anglo-Saxon name, and became naturalized. Although far from its homeland, it prospers, grows from seed, and mingles with native woodland.

The medievals valued chestnut for its nuts, but seem to have been unaware of the excellence of its wood. Much later it was planted as a source of coppice poles, used by growers of hops; but there are also woods with ancient stools, such as Stour Wood (Essex) and Chestnuts in the Forest of Dean, which could even represent original introductions.

Sycamore, native of central Europe, was introduced in the late sixteenth century. It became a fashionable garden and churchyard tree, which may explain its peculiar English (and Welsh) name. 'Sycamore' is a Hebrew word for a quite different Palestinian tree. This word for an unknown tree was becoming familiar to the public through the King James Bible at the same time as a new tree, lacking a name, was becoming familiar in gardens.

**Is Sweet-chestnut Native?**
Historical ecology began in 1769 with a controversy in the Royal Society over whether chestnut was native. Daines Barrington, friend of Gilbert White, gave reasons why (he supposed) it was not native. Hasted, the Kentish antiquary, claimed that it was: it grew from seed and was not always planted; woods contained different ages of trees. He produced references to chestnut in documents dating back to the twelfth century; place-names supposedly derived from it; ancient buildings in which its timber had supposedly been identified; and ancient trees then alive or mentioned in earlier works.

Neither argument was perfect. Barrington was wrong in asserting that all native trees grow freely from seed. Not all Hasted's place-names were genuine. Most 'chestnut' timbers in ancient buildings are really oak. Despite these imperfections, the logic of Hasted's arguments is overwhelming. He properly concluded: 'These chestnuts are undoubtedly the indigenous growth of Britain, planted by the hand of nature'. But unreason triumphs in arguments about trees. Barrington was the more famous man, and his views gained credence: people even believed that chestnut is not native anywhere in Europe and does not produce nuts in Britain.

The reality, that chestnut is an introduction but a very early one, was unsuspected by Barrington or Hasted and emerged only from pollen analysis long after.

*A famous ancient tree: the Tortworth Chestnut (Gloucestershire) as shown in Strutt,* Sylva Britannica, *in 1827 and as photographed (by the author) in 1977. It stands by a churchyard; the deer would be a less unlikely embellishment today than in 1827. (Left: RBG)*

*Poppies and corn-marigold are cornfield weeds (here relegated to a roadside verge) from the homelands of agriculture. With declining use of weedkillers they have become somewhat less rare. (BG/NI, Breamore, Hampshire, June 1989)*

### Weeds

Weeds are very specialized plants, intimately linked to farming. Many weeds could not survive on their own. Although traditionally listed as 'native', they came with agriculture in Neolithic times. Plantains, mugwort, shepherd's purse and the like were arctic plants, from the tundra of late-glacial Britain, which in Neolithic times found a new lease of life as weeds. Poppies, corn-cockle and shepherd's needle came from the homeland of agriculture in the Near East and Crete.

Our ancestors were less certain than we about which plants were weeds and which were crops. Ground-elder, introduced by the Romans, was grown in gardens until recently. Tollund Man, of the Danish Iron Age, had porridge of goosefoot and persicaria for his execution breakfast.

Weeds began to decline with the shrinking variety of crops. Vastly less flax and *Cannabis* are grown, and we have lost the weeds that go with these crops, such as gold-of-pleasure (*Camelina sativa*), itself once a crop, and hemp broomrape (*Orobanche ramosa*). Corn-cockle and cow-wheat declined through seed-cleaning. Arable weeds have become the most severely threatened part of the flora, which is a pity. Weedkillers tend to kill the wrong weeds, almost exterminating Venus's looking-glass, shepherd's needle, and many other beautiful and harmless plants, but leaving the prosaic and pernicious blackgrass and wild oats.

In Britain (unlike its alpine homeland) sycamore is an aggressive tree forming new woodland and invading native woods. It is difficult to destroy, and most of the trees ever successfully planted must still be alive, at least as coppice stools. Most conservationists disapprove of it: it displaces native trees and is supposedly a poor habitat for wildlife. Nobody should plant it without considering the long-term consequences.

### Other Naturalized Plants

Not many of the thousands of species introduced into Britain, often centuries ago, have become naturalized. Trees include Turkey-oak, Corsican pine and (occasionally) Douglas fir. Scots pine is native to the Scottish Highlands, naturalized in England. Beech, native in the south-east of Great Britain, is naturalized and spreading far into Scotland.

*Rhododendron ponticum* was introduced from southeast Europe to the British Isles, and became abundant in the nineteenth century. Its inhospitable evergreen shade and extreme tenacity of life make it a menace to conservation, especially in Ireland and west Britain.

Oxford ragwort is a typical naturalized herb. Originally from Mount Etna, it escaped from Oxford Botanic Garden in the eighteenth century, but spread slowly at first. The coming of railways gave it a means of spread and a new habitat; its climax came with World War II, which presented it with ruined buildings on which it flourishes.

Rosebay willowherb, an arrestingly beautiful plant, has a curious history. Originally it was a relatively rare mountain plant in northern England and Scotland. From the early nineteenth century it began to appear in southern England and to spread north and west. It, too, was a plant of railways and later of bombed buildings. It also spread into woods after felling. The most popular 'explanation' of the sudden rise was the felling of woodland during World War I, as if woods had never been felled in previous centuries! The reality may be that the new rosebay was an introduction, probably from North America, of a plant looking identical to the old rosebay but behaving very differently.

## Naturalized Fungi

These can have catastrophic human or ecological effects, for example potato-blight causing the Irish famine of 1845, or chestnut-blight and Dutch Elm Disease in North America.

Oak mildew, the fungus *Microsphaera alphitoides*, covers the leaves of oaks with a white film. It affects almost every oak in Britain except perhaps where severe air pollution acts as a fungicide. It is very conspicuous, and it came from America in *c.*1908 and spread like lightning through Europe. This may explain why oaks no longer grow easily from seed in existing woods. It is extremely easy to grow an oak from an acorn in an abandoned field, but it has become very difficult to do so in most woods. An oakling, partially shaded by tall trees, may succumb if it has to contend with mildew as well as shade.

*A mildewed oak. The white film on the leaves is the fungus* Microsphaera alphitoides. *(TM, Newlands Corner, Surrey, August 1993)*

### The Creation of Species

As well as redistributing existing plants, human activity creates new species. Plants are less reluctant than animals to form hybrids between species. They can also form new species suddenly, as well as slowly by natural selection.

In the last century the native salt-marsh grass, *Spartina maritima*, met its American cousin, *S. alterniflora*, accidentally introduced to Southampton Water. The two species crossed to produce a hybrid, which was sterile (like a mule). About 1890, something went wrong with the division of a certain cell in that hybrid. The nucleus divided but the cell itself failed to split. From it grew a plant – a polyploid – with double the usual number of chromosomes. This created a new, aggressive, fertile species, cord-grass, *S. anglica*, which has spread throughout Britain, assisted by people who, unwisely, have planted it as a sea-defence. It has proved catastrophic to the ecology of salt-marshes by crowding out other plants.

Many British plants have apparently arisen in this way. Human activities have brought plants together which would not otherwise have hybridized. Many crop plants, such as wheat and apples, have been created thus by the unconscious genetic engineering of prehistoric men. Polyploids tend to do well in the habitats which human activity provides. They include 'common-or-garden' wild plants of hedgerows and meadows and around habitations. Examples are *Poa annua* (probably the commonest garden weed grass), white clover and hemp-nettle.

*Cord-grass invading salt-marsh at Barnaby's Sands in Lancashire. (DW/WI, August 1986)*

28

# WOODLAND

In the beginning, and for millennia after the end of the last Ice Age, the British Isles were covered with natural forests known as *wildwood*. There is no wildwood in Britain today, nor any records or native legends of it: our pioneering days were far too long ago to be remembered. On the Continent, wildwood survived in places into historic times.

Throughout history, trees have been part of the cultural landscape. They have been managed and used in six traditional ways:

**1.** *Woodland* – land on which trees have arisen naturally. They are managed by the art of *woodmanship* to yield successive crops of produce in a perpetual succession. When cut down, the trees replace themselves by natural regrowth.
**2.** *Wood-pasture* – land-use involving grazing animals and trees.
**3.** *Non-woodland* – trees in hedgerow and field.
**4.** *Orchards.*
**5.** *Trees of gardens and streets.*
**6.** *Plantation* – here the trees are not natural vegetation. Plantations are usually of just one or two species, often conifers or other exotic trees. They usually die when felled and are replaced by a new plantation. This is the basis of modern forestry.

The first five traditions go back at least to Anglo-Saxon times.

Right: *Ancient beech stools in Coed-y-Person near Abergavenny. Beech was much less common before it became a fashionable forester's tree in the eighteenth century. It is native only in southeast England, the Chilterns, and certain outlying areas, of which the mountains of southeast Wales are one. (TM, July 1993)*

Orchards, garden trees, forestry plantations and other formal plantings are outside the scope of this book.

Among the treasures of the Suffolk Trust for Nature Conservation, in the Bradfields near Bury St Edmunds, are two adjacent woods called Felshamhall Wood and Monks' Park. They are of ash, maple, hazel, lime, several different elms, two birches, alder, two species of sallow, oak, two hawthorns and many more. Every year part of the wood is cut down, leaving the oaks standing, but the wood grows again and is not diminished. No trees are planted. The produce consists of poles, partly used by woodworking concerns, and partly for stakes and firewood. Every spring, in areas felled the last winter but one, there are countless oxlips, anemones, violets, water-avens and wood-spurge. Different stages of regrowth are full of nightingales and other birds, summer flowers, bush-crickets and other insects. The Bradfield Woods are a place of gnarled tree-stools and mysterious ponds, and of rare and difficult fungi. In the 1960s they were saved from destruction by the energetic opposition not of the scientific world, for the Bradfield Woods were almost unknown, but of local people who loved them.

These woods were owned by the great Abbey of Bury St Edmunds. They are well documented back to 1252, and would still instantly be recognised by Abbot Symon of that year. Their outline is demarcated by a mighty bank which may have been old in his time. The woodland is managed almost exactly as it was then, and some of the very trees may still be alive and productive.

The Bradfield Woods are as important an antiquity as the Abbey ruins themselves. They have doubtless always been especially beautiful and rich in plants and animals, but until recently there was nothing unusual about their survival. In 1910 there were thousands of woods which had been part of the England of George Sturt, who wrote of the late-Victorian heyday of woodworking crafts. Sturt's countryside had inherited these woods from the different Englands of William Cobbett, Oliver Goldsmith, John Evelyn, Shakespeare, Chaucer and Abbot Symon. Even to Symon such woods were relics of the unwritten past of King Alfred and Guthrum the Dane. Some things are inherited from a more remote past still: Mesolithic men hunted beneath lime trees and drank from the mysterious ponds.

Woods result from long-running interactions between human activities and natural processes. Their history should never be based on written records alone. I have never seen a wood – not even Gamlingay Wood, the best documented wood of all (p. 42) – which has not produced surprises when visited for the first time. Earthworks and surface features, trees, other plants, pollen analysis, timber and wattle in ancient buildings, all complement the written record.

The history of woods is infiltrated by factoids. Trees arouse strong feelings and give rise to complaints, regulations, policy statements, textbooks, laws and Letters to the Editor. Things people have said about woods have an unreasonable fascination for scholars, who retail them at face value without investigating the woods themselves.

## THE COPPICING CYCLE

*Buff Wood, Cambridgeshire - newly felled. (OR, April 1983)*

*The same scene one year later: note the profuse blooming of oxlip and primrose. (OR, May 1984)*

*After two years' growth: the underwood is starting to shade out the coppicing plants. (OR, May 1985)*

*After seven years' growth: the underwood forms a dense thicket suitable for nightingales. (OR, March 1990)*

## Coppice Management

Coppicing is an efficient, reliable method of harvesting wood. The new shoots can grow at more than 2 inches a day – even oak can stand 7 feet high and 1 inch thick after a season's growth. The diagram (right) shows three stages of a coppiced tree such as ash. The stool is shown before cutting, after cutting, and one year after cutting.

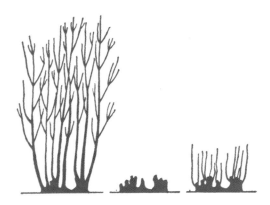

**What a Coppiced Wood Looked Like**
This map shows Link Wood near Bury St Edmunds in the summer of 1736. The whole wood had been felled in the previous ten winters. The very irregular arrangement of panels is typical of traditional coppicing. Note the scatter of timber trees. Reconstructed from a contemporary map in Suffolk Record Office.

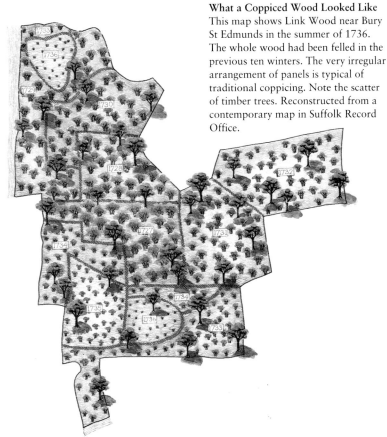

Almost all natural woods in Britain have been managed. Woodmen exploit the self-renewing power of trees. Some trees such as pines die when cut down, but ash, elder, oak, hazel, wych-elm, lime, hornbeam and many others *coppice* – the stump sends up shoots and becomes a stool from which successive crops of poles can be cut for ever. Aspen, cherry and most elms *sucker*; the stump dies but the root system remains alive and sends up successive crops of poles, forming a patch of genetically identical trees called a *clone*. Coppice and sucker shoots are a favourite food of cattle, sheep and deer, and in places accessible to livestock it was the practice to *pollard* trees instead. Pollards are cut at between six and 15 feet above ground, leaving a permanent trunk called a *bolling* (to rhyme with 'rolling'), which sprouts like a coppice stool but out of reach of animals. Pollarding is typical of wood-pasture and some non-woodland trees.

## COPPICING PLANTS

Magnificent and spectacular displays of primroses, oxlips and anemones are a result of coppicing. Most woods have had years of light followed by years of shade, going back in cycles to beyond the memory of records. Their plants, on the whole, do not like continuous shade. Primroses and other spring flowers flourish in the years of light; they also require years of shade to suppress the tall grasses and other non-woodland plants which would overwhelm them outside woods. There are different kinds of response:
**Spring-flowering perennials** are present all the time, but flower profusely only in the second or third year after felling.

Primrose
(*Primula vulgaris*)

**Summer-flowering perennials** are present all the time, but are induced by the extra light to grow tall and bloom. (Light is increased about twentyfold in summer when the trees are in leaf; about twofold in spring when they are leafless.)

Meadowsweet
(*Filipendula ulmaria*)

**Buried-seed plants** die out in the years of shade, leaving long-lived seeds to wait for the next felling when they can germinate.

Wood-spurge
(*Euphorbia amygdaloides*)

## WOODS, THEIR MANAGEMENT AND BEHAVIOUR

The trees of a wood are divided into *timber trees* and *underwood*. Every so often an area of underwood is felled and allowed to grow again by coppicing or suckering. Scattered among the underwood are the timber trees, which are allowed to stand for several cycles of regrowth and are felled when full-grown. Timber trees are usually replaced by seedlings. The whole wood is surrounded by an earthwork called a *woodbank* with a ditch on its outer side, traditionally set with a hedge to keep out livestock and with pollard trees at intervals to define the legal boundary.

The wood yields two products, *timber* from the trunks of the timber trees, and *wood* from coppice stools or suckers (plus the branches of felled timber trees). *Timber and wood had different uses and are not to be confused*: we still talk of 'timber' buildings and 'wood' fires. Wood is rods, poles and logs, used for fencing, wattlework and many specialized purposes but in large quantities for fuel. Woodland was traditionally regarded as a source of energy. Timber, the stuff of beams and planks, is too valuable and too big to burn.

Woods do not cease to exist through being felled. A wood is self-renewing, and is no more destroyed by being cut down than a meadow is destroyed by cutting a crop of hay. The Bradfield Woods have been cut down at least 70 times without disappearing. Woods cease to exist through being grubbed out to use the land for something else, or through long-continued grazing.

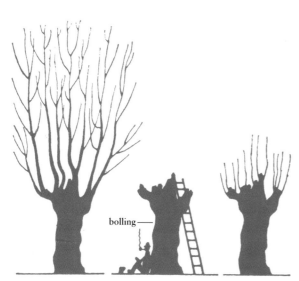

*A pollard tree before cutting, after cutting, and one year after cutting. Pollarding is harder work than coppicing. Its function is to protect the young shoots from browsing animals. It is not typical of woodland, except to mark boundaries. Pollards often become ancient trees.*

bolling

*Ashes and maples formerly coppiced, and now pollarded for the second time, in Hayley Wood, Cambridgeshire. This is not normal practice but a response to the coming of fallow deer, which have turned this wood into a wood-pasture. At the previous coppicing, deer eliminated any ash that was not pollarded. (TM, June 1993)*

Some woods are believed to be derived from the original wildwood; others (*secondary woods*) have arisen on land that has at some time not been woodland. Let a field be abandoned, and within a year it will be invaded by oaks springing up from acorns dropped by passing jays, or birches from wind-blown seed. In 30 years it will have 'tumbled down to woodland'. The same happens to chalk downs, heaths, fens, and some moorland whenever grazing and burning cease.

Secondary woods may be of any age from prehistory onwards. They are composed of those pioneer trees – oak, birch, hawthorn, ash – which easily invade vacant ground. They also lack many of the herbaceous plants of ancient woodland.

Secondary woodland is familiar on railway land and old quarries; its spread threatens the conservation of heath and old grassland. In the eastern United States, an area much greater than the whole British Isles has tumbled down to woodland since 1800. Once the subject of many scientific studies, secondary woodland is now unfashionable: recent writers call for expensive tree-planting as if it were the only way to create new woodland. Like all gradual changes which cost nothing, succession to woodland often goes unnoticed.

## Wildwood

Woodland history begins for practical purposes about 12,000BC, when the last glaciation ended. The story is known chiefly from pollen analysis. The trees which had retreated to southern latitudes during the Ice Age slowly migrated north again. Birch, aspen and sallow were followed by pine and hazel; then alder and oak; next lime and elm; then holly, ash, beech, hornbeam and maple. Birch, aspen and sallow are relatively arctic trees. Late-comers were either trees of warmer climates (hornbeam, maple) or bad colonizers (lime).

After the changes of the first millennia there came a long period of apparently stable climate, about 7,000 to 5,000BC. Tree species fought one another by natural processes of succession to form a series of 'climax' woodland types. They covered all the British Isles except for small areas of moorland and grassland on high mountains and in the far north, and for coastal dunes and salt-marshes. Such was the natural wildwood before the beginning of large-scale human activity.

Wildwood was far from being the monotonous 'mixed oak forest' which earlier pollen analysts supposed. There were many local variants, which can be grouped into five 'provinces' where many different types of woodland could be found. These 'provinces' have some expression in ancient woodland today.

A Mesolithic inhabitant, returning to the British Isles after 7,000 years, would find that we have got rid of 99 per cent of the original woodland, and even the remaining 1 per cent is longer wildwood; for instance, its management history has deprived it of old trees. But that 1 per cent would not be utterly unfamiliar. There are still eastern Scottish pinewoods and western Scottish birchwoods. Oakwoods are still a speciality of the north and west, even though 6,000 years of human intention and default have favoured oak relative to other trees

*To see what wildwood looked like, we go to America. Sometimes it consists of mighty trees: here in Tennessee a hemlock 5 feet thick and about 150 feet high has rotted at the base and crashed down, making a gap which will be filled by shorter-lived trees until hemlock takes over again. Some of the 'bog oaks' buried in English fen peats were on this scale, but may have been peculiar to this habitat. American wildwoods are very varied: some are of one species of tree, some of mixtures; on exposed mountains they may be less than a man's height. They tend to be full of saplings, but this may not have been so in Britain, where there were few shade-bearing species of tree. Before the great English storm of 1987, people assumed that the normal habit of a tree is upright, but this may be wrong. Wildwood could have been full of horizontal, living trees – perhaps the reality behind the phrase 'impenetrable forests'? (OR, Great Smoky Mountains National Park, May 1981)*

**Wildwood Regions**
in 5,000BC. In the Lime
Province the commonest tree
was small-leaved lime, but
there was much local
variation; as well as
limewoods, there were areas
of hazelwood, elmwood,
ashwood and probably
oakwood. In the Oak
Province the commonest tree
was oak, followed by hazel;
there were areas of oakwood
and hazelwood, with patches
of elmwood, pinewood,
limewood and others. The
Hazel-Elm Province included
hazelwoods, elmwoods, and
areas of oakwood. The Pine
Province involved pine-
woods with areas of birch,
oak and elm. The Birch
Province was mainly
birchwood, with patches of
pine and oak to the west. In
the extreme north there was
tundra, with woods confined
to sheltered ravines.

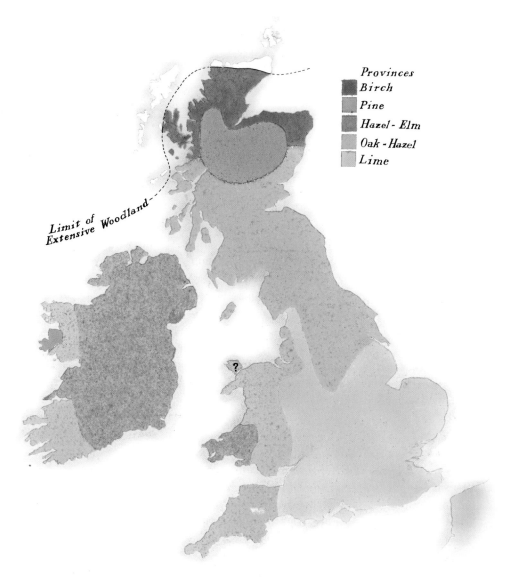

in the English lowlands. Rare though native lime now is, by careful
search our visitor could still find it, here and there, within exactly that
region in which it grew in 5,000BC. Ash and beech are now
significantly commoner, though much of the increase of beech is as a
planted tree, and very recently birch has also increased. What the
visitor would make of maple-woods and hornbeam-woods I cannot
say: their Mesolithic distribution is unknown.

**Destruction of Wildwood**

It is usually assumed that until men began to till the soil they had no
more effect on vegetation than the beasts on which they preyed.
Mesolithic and even Palaeolithic men made temporary clearings, but
they were so few that they could have made little impact merely by
cutting down trees, even if they had nothing else to do.

However, hunting and gathering may have involved some definite
management of land and vegetation. Some North American Indians,
whom we would call Mesolithic, produced a kind of wood-pasture by
periodic burning, but this would seldom have been possible in
incombustible British wildwoods. It has been conjectured that

Mesolithic men, who were great eaters of nuts, may somehow be responsible for the great abundance of hazel in prehistory.

There is no doubt about the 'Neolithic revolution'. Farmers – whether actual settlers, or people who had acquired the crops, domestic animals and weeds, and had learnt how how to use them – arrived about 4,500BC. They set about converting Britain and Ireland to an imitation of the dry open steppes of the Near East in which agriculture had begun. They attacked elms and caused a sudden drop in elm pollen production, perhaps by letting loose Elm Disease (p. 90). This 'Elm Decline' is associated with early pottery and Neolithic tools, with an increase in plants of non-wooded country, and with crops such as emmer wheat and weeds such as plantains. Within 3,000 years large tracts were converted to farmland or heath. Wildwood vanished from terrain as diverse as the chalklands, the Somerset Levels, and the coastal Lake District.

During the Bronze Age (2,400-750BC) most wildwood disappeared from high altitudes and river valleys. Inroads were made on some of the heavy soils. I shall hazard the guess that half of England had ceased to be wildwood by the early Iron Age (500BC); some archaeologists would put it earlier.

## Origins of Woodmanship

It is unlikely that farmland resulted from people felling trees for use. This has rarely happened in history; trees felled to make farmland have normally been wasted (as they are today). Woodmanship is part of civilization, and is separate from destroying wildwood. By the earliest Neolithic period, someone had discovered that regrowth shoots from a stump are of more use than the original tree.

The world's earliest evidence of woodmanship comes from wooden 'trackways' buried in the peat of the Somerset Levels. Even the earliest, the Sweet Track, is an elaborate structure of oak timber, large underwood poles of ash, lime, elm, oak and alder, and small poles of hazel and holly. Many of the poles were grown for the purpose in a mixed coppice-wood not unlike the present Cheddar Wood nine miles away.

Later trackways were made of wattle hurdles woven from thousands of hazel rods, grown in an elaborate coppicing system. The rods had to be of exactly the same size (and therefore of different ages, as rods from individual trees would have grown at different rates), because there were no metal tools with which to split the thick ones. Such hurdle-ways continue into the Bronze and Iron Ages; the wattle hurdles still made in Somerset are a 6,000-year-old industry.

Wattle-work, and the woodmanship which grew the materials, were of immense importance up to Anglo-Saxon times and beyond. Remains have been found, though only recently adequately recorded, in innumerable excavations in England and Ireland. Large wattle-work houses have been reconstructed at the Iron Age farm at Butser Hill (Hampshire).

**How Was Wildwood Destroyed?**
To convert millions of acres of wildwood into farmland was the greatest achievement of our ancestors. It belongs to an age far beyond record or memory. We know nothing of how it was organized, how many man-hours it took to clear an acre, or what people lived on while doing it. Experiments on 'clearing' woodland with prehistoric tools should not be hastily extrapolated to prehistoric Britain. Most British trees are difficult to kill; they survive felling or ringbarking, though their regrowth is eaten by cattle and sheep. In the twentieth century, Amazon wildwood is easier to destroy (acre for acre) than ordinary English coppice.

A persistent myth claims that prehistoric people 'cleared wildwood by fire'. This is not possible in Britain or Ireland, where woodlands (except pine) burn like wet asbestos. As Dr James Dickson tells me, the frivolous youth of Glasgow try every year to burn down the oakwoods around the city, and have never succeeded. To burn trees, one has to cut them down, cut them up, and stack the pieces, a far more laborious task than merely felling them. A log of more than 10 inches diameter is almost fireproof and is a most uncooperative object. There are the bigger problems still of digging up or ploughing round the stumps and preventing regrowth.

Cattle, sheep and goats probably helped by browsing regrowth and killing the stumps. This has been done in historic times, but it takes a great deal of grazing to go on consuming all the saplings year by year for centuries. How often was there enough livestock to do this in prehistory?

## ROMAN AND ANGLO-SAXON WOODLAND

### Roman Woodland

Roman Britain was not a frontier country, with boundless wildwoods surrounding occasional precarious clearings. On the contrary, it was so full of villas, small towns and the lands of British farmsteads that it can hardly have been much more wooded than it is today. The Romans – and sometimes their Iron Age or even earlier predecessors – lived in some places that the medievals thought to be uncultivable. Settlements extended deep into what were later to be great woods; for instance Wychwood Forest (Oxfordshire), Rockingham Forest (Northamptonshire) and Grovely (Wiltshire). Roman England probably had two types of terrain: regions where there was a patchwork of woodland and farmland (for instance, Hertfordshire and Essex), and regions with little or no woodland at all (the great river-valleys and most of the chalkland).

Roman woodmanship had apparently developed into something like its medieval and modern form. Not merely was it necessary, as in Neolithic times, to grow poles and rods of sizes difficult to get from wildwood. The Romans needed to conserve a limited resource and to organize supplies to woodless places. They dwelt in cities and had timber-framed buildings, bridges and ships; they needed a permanent supply of wood as well as timber, for they indulged in baths, bricks, hypocausts, corn-driers, iron, lead and glass. They apparently used great numbers of small oak-trees for buildings. The ironworks of the Weald used tens, if not hundreds, of square miles of coppice-wood.

### Dark Ages and Anglo-Saxon Period

If, as we used to suppose, Roman Britain went down in the fifth century in a cataclysm of battle, murder and sudden death, then within 50 years it should have reverted to woodland. England in the seventh century ought to have looked like New England in the twentieth, with thousands of miles of field-walls lost in the woods, and cellar-holes where thousands of farmsteads had rotted back into the ground. In America there was merely an economic recession, and only pots lie under the bushes; in England there ought to have been skulls as well. Out of this the Anglo-Saxons (we once supposed) laboriously hewed a new landscape, but had not got far by the time of the Norman Conquest.

Is this true? Neither pollen analysis nor archaeology gives any hint of a massive return of secondary woodland, invading even the good land. At Shakenoak (North Leigh, Oxfordshire) the lands of a Roman villa did tumble down to woodland, but not until three centuries after the legions left. This was not the effect of a national catastrophe but of a local retreat of cultivation in the Wychwood area. Other evidence is best approached by working backwards from the end of the Anglo-Saxon period, when we know (for England) reasonably well where the woods were.

Domesday Book makes it perfectly clear that England was not a very wooded land in 1086. The landscape of Norman England was very unlike that of modern Borneo but rather like that of modern France. The modern Vosges, like the Norman Weald, are well over half tree-covered, but full of roads and villages and hamlets in clearings. At the other extreme, the vast woodless cornlands of Champagne or around Chartres correspond to the environs of Rugby or Cambridge in 1086.

Anglo-Saxon charters tell of an earlier state of England which we might expect to have been more wooded. In practice this is not obviously so; many features (such as downs) are specifically non-woodland, and others, such as trees, would have been of no value as landmarks within a wood. The Anglo-Saxons had many words for woodland, some still in use, such as *wudu* 'wood', *graf* 'grove', *scaga* 'shaw', *hangr* 'hanger'.

Woods in the charters had individual names and were permanent; at least one wood in four was still there in the twentieth century. The bounds of Long Itchington (Warwickshire), dated 1001, pass through 'a high oak in the middle of Wulluht grove'. Mr David Morfitt has shown me the very spot, on a great bank bisecting a 200-acre wood. Wayland Wood (Watton, Norfolk), anciently Wanelund, is one of many wood-names based on the Old Norse *lúndr*, a grove or sacred grove, which go back to Viking times. Domesday refers not directly to the wood but to Wayland Hundred, a division of the county named after it. This was a grove of assembly, perhaps even of heathen worship, long before the Conquest. Much later it was to become the Babes-in-the-Wood wood, and by some miracle of continuity it is still intact and now belongs to Norfolk Naturalists' Trust.

The location of woods in the charters agrees quite well with that in Domesday. For example, in both the almost woodless eastern Cotswolds contrast with the very wooded western Cotswolds; and the moderately wooded Marlborough area (Wiltshire) contrasts with the almost woodless claylands to the north.

Woodland was not always situated in the place to which it belonged. The charter for Benson (Oxfordshire) in 996, having traced the main boundary, then says 'These are the bounds of the wood that belongs to the land', and goes on to perambulate a separate piece of land some miles away in the Chilterns. Almost the whole of the Weald was parcelled out into dependencies of places lying outside it. Originally this had been connected with the seasonal pasturing of pigs, much more important in the economy of the Weald than elsewhere. By 1086 the pig economy was being replaced by conventional settlement and agriculture, but most of the settlements were still regarded as part of their parent manors. Tonbridge, for instance, though quite an important place, was subsumed in Otford, 10 miles away.

Charters do not set out to record the uses of woodland, but they let slip many incidental details of coppicing and the supply and transport of rods, charcoal and wood, less often of timber. The woodland pig economy and its undependability are mentioned. Wood-pasture was differentiated from other woodland, and common

**Pannage**
Pannage is the practice of driving tame pigs into woods in autumn to fatten on acorns before being slaughtered and salted down. In eastern and south-eastern England Domesday Book records woodland as 'wood for so many swine' or 'wood rendering so many swine for pannage'. This is not a down-to-earth method of estimating the area of a wood. The acorn crop is (and was) very undependable. By 1086 the wood-swine had become swine of the imagination; real pigs were counted separately and fed in other ways. We cannot objectively tell whether a wood for only a few swine was a small wood, a hornbeam wood (not yielding acorns), a coppice wood (lacking big oaks), or a wood owned by a pessimist. For the later history of pannage see p. 58. (illustration from *English Forests and Forest Trees*, Ingram, Cooke, and Co., 1853)

*Places possessing woodland in 1086, according to Domesday Book. Out of 12,580 settlements, only 6,208 had any woodland. Note the concentration of woodland around London. In the Breckland, Fens, the Cambridge area, and much of the Midlands there was no woodland at all, either in Domesday or in documents from the next centuries. This map takes no account of the area of woodland.*

**Woodland in Domesday Book**

Domesday covered 27 million acres of land; of these I estimate that 4.1 million, that is 15 per cent, were woodland (including wood-pasture). England was not well wooded even by the standards of twentieth-century, let alone eleventh-century, Europe. It had a proportion of woodland between those of modern France (20 per cent of the land) and modern Denmark (9 per cent).

Most of England consisted of farmland with islands of wood, ranging in size from over a thousand acres to fractions of an acre. Woodland in the eleventh century was much less evenly distributed than its remains are now. A few areas were still mainly wooded with large islands of farmland. The biggest wooded area was the Weald, some 75 miles by 30. The second largest was the Chiltern plateau, 40 miles by 25, immediately north of London; there were others in north Worcestershire extending into Warwickshire, in east Derbyshire, and in the Forest of Dean. Even these areas were not uninhabited wildwood; it was nowhere possible in eleventh-century England to penetrate into woodland further than four miles from some habitation. Conversely, many villages were over four miles from any wood and a day's journey from any substantial woodland.

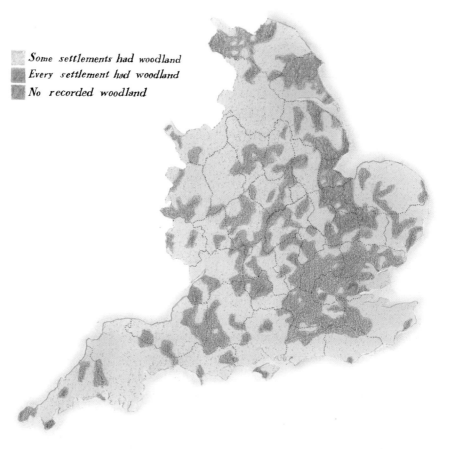

Some settlements had woodland
Every settlement had woodland
No recorded woodland

woods were separated from private woods. Here are some examples.

> Pasture for 70 pigs in that wooded common ... which the country-folk call Wulfferdinleh [Wolverley, Worcestershire] and 5 wagons full of good rods and every year one oak for building ... and wood ... for the fire as necessary.
>
> *Grant by Burgred, king of Mercia, 866*

> A place in which salt can be got and with [right of] access for 3 carts into the wood which is called Blean.
>
> *Grant at Lenham, Kent, 850 [The Blean, still the second largest woodland area in Kent, is 15 miles from Lenham.]*

> I give the lands at Brycandune to St Peter of Westmenstre, except that I will that they fatten two hundred swine for my wife, if there be mast.
>
> *Brickendon, Hertfordshire, 989*

Woods were valuable private property; a wood near Powick (Worcestershire) was the subject of a complicated lawsuit in 825. Their boundaries could be demarcated by a linear feature called a *wyrtruma*, probably a woodbank.

An earlier stratum of evidence still is that of place-names; not, for this purpose, the names of woods themselves, but of settlements implying substantial woodland. The hundreds of villages and hamlets named -*ley* and -*hurst* (for instance, Bromley, Stoneleigh, Stoneley, Leigh-on-Sea, Hawkhurst) appear to mean an inhabited clearing surrounded by woodland. Names ending in -*feld*, such as Beaconsfield, appear to mean not a 'field' as we know it but an open space in sight of woodland with which to contrast it. Most such places already existed in Anglo-Saxon times, many of them early in that period. Do not *Tues*ley, *Wednes*field and *Thor*ley go back to the twilight of the heathen gods?

These place-names, again, match unexpectedly well the distribution of woodland in Domesday. Woodland place-names are thick on the map in the Weald, the Chiltern plateau, north-west Warwickshire and adjacent Worcestershire, east Derbyshire, etc. Areas which were woodless in the eleventh century, such as the Breckland, the Fens, Lincolnshire, south-east Warwickshire, north Oxfordshire and east Gloucestershire have few or no such place-names.

Had the Anglo-Saxons started with boundless woodland, place-names and charters would have recorded earlier stages in its destruction than Domesday. In reality, with small exceptions, the three sources, despite their different dates, agree on what were the wooded and woodless regions. It follows that that distribution was not the work of the Anglo-Saxons but was taken over from the Romano-Britons. The Anglo-Saxons in 600 years probably increased the area of farmland, managed the woodland more intensively, and made many minor changes; but did not radically reorganize the wooded landscape.

There is nothing to suggest that Anglo-Saxons were pioneers, spending their lives digging up trees among boundless woodland. Such may have been the business of folk in the Weald or around Birmingham, but not of the country as a whole. As far back as records go, most of England had a stable, predominantly agricultural countryside. The glimpses we are given of the Anglo-Saxon way of life show woods having a place in the landscape and in human affairs not very different from that which they were to hold in the Middle Ages. The whole of Anglo-Saxon writing contains remarkably few allusions to the destruction of woodland.

**Wales, Scotland and Ireland – the Dark Ages**

For Wales and Scotland there is much less evidence. In Wales charters (and some Domesday evidence) indicate rather more woodland than in England. In Scotland the archaeological evidence shows that by Roman times there was a landscape of moorland and farmland, with probably less woodland than contemporary England. It used to be thought that there was a 'Great Wood of Caledon', extending for 100 miles across the central Highlands and persisting into historic times. This idea, suggested by vague allusions in Roman historical writers, was nourished by people finding logs buried in peat (see p. 156). Dr Dickson and others have shown that this cannot be true. The buried logs are thousands rather than hundreds of years old. If there was a Great Wood of Caledon somewhere, it would have covered at most a few square miles, like the Glen Tanar woods today (Walk II, pp. 102-105).

In Ireland the dense population and cultivation of the Iron Age are evident from tens of thousands of earthworks called *raths*, which represent farmsteads. Up to the Viking period Ireland was a civilized and populous land, with no room for great tracts of wildwood; indeed many later well-wooded areas contain raths.

## MEDIEVAL WOODLAND

From the thirteenth century onwards the records become much more copious. Hundreds of specific woods are mentioned in surveys of lands. The earliest is the *Ely Coucher Book*, an inventory of the Bishop of Ely's lands in 1251. This is a sample entry:

> The Wood. There is one wood which is called Heyle which contains fourscore acres. Item, there is one wood which is called Litlelund, which contains thirty-two acres ...

> William Clark holds one virgate of arable ... he has to cut one cartload of underwood for one work, but not to cart it. And he has to cut rods and collect them and make from them two fold-hurdles for one work, or three hurdles if he finds the rods ready ...
> [A 'work' is a unit of labour-service, to be done by way of rent.]

Woods had definite names, boundaries and acreages, were private property, were intensively managed and were permanent. Hayley

Wood and a wood then called Bradeleh, now Hardwick Wood, are still with us after 743 years; they are copiously documented for the intervening centuries, and there can be no question that they are the same woods. Hayley is exactly the same apart from minor changes due to the making of a railway; its companion wood, Litlelund, was grubbed out in the 1650s. Hardwick Wood has had a more complex history and only half the present wood is original. Both woods are now nature reserves of Cambridgeshire and Bedfordshire Wildlife Trust; so are several woods recorded in the Hundred Rolls of 1279.

Many other woods in the *Coucher Book* still exist, such as the five woods of Barking (Suffolk), in area from 5 to 130 acres. Roughly half the woods named in thirteenth-century surveys were still there in 1945. (More than half the Bishop of Ely's estates, scattered from Norfolk to the Thames, had no woodland in 1251.)

Most medieval woods were shared by timber trees and underwood. Both were self-renewing and produced a sustained yield. This was usually taken for granted, but occasionally stated in writing:

A certain Wood called Heylewode which contains 80 acres by estimate. Of the underwood of which there can be sold every year, without causing waste or destruction, 11 acres of underwood which are worth 55s. at 5s. an acre ... A certain other Wood called Litlelond which contains 26 acres by estimate. Whose underwood can be sold as a whole every seventh year. And it is then

Right: *The woodbank to King's Wood, Gomshall, Surrey. The wood was once much smaller. The ditch lies on the right, showing that the part on the left is the original wood and that on the right an addition. (TM, August 1993)*

Below: *The woodbank to Felshamhall Wood, Bradfield Woods. Coppicing is in progress. One of the pollard trees that define the boundary has just been pollarded. (BG/NI, April 1986)*

A medieval picture of a wood in Flanders: a miniature painted by Simon Benninck, one of the few artists who have been able to draw convincing trees. This is a limewood. The foreground was felled last year, leaving standing most of the timber trees of elm, oak and aspen. The lime stools are of one year's growth, and keep their leaves later than those of lime of about twenty years' growth in the middle distance. Coppicing plants include broom, male fern, bramble and (this being Belgium) the shrubby honeysuckle Lonicera xylosteum. The whole scene, including the hedges, hedgerow trees, and scattered farmsteads in the background, could have been repeated in south Suffolk or north Essex at the time. (Ignore the persons and animals: a pigsticking was the conventional Continental way of saying that the month is November.) (BL Add. MS 18855, f.108v)

worth in all £6.10s. at 5s. an acre.

*Survey of the Bishop of Ely's estates, 1356*
[occasioned by the Bishop being wanted for murder]

Underwood was usually the regular and more important product. Surveys either state a felling rotation (seven years for Hayley Wood, five for Hardwick) or state the annual return expected. Coppice cycles were usually from four to eight years, though some rotations of 16 to 20 years are known. Timber trees were felled at irregular intervals when it was considered necessary.

By 1270 woods were valuable property: the return from underwood alone – leaving out timber, hazel-nuts, and other produce – was more than from arable land. Their boundaries were carefully defined by a great bank and ditch, usually with a hedge or a fence. This prevented encroachment by neighbours and kept out livestock which would eat the young shoots. Most woodbanks appear to have been already in existence: that of Knapwell Wood (Cambridgeshire), which still exists, is mentioned in the twelfth century. Contractors' accounts exist for making three miles of new woodbank round the Norwich Cathedral woods at Hindolveston, Norfolk, in 1297-8. This included planting a hedge on the banks and providing bridges, gates and padlocks at the entrances.

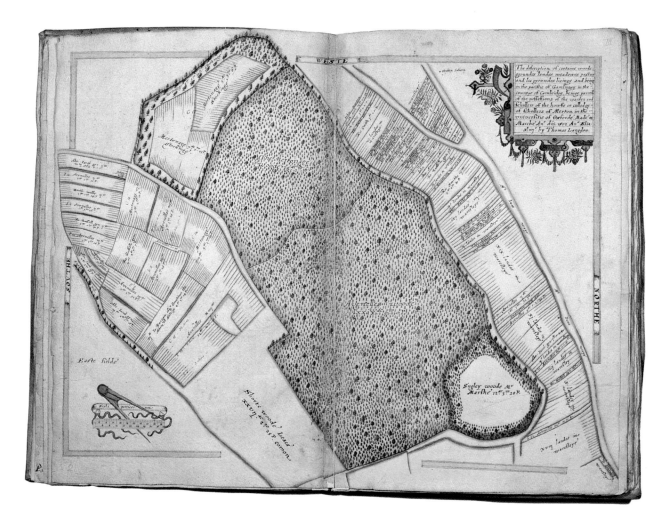

### Gamlingay Wood

This Cambridgeshire wood is perhaps the best documented wood in England. Part of it belonged to Merton College, Oxford, from 1268 to 1959. The map above was made for Merton in 1601. *North is to the right.* The field to the southwest was called Stocking, a place of stocks or tree-stumps; it had been grubbed out from the wood in the twelfth century. The belt of trees round the field is not a remnant of the wood, but an enlargement of a hedge which had been planted round the field some 300 years earlier. Note the open-field strips around the wood, separated by a narrow headland on which to turn the plough. In the twelfth century the principal manor, and the wood, had been divided into two unequal parts; the map was made to commemorate the re-amalgamation of the ownerships. *(Merton College, Oxford/TP)*

### Timber and Wattle

Over 90 per cent of building timbers are oak, which was the commonest and most expensive timber tree. Other species – elm, ash, aspen – are most often found in houses of the relatively poor.

Although saws had been invented long before, recent excavations show that the Anglo-Saxons and Normans split big logs with wedges. This specialized craft demands a rare type of tree – a big, slow-grown woodland oak lacking side-branches. There was evidently a source of such trees, at least near London (where most of the excavation has been done). The date is too late for wildwood; a more likely source would be post-Roman secondary oakwood growing through the Anglo-Saxon period. The diminishing supply of such trees may account for records of trees transported hundreds of miles.

By the thirteenth century, technology used small, fast-grown trees from coppice-woods and hedges, used whole or sawn into planks. Most medieval buildings are made from large numbers of small oaks; every timber was made from the smallest tree that would serve the purpose. The carpenter chose trees of the sizes required and squared them up, usually leaving the corners rounded (*waney*). Oaks, then as now, were crooked, and carpenters made ingenious use of their irregular shapes.

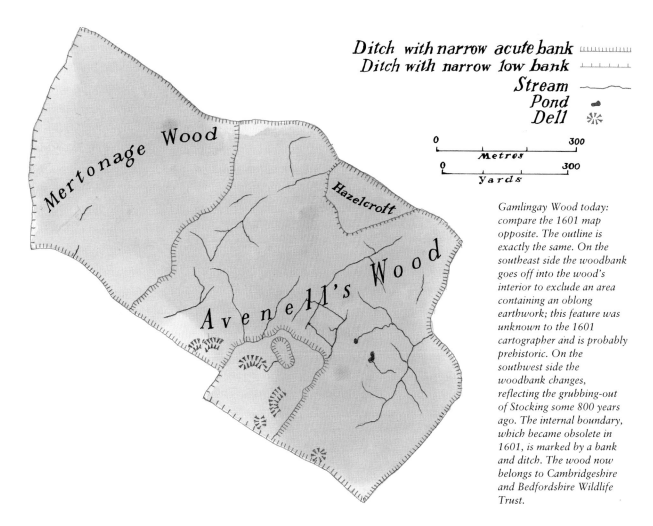

Ditch with narrow acute bank

Ditch with narrow low bank

Stream

Pond

Dell

0      Metres      300

0      yards      300

*Gamlingay Wood today: compare the 1601 map opposite. The outline is exactly the same. On the southeast side the woodbank goes off into the wood's interior to exclude an area containing an oblong earthwork; this feature was unknown to the 1601 cartographer and is probably prehistoric. On the southwest side the woodbank changes, reflecting the grubbing-out of Stocking some 800 years ago. The internal boundary, which became obsolete in 1601, is marked by a bank and ditch. The wood now belongs to Cambridgeshire and Bedfordshire Wildlife Trust.*

A typical fifteenth-century Suffolk farmhouse, rather larger than average, turns out to be made of some 330 trees. Only three trees were as much as 18 inches in diameter, a usual size for a 'mature' oak nowadays; half of them were less than 9 inches in diameter. Such sizes, typical of medieval houses, barns and colleges, imply woodland with a rapid turnover of small oaks and no difficulty in replacing them. This is just as true of the well-wooded Weald – see the buildings in the Weald and Downland Museum at Singleton (Sussex) – as of East Anglia. Oaks grew among underwood which suppressed their lower boughs, producing a trunk about 20 feet long, above which the crown of the tree branched out.

Examining the timber and underwood of a medieval building may bring back to life the trees and the men of a long-vanished wood. But let us be cautious. Building materials are not always local; the medievals had good roads and used them. Trees more than about 25 feet in usable length or 18 inches in diameter did not normally grow in the local woods; they were rare and expensive and were brought from a distance to be used in the king's castles, the great roofs of cathedrals, and the posts on which windmills turned. They came mainly, not from woods, but from hedgerows, parks and Forests. Not only outsize trees, but ordinary timber and even underwood were moved about the country to supply woodless areas – not only in England, but in the Scottish and Irish midlands and in Anglesey in Wales.

There was a large import trade from Norway and eastern Europe. Pine did not grow in England, so when, as in a building in Ely, we find a thirteenth-century roof largely made of small pine trees, we are reminded of the pine scaffolding-poles which the fabric rolls of Ely Cathedral record as having been brought from Norway. Pine boards survive in the thirteenth-century doors of the Chapter-house in York Minster. The documents also speak of a large trade in oak boards. Imported 'wainscot' boards survive most often in medieval church furniture and doors. They do not carry the stamp NOT MADE IN ENGLAND so obviously as do the pine boards; yet with practice one can distinguish the giant, straight-grained, slow-grown oaks of Central Europe, accurately cut in a board factory, from the small, crooked, fast-grown, local oaks used for the structure frames of the same buildings.

Medieval Wales had coppice-woods much like those of England. So did southern and middle Scotland, to judge by field evidence. The pine and birch woods of the Scottish Highlands, however, lacked definite boundaries and management; they functioned in a different way (Walk II, pp. 102-105). Ireland was less wooded than England, but woods were concentrated in mountain areas and impressed travellers with their extent and impenetrability. The first extensive information is from the mid-seventeenth century, when woodland covered a little over 2 per cent of Ireland (about one-third of its extent in England). The prehistoric elmwoods on good soils had vanished, as had most hazel-woods. This left oak as the commonest species, growing on poor soils. Celtic and Viking Ireland had had a strong coppicing tradition, whole buildings being made of underwood. By the seventeenth century this had declined, although some 'copps' is still recorded.

## WOODS DOWN THE CENTURIES

The woods of 1250 were relics of an Anglo-Saxon and Norse landscape. In between there had been a time of rising population and of such land-hunger as England has never experienced since. Woodland was to shrink from 15 per cent of England in 1086 to perhaps 7 per cent by 1350, an average destruction of 27 acres a day. This was mainly in well-wooded areas, most of which became no more wooded than the rest of the country, although in almost every county some encroachment is known.

This period was cut short by the Black Death in 1349. The surviving population made less use of the land. Any wood then remaining had a good chance of surviving the next 500 years. Some land probably reverted to woodland: all over Eastern and Midland England there are woods which show evidence on the ground of having been smaller at some time.

## MEDIEVAL BUIDINGS

*The thirteenth-century Wheat Barn, Cressing Temple, Essex. This immense structure contained about 470 oaks, most of them quite small. (OR)*

*Wattle-and-daub in a fifteenth-century house at Lavenham (Suffolk). The bark is missing from the rods because they are of lime, whose bark was stripped off for use as fibre. Small-leaved lime still grows in Lavenham Wood. (OR)*

Buildings were the biggest single use of timber and tell us much of the management of woods in general, though they can rarely be related to particular woods. Timber is not inherently perishable: many thousands of timber-framed buildings survive from the fifteenth century, and those that have come down to us from the twelfth, though few, are not in a worse state of decay than those of the eighteenth.

Medieval timber-framed buildings were not just the poor man's substitute for stone. Timber was an architectural medium; a 'wealth of exposed beams' looked picturesque and expressed prestige. Although every building contained some timber, wholly timber buildings are confined to certain parts of the country, for reasons of fashion and etiquette which we cannot now explain. Cambridge had abundant easily-worked stone and no local woodland, but apart from colleges it was an almost entirely timber-framed

town. In many areas timber-framing was a mark of urban building.

The panels between the timbers of framed buildings are usually filled with wattle-and-daub made of interwoven underwood rods. Underwood, where it has not been thrown away by 'restorers', is often excellently preserved, down to the very lichens which grew on the rods when alive (p. 22). Hazel and sallow are the commonest species. I have encountered elm, aspen, birch, maple and lime (also the bast fibre of lime used as string).

Rods were commonly cut at five to nine years' growth – the evidence of woodland records is vindicated by the produce itself – and had grown to about 2 inches in diameter at the butt.

Outsize timbers are still to be admired in the twelfth- and thirteenth-century timber church towers of Essex and Hertfordshire. By the fourteenth century they were rarer than at any time before or since.

Top and above: *The grandest of all medieval timber structures, the Lantern of Ely Cathedral, built c.1330. It contains timbers 42 feet long by 13½ inches square, which were hewn from trees not really big enough for the purpose, though they are not impossibly huge by modern standards. How the immense curved ribs of the timber vault were achieved is a mystery. (Both photographs: MH)*

*A charcoal-burning blast furnace at Gun's Mills, Forest of Dean. The date 1683 is cast into iron beams in the masonry. Charcoal was fed in through the timber-framed superstructure. (OR, October 1993)*

**Did Industry Destroy Woodland?**
The theory that industry destroyed woodland fails to pass a simple test. If it is true, less medieval woodland ought to survive in areas where there was industry than where there was not. Exactly the opposite is the case. The woods did not disappear from the Weald – the chief home of the iron industry – or the industrial Lake District, the Forests of Dean or Wyre, or South Wales. It was non-industrial Norfolk, the land of agricultural innovation and prosperity, that lost three-quarters of its medieval woods between 1600 and 1790.

In Scotland too, woods tended to survive where industrialists cut them down. For example, the ironworks at Lorn (Argyll), which went on until 1876, maintained some 10,000 acres of coppice.

Woods were more valuable than most other land, in terms of the regular income from underwood. In addition, timber provided capital growth, and could be sold when the owner needed money. Unlike modern forestry, woodland cost almost nothing to maintain. Expenses, chiefly in maintaining boundaries, could be passed on to the purchaser of the wood. For at least 600 years prices of trees, both timber and underwood, either remained steady or rose in real terms. The economic and social value of woods, plus the expense of destroying them, tended to preserve woodland against other land-uses from 1350 to 1850.

**Woods and Industry**
Woods attracted specialist craftsmen, and their owners often preferred to sell finished articles rather than trees. Already in the thirteenth century many estates, though having woods, bought in things like wheels, hurdles and boards.

There were also the heavy industries that made iron, glass, leather and ships. Economic historians have built an inverted pyramid of argument on the belief that woods were destroyed by felling for fuel, especially by the charcoal iron industry between 1550 and 1700. Woods felled are supposed to have ceased to be woodland, leading to a 'timber famine', high prices, restrictive legislation, industries moving further afield, and even the invention of coke as a substitute for charcoal. Finally the ironmasters, having 'used up' the woods of England, are supposed to have committed economic suicide in the flames of the woods of Scotland and Ireland.

The argument rests on the ignorant belief that timber was used for fuel and did not grow again. In reality, ironworks used mainly underwood, often from their own woods, and protected their supplies. Their fortunes were not determined by the relatively small cost of standing trees but by labour costs or by foreign competition. Ironmasters who moved into Scotland were expanding their production, not abandoning England. Coal and coke were substituted for wood because their labour costs were less.

Throughout history the bark of oak – other trees will not do – has been used for tanning leather. After 1780 there was a sudden boom in leather which followed the same course as the contemporary boom in shipping. From 1780 to 1850 the tanyards were a gigantic industry, a much bigger consumer of oak-trees than the naval dockyards and almost certainly a bigger consumer than the merchant shipyards. The supply came mainly from the historic oakwood regions – Scotland, Wales, northern England. Thousands of acres were maintained as oak underwood, in which timber production was sacrificed for a greater yield of bark.

What effects have the industries left? Most of the woods that supplied the iron industry outlived its decline. In oakwood regions, the tanbark trade took over these woods. Elsewhere, the abnormally high prices for oak bark and timber from 1820 to 1850 disrupted the balance between timber and underwood. Many landowners encouraged the growth of an unreasonable number of oaks. In the 1850s the booms in oak-bark tanning and timber shipbuilding both collapsed; the oaks were not felled in due time but went on growing bigger, spoiling the underwood by their shade.

Irish woods met with disaster. Prosperity and agricultural expansion in the eighteenth century were followed by tragic overpopulation which culminated in the famine of 1845. Almost every scrap of possible land, even islands in bogs, was grubbed out and farmed. It was rare for a wood listed in the seventeenth century to have been still there in the nineteenth. Industry, though often blamed as a destroyer of woodland, seems to have given a little protection; the rare survivals were in industrial Counties Wicklow and Kerry rather than in non-industrial Tipperary.

## Woodland in Decline

Until the early nineteenth century, woods had outlived many changes in society and economics, but had themselves changed only in detail – lengthening coppice rotations, letting timber trees grow bigger, and such natural processes as the spread of elm.

Since 1800 woodland has become linked to the boom-and-bust cycles of the modern economy. Because of the long time-scale, woods tend to perpetuate economic fashions of at least 50 years earlier. The first major change came with the high prices of oak bark and timber at the same time as the coming of the railways brought cheap coal to the countryside. The habit of mind therefore grew up of regarding woods as sources of timber rather than energy.

Next there came a short-lived boom in agriculture after 1840. Ancient woods were grubbed out more than ever before. At the same time commons and heaths, where not destroyed, often fell into neglect and became secondary woodland. The slump which followed after 1880 created yet more secondary woods without, of course, bringing back the ancient woods.

The nineteenth century brought the first large-scale attempts to apply modern forestry to existing woods. The distinction between woods and plantations began to be forgotten, and many landowners planted conifers and fashionable trees (sycamore, rhododendron, horse-chestnut) in woods. Often these failed, although the underwood, particularly on acid soils, was damaged in the attempt. It was probably replanting, followed by the death or felling of the planted trees, which replaced woodland by moorland in the South Welsh mining valleys, which up to 1900 had been one of the most wooded parts of Britain.

A great deal of timber was felled to meet the sudden demands of two World Wars. Probably more was felled in the social upheavals between the wars. It is not true, as many writers tell us, that these fellings destroyed woodland; almost all the ancient woods surviving in 1870 were still there in 1945. Ancient woods have great powers of recovery; the 1914-45 fellings did little more than catch up, for some woods, with the neglect of timber felling between 1860 and 1914.

Coppicing declined. The specialized underwood trades did not

**Shipbuilding**
A well-worn belief is that the history of woodland has been dominated by the influence of the sea. We are told that shipyards were chronically short of timber, and in their search for suitable trees destroyed the ancient forests, or (in another version) maintained the ancient woods.

As the Greeks and Dutch bear witness, it is not necessary for a nation with a proud seafaring tradition to have had much woodland. In Britain, in medieval and Elizabethan times, shipbuilding had been insignificant compared to other uses of timber. Not until about 1780 did its growth – through the growth of intercontinental trade and the arms race – begin to catch up with the supply of trees. Had there been the slightest difficulty in finding timber for the tiny fleet that defeated the Armada, it would have been utterly impossible to build the sixtyfold larger fleet that defeated Napoleon. The output of timber-built ships between 1800 and 1860 was probably equal to that in all the rest of history put together. Much shipbuilding timber, especially in large sizes and special shapes, came from hedges and parks, not woodland.

Complaints of shortage of timber come from naval dockyards, which were wasteful and penurious, rather than from commercial shipbuilders who could pay the market price. Rising prices of oaks are evidence of inflation rather than shortage. In relation to prices in general, the price of oak-trees rose only slowly during the eighteenth century. It nearly doubled during the Napoleonic Wars, but went on rising after the war ended. Much of the rise in price was in the bark, not the timber.

**Lost Woodland in Essex**
The diagram shows what has happened
to the ancient woods of north-west Essex
since 1800. About one-quarter of the
area was destroyed by nineteenth-century
agriculture, mainly between 1840 and
1870. Then came eighty years of stability,
broken only by the loss of 4 per cent of
the woodland to airfields in World War
II. From 1950 to 1973 agriculture and
forestry, in roughly equal shares, ate up
a third of the remaining ancient woods.
Only 3 per cent of the 1800 area went
to roads and housing. The larger woods
survive less often. Northwest Essex
has fared relatively well, as anyone
can see who visits Oxfordshire or
Nottinghamshire. In large woods and
well-wooded areas modern forestry
was usually more greedy.

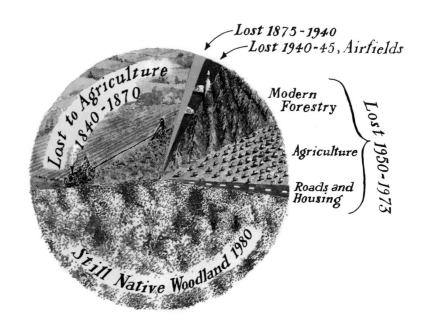

become obsolete – their heyday may have been as late as 1900 – but
suffered from disorganization and lack of capital and machinery.
Renewable fuels became forgotten in the successive fashions for coal,
atomic energy and heating oil. The timber trade adapted itself to
handling foreign imports. Paper-pulp and even charcoal were got from
overseas: we ground up other nations' wildwood while neglecting our
own woods. By 1950 it was rare for a wood still to be coppiced
outside south-east England and Essex.

There was the rise of organized gamekeeping. Gamekeepers and
their employers kept alive (as they still do) many woods that might
otherwise have been grubbed out. But they took it upon themselves
to persecute beasts and birds of prey and to exclude the public from
woods. This need not have been so. In France, Germany and
Switzerland, ancient woods are everyone's heritage; in Britain alone
have we lost that birthright, and with it the knowledge and love of
woods. A generation of people grew up who had never been in a
wood and could be persuaded that woods had merely an economic
function. People who have been rudely expelled from a limewood are
unlikely to oppose its later destruction.

The greatest threats for a thousand years came from the destructive
courses which agriculture and forestry took in Britain after 1945.
Many hundreds of woods were grubbed out to make farmland (after
the wartime need to plough every acre had disappeared), and
thousands more were wrecked by replanting.

For its first 25 years, the Forestry Commission had little direct
impact on woodland; but after 1945 foresters acquired woods and
treated them as moorland, trying to poison or otherwise destroy the
existing vegetation and to replace it by plantations, usually of conifers.
This was justified by a crude kind of cost-benefit analysis, which
gained acceptance, even among conservationists, who did not dare to
dispute 'the hard facts of economics'. It did not occur to them that

even financial calculations can be wrong.

Successful replanting destroys not only the trees of a wood but the herbaceous plants as well, which succumb to evergreen shade or are buried by heavy leaf-litter. Like other plantations, those on the sites of woods are meant to be replanted every few decades for ever; after two replantings it is unlikely that anything but the woodbanks will remain to show that there was once a wood on the spot. Not that this is as easy to achieve as was expected, as many ancient woods simply refuse to die. As much ancient woodland was destroyed in 28 years as had been in the previous 400 years.

Modern forestry was the parting gift of the British to Ireland, and the latest in the chain of disasters to Irish woods. Most of the remaining scraps of the woodland that St Patrick would have recognized have vanished under plantations.

Things are different now, partly owing to the agricultural recession, the growth of interest in woodland conservation, and the very different new attitudes of Forest Enterprise and Forest Authority and of the National Trust. The 'hard facts of economics' have been defeated by natural events. Many ancient woods have refused to die; the native trees have come back, or the planted trees may have died as well, leaving self-sown ash or birch to take over the site. The great storm of October 1987 plucked out hundreds of thousands of planted trees from ancient woods. The droughts of 1989-91 have taken their toll of others, leaving the wild trees in possession.

*A large, complex ancient wood: Hockley Woods, SE Essex. The banks range in date probably from the Iron Age to the twentieth century. The original (Anglo-Saxon?) perimeter woodbank has been much destroyed by encroachments into the wood margins. Within it are banks and ditches made when the ownership of the wood was divided among various manors and farms, some of them situated at a distance (for example, Beaches, three miles away). The subdivision was already well advanced by the twelfth century: parish boundaries have been made to conform to it. Since the end of the Middle Ages the ownerships have gradually become amalgamated again. Underlying these earthworks are faint banks which seem to indicate a different, much earlier, distribution of woodland and non-woodland. (DW/WI, October 1987)*

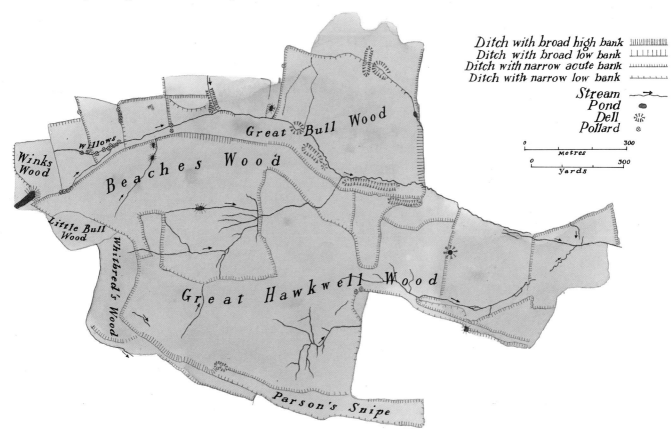

Ditch with broad high bank
Ditch with broad low bank
Ditch with narrow acute bank
Ditch with narrow low bank

Stream
Pond
Dell
Pollard

0   metres   300
0   yards   300

Above: *An East Anglian elmwood: Overhall Grove, Boxworth, Cambridgeshire. (OR, May 1991)*

Right: *An ancient ash stool, about 400 years old, in ash-maple-hazel woodland. (TM, Hayley Wood, June 1993)*

*A giant oak stool, or 'moot', typical of ancient oakwood. Merthen Wood, Constantine, Cornwall. (OR, May 1980)*

## WOODS AS THEY ARE NOW

### Woods on the Map

In England woods are individual places, like towns and villages. Even the smallest has its own name, often of Anglo-Saxon antiquity. A wood now called The Frith or Free Wood or Beare Wood is almost certain to be pre-Conquest, from Old English *fyrhþ* or *bearu*. Woods composed of particular trees have names ending in *-ett*, such as Birchet, Haslet, Oket; the only frequent name so derived is Spinney, a wood of thorns (Medieval Latin *spinetum* from *spina* 'thorn'). *Way*land, *Lound* and *Lownde* Woods are modern spellings of Old Norse names involving *lúndr*.

Wood-names referring to management include Coppice (also spelt Copse), Spring, and the northern Hag; all these mean a wood managed by coppicing. The Anglo-Saxon equivalent is *hris* 'underwood', which gives rise to names such as Royce Wood; the Norman-French word is *tailz* (Modern French *taillis* 'coppice'), now spelt Tails Wood or Taylor's Wood. Some woods are named after historic persons; Robin's Wood in eighteenth-century Hindolveston commemorated John Robynes, who 400 years earlier had leased the wood for a hurdle-making business. 'Park Wood' and 'Out Wood' are connected with a

## Kinds of Ancient Woodland

At least 75 types of ancient woodland have been recognized in Great Britain: for example the ash-maple-hazel woods in the Midlands, the hornbeam-woods around London, the native beechwoods of SE Wales, and the different kinds of Scottish Highland pinewoods. Many of these have their own histories, and still perpetuate the provinces and some of the variants of prehistoric wildwood.

Lime is well-documented; people took notice of it because it produced bast (a low-grade fibre) as well as being a tree of romance. In prehistory small-leaved lime had been the commonest tree of Lowland England. It is still the commonest of ancient woods in certain sharply-defined areas of Lowland England, such as between Lavenham (Suffolk) and Braintree (Essex). Why this should be so is a mystery, but it is known that lime has hardly changed in the last thousand years. One of the Essex limewoods was called in Old English Lindris (*linde* 'lime tree' + *hris* 'underwood'); a thousand years later, part of it is still there (Paul's Wood, Black Notley) and has great stools of lime underwood.

Left: *Ancient coppiced beechwood: a rather rare type of woodland (most beechwoods are modern) in SE Wales. (TM, Govilon, Abergavenny, July 1993)*

*Ancient limewood (note coppice stools) with anemone. (DW/WI, Great West Wood, Goltho, Lincolnshire, May 1990)*

*Scottish Highland birchwood. Although there have been birchwoods in the Scottish Highlands since wildwood times, individual woods appear to be impermanent and hardly constitute ancient woodland. (TM, Glen Tanar, Aberdeen, October 1993)*

medieval deer-park. Modern wood-names include Plantation, Cover, Jubilee Wood, and Furze (or Firs) Wood – occasionally these are re-namings of ancient woods.

Woods are not on land good for growing trees, but on land that was bad for anything else. The bad lands of the Middle Ages were not quite the same as now. Fertility mattered much more, for it could not then be brought back in a sack, but steep slopes and poor drainage were then less severe obstacles to cultivation. Ancient woods tend to be on steep slopes or on high ground, on flat hilltops and plateaux, patches of infertile sands and gravels, or specially wet clays. Woods avoid land liable to flooding by rivers, which was the most valuable land of all as meadow. Where a medieval wood adjoins a road, a clearing called a *trench* was usually made to deter highwaymen, with the woodbank set back from the road (p. 126).

Ancient woods have a sinuous or zigzag outline visible on the 1:25,000 map. Such outlines date from a period before 1700, when the landscape was set out on the ground rather than in the draughtsman's office, and when the countryman saw no purpose in straight lines. Sinuous outlines may result from having to take a boundary ditch round individual large trees. Zigzags may represent successive grubbings-out of woodland, acre by acre, until the Danes or the Black Death intervened and no more acres were taken. When a wood has been altered — enlarged or partly grubbed out — since 1700, the new edges are usually straight or regularly curved. In Ancient Countryside, the ghost of a grubbed-out wood may haunt the map as the irregularly-shaped perimeter of a 'Wood Farm' whose internal hedges are anomalously straight.

### Trees

A normal wood consists of underwood and timber trees. The latter are usually oak, whatever the underwood, but that does not make nearly every wood an oakwood. Timber trees are the most artificial part of a wood; they reflect merely the decision of past woodmen to treat oak as timber and other trees as underwood. The continuity of a wood, its connection with the natural vegetation, and its distinction from other woods reside in the underwood and herbaceous plants.

Annual rings (in felled or cored trees) are the primary evidence of what has happened in a wood within the lifetime of the present trees. This record may be extended back for about a century by stumps (and branches if left lying about) of the previous crop of timber trees. Occasionally we can cut a section through the above-ground base of a coppice stool, from which we can estimate the age of the stool itself. Previous coppicings are recorded in the stool base by cycles of suddenly narrowing rings followed by gradual recovery.

A minimum limit to the age of a wood is normally the age of its oldest trees, which will usually be the coppice stools. There are exceptions. Secondary woodland may incorporate park or hedge trees that are older than the wood; these may be recognized by their low spreading branches now hemmed in by younger trees. Pollard trees

### Ancient Stools

An ash when cut down sprouts to form a stool, which gets bigger on successive fellings. Stools do not die of old age or wear out; they are among the oldest living things in Britain, but continue to produce good crops of poles. Ancient stools of ash spread into rings which may be 18 feet across; sometimes these are on waterlogged sites, such as the Bradfield Woods, on which they grow slowly, and are at least 1,000 years old. (An ash-tree if not cut down falls to pieces in about 200 years and disappears.) Similar giant stools are produced by lime, oak, hornbeam and maple.

that are not on earthworks arouse suspicions of secondary woodland.

These features are present, though usually less well preserved, in ancient woods in Wales. In Scotland they are more elusive, but ancient stools demonstrate the existence of medieval coppicing, despite the apparently poor written evidence for it. In Ireland most of the features were once present, but have rarely survived the chain of disasters. Even the famous Killarney woods have suffered from replanting, rhododendrons and deer, which have obscured their earlier coppicing and industrial history. An apparently unique survival of a well-preserved coppice is St John's Wood by Lough Ree.

Every ancient wood is uniquely different from every other. Most contain several different types of woodland; for instance Tarecroft Wood (Rivenhall, Essex) has within 16 acres areas of seven kinds of woodland. The variation appears to be natural: the boundaries between tree communities (some of which are abrupt, while others show gradual transitions) are irregular, eschew straight lines, and disregard rides and management boundaries. The natural properties of trees, and their reactions (past and present) to soils, spring-lines and other aspects of the environment, still shape the character of woods despite the levelling-down effects of centuries of management.

## Earthworks

The visitor to an unknown wood should first walk the boundary. A typical medieval wood edge has a strong bank with an external ditch, 20 to 40 feet in total width, which follows all the sinuosities and zigzags. The profile is usually rounded but may be steeper on the outer face. There are often pollard trees halfway down the outer slope.

There are many variations. Banks change with time: the ditch may be cleaned out and the spoil dumped on top of the bank. Sheet erosion may cause several feet of the adjacent field to creep away downhill, effacing the ditch and leaving the bank at the top of a miniature cliff. In west England and Wales woodbanks are faced, and sometimes replaced, by dry-stone walls. Banks and walls are often left unfinished.

Early woodbanks are massive earthworks. New wood edges formed in later centuries can be detected by successively weaker earthworks. Where part of a wood has been destroyed, the original outline may be preserved as a ghost hedge, or be visible from the air as a soil mark in fields. Where a wood has been added to, the original woodbank is left behind in the interior. New boundaries of the nineteenth century are straight, with feeble banks and ditches bearing flimsy hawthorn hedges, like contemporary field boundaries.

Inside woods, there are features peculiar to woodland as well as others known outside woods. Many ancient woods are full of ponds and depressions (pp. 181-2). Some of the depressions are mysteriously filled up with sand to slightly above the surrounding surface level. Ponds and 'sand-lenses' are among the obstacles to cultivation which have kept places as woodland. Woods also preserve minor streams which elsewhere have been straightened and made into field ditches. Within woodland there are banks which separate two contiguous

### Natural Changes in Woodland

I have emphasized continuity, but let us not suppose that woods are unchanging. There can be little doubt that much of what is now hornbeam-wood, beechwood and chestnut-wood was originally limewood. One of the best historic chestnut-woods is Stour Wood near Harwich (belonging to the Woodland Trust), yet this still has a few surviving lime stools.

Elms, birch and ash have increased. Those kinds of elm with suckers (p. 88) tend to spread into existing woods and turn them into elmwoods. Birch had its heyday in the early post-glacial period. In later prehistory it was squeezed out by more competitive and longer-lived trees. In the last 100 years it has returned on a large scale. Birch has been helped by the fashions for growing abnormally large numbers of oaks and then felling them, and for planting conifers which often die. Both practices damage the underwood and make room for birch, which is now increasing even on clay soils on which it was once thought incapable of growing. Ash has recently increased in many woods from Shropshire to Somerset and Lincolnshire. Woods have a life of their own, and we should take warning not to guess at facile explanations of similar changes in prehistory.

## Woodland Vegetation and Coppicing

The *flora* of a wood – the plant species present – is influenced by a wood's continuity. The *vegetation* – the plant communities and their relationships to each other – is partly determined by the history of management.

Coppicing plants are gloriously unpredictable, and each wood has its own specialities. The wetter parts of Hayley and Hardwick Woods are yellow with oxlips in the second and third springs after felling. Norsey Wood (Billericay, south Essex) has one of the greatest concentrations of bluebells in the world. In the Mendip Woods there is the brilliant blue *Lithospermum purpureocaeruleum*. These plants survive the shade years in an attenuated form, but flower in abundance in the years of release. Many other plants come up from buried seed waiting since the last coppicing. In Chalkney Wood (Essex) red campion and wild raspberry are completely killed by the shade of tall lime and hornbeam, but come up in tens of thousands after each felling.

Stinging-nettle, elderberry and goosegrass are significant because they live on phosphate, and mankind is a phosphate-accumulating animal. Most ancient woods are short of phosphate (which is one reason why they are still woods), and plants will not grow in them. Phosphate plants grow where people have lived (and especially where they have died), and where they have thrown bones and the ashes of faggots. The phosphate thus accumulated lasts for centuries in non-acid soils. Little Gidding (Huntingdonshire), the famous deserted village forgotten by 1640, is still marked by an elm-grove full of ear-high nettles.

Woodland rides and the lanes around the edges of ancient woods often have a special suite of plants, such as ragged robin, devil's-bit, and the umbellifer *Pimpinella major*. The 'woodland grassland' which contains these plants may seem to be a relatively artificial component of a wood; yet the pollen record shows that such permanent glades were a feature of wildwood too.

woods or which divide a wood among several owners.

Woods may contain hillforts, barrows, territorial ditches, Roman roads, mounds of debris left by potteries, and many other prehistoric and Roman antiquities. Some of these prove that the site was not woodland at the time; others, such as the pottery debris, that there was a wood-using industry on the spot. It can rarely be proven that woodbanks are not of Roman origin, although sometimes medieval banks overlie faint earthworks which suggest a different distribution of woodland in the more remote past.

Charcoal-hearths are a feature occurring in woods with an industrial history, as in the Forest of Dean and Cornwall. They are circular platforms, some 20 feet in diameter, scooped into hillsides. On the flat floor a stack of wood was built, covered with earth, and ignited from within to smoulder into charcoal. A layer of charcoal fragments will still be found under the leaf-mould and can be used to identify what kind of wood was being charked.

Among medieval non-woodland earthworks, the ridge-and-furrow of arable cultivation (p. 79) conclusively proves that many woods in the Midlands were once smaller. Moats (pp. 176-7) have often become woodland, perhaps by the suckering of elms planted around the original house.

## Plants of Ancient Woodland

Ancient woods have distinctive floras. Small-leaved lime now grows from seed with difficulty, and until recent years has seldom been planted. It is largely confined to ancient woodland. In south Suffolk it grows, often in abundance, in about thirty woods, all of them known or suspected on other grounds to be ancient. Where woods have increased in size, lime faithfully picks out the parts of the wood inside the original woodbank.

Oxlip, *Primula elatior*, is a plant confined to a well-defined area in Cambridgeshire, Suffolk and Essex. Here it grows, usually in abundance, in nearly every wood (over a hundred) known on documentary or topographical grounds to be ancient, but very rarely in secondary woods, even those that are at least 350 years old. When an ancient wood increases in size, oxlip spreads slowly into the addition (at about four feet a year). It is very reluctant to jump across even a hundred yards of open country to colonize an isolated secondary wood.

Other plants strongly and widely associated with ancient woodland include service, woodland hawthorn (*Crataegus laevigata*) and herb paris. Dr George Peterken has listed 50 indicator species of ancient woodland in Lincolnshire, including such quite common plants as anemone, wood-sorrel and barren strawberry.

Recent woods contain plants that have no particular connection with woodland but are widespread in hedges and other habitats, such as ivy (seldom abundant in ancient woods), cow-parsley, hedge-garlic, and lords-and-ladies.

Floras are valuable evidence of woodland history but should be

used intelligently. Woodland plants can, on occasion, survive in old grassland. Evidence should be based on a suite of indicator species rather than a single one. The presence of small-leaved lime is strong evidence that a wood is ancient, and is almost conclusive if the lime forms giant stools; but lime is missing from much of the country, and its absence does not prove a wood recent. Lime indicates ancient woodland throughout its English range, but not all species do so. Spindle is a plant of ancient woodland in Lincolnshire but is only a weak indicator in Suffolk. The investigator should make a regional list of ancient woodland plants. A good beginning is to find out what plants grow in woods known to be ancient but not in hedges. Hayley Wood used to have four million oxlip plants, but there was not one in the hedges abutting on the wood, some of which were already 'antient' in the early seventeenth century. Dog's-mercury is much commoner in hedges, and is a less good indicator of ancient woodland in Suffolk than in the Midlands.

*A hornbeam wood, with bluebells. This is the commonest type of ancient woodland around London. Hornbeam is a non-distinctive tree and is much less well documented than lime. (DW/WI, Hurst Wood, Kent, May 1993)*

*Oxlip, a plant of ancient woodland and also a coppicing plant. (OR, Hayley Wood, Cambridgeshire, April 1985)*

# WOOD-PASTURE

In many parts of England we find the remains of a tradition of using the same land for trees and for grazing animals. 'Wood' and 'pasture' are self-contradictory, indeed mutually exclusive. Livestock are fond of tree leaves but cannot climb for them. Little sustenance is to be got from woodland herbs, many of which are poisonous or distasteful. Grasses that grow in shade are so attenuated as to be hardly worth eating. The more trees there are, the worse will be the pasture; the more animals there are, the less likely saplings or coppice shoots are to survive to produce a new generation of trees. Woods that are pastured are, therefore, different from those that are not, and are managed so as to separate the grazing from the regrowth of trees.

Wood-pasture, although perhaps uniquely complex in England, has been reinvented many times. In North America it was practised both by American Indians and by early European settlers. Nineteenth-century explorers in Michigan found a landscape of great oaks set in grassland; the American Indians had managed the vegetation, mainly by burning, to encourage the native game animals. This was an example of *savanna*, the grassy wood-pasture that is widespread in hot countries including Spain and Portugal.

From these examples, we can hardly doubt that Neolithic men would have practised wood-pasture as soon as they took domestic livestock into the wildwoods of northern Europe, where there was little grass. There is some definite evidence for this from small pollards incorporated into the Somerset trackways (p. 118). The wood of the trackways had been cut in summer, probably to use the leaves as hay to feed cattle, as is still done in the Alps, Greece and Nepal. In the British Isles holly was pollarded as fodder until recently.

*Ancient hornbeam, a pollard (p. 32), repeatedly cut to produce successive crops of wood. Most old pollards are hollow, and occasionally (as here) the shell of the trunk has partly rotted away, leaving two separate living parts. Decay is not a disease. The wood of an old tree divides itself into compartments. The compartments which still take part in the functioning of the tree remain sound, while superfluous ones rot and disappear. (TM, Hatfield Forest, Essex, May 1993)*

*Feeding pigs in what was probably wood-pasture – the trees seem to be meant as pollards. In medieval art, and in modern popular myth, pigs are associated with woodland. In practice woodland played only a small part in pig-keeping. (BL, Cott. Tib. BV f.7)*

*Black Berkshire sows in Burnham Beeches, Buckinghamshire. This is a splendid common with pollard beeches and oaks, grassland, heath and juniper. After a hundred years of decline, the City of London Corporation has restored traditional features including pigs and new pollards. (TM, September 1993)*

## WOODED COMMONS

Wooded commons, like other commons, belonged to the lord of the manor; but the right to use them belonged to commoners who occupied particular properties. Usually the grazing belonged to the commoners and the soil to the lord. Often timber belonged to the lord, and wood (pollards or underwood) to commoners. Anglo-Saxon charters sometimes distinguish wood-pasture commons from woodland.

By the Middle Ages common-rights already dated from time immemorial. They were administered, and could be revised, by the manorial courts, composed mainly of the commoners themselves. The number of livestock allowed to each commoner was limited.

Domesday Book often distinguishes wood-pasture from underwood; most wood-pasture was communal. By 1300 wood-pasture commons had greatly diminished. In some, grazing had got the upper hand and they had become heath or grassland. Others had been encoppiced and made into private woods.

A typical wood-pasture common was grassland or heather with more or less thickly scattered trees and bushes. The grass was grazed by livestock ranging from horses to geese. Trees were pollarded to produce repeated crops of wood (or occasionally leaves) without the animals eating the regrowth. Fuel could also come from cutting bushes. Only rarely was there coppicing, the regrowth being protected by compartmentation like that used in parks and Forests (see later).

A famous, though not very important, use of wood-pasture, and of woodland and non-woodland trees, was the pannage of pigs. Tame swine were fed in autumn on acorns (or beechmast if any) before being slaughtered and salted down. For this common-right the lord received a rent of one pig in ten. Pannage customs could be jocular: at Hatfield Broad-oak (Essex), where every pig-keeper was supposed to give the lord two swine for 'avesage':

> If he has [only] two pigs he shall give them for Avesage. And if he had [only] one pig he shall buy another identical pig and give both for Avesage. And if he has no pigs he shall give nothing for the same.

Pannage was never very practical, because the acorn crop was erratic and undependable. It is still to be seen in the New Forest.

Economists expect commons to be unsustainable because of the 'Tragedy of the Commons': the system is supposed to collapse through over-use, because each individual participant over-extends his own rights, regardless of the welfare of the whole. In practice this did not happen: manorial courts were aware of the danger and made rules to avert it. However, they did not always successfully preserve trees. If trees disappeared, the common remained a common, and trees could return if grazing diminished.

## PARKS

A park in this book means a deer-park; a piece of private land surrounded by a deer-proof fence called a *park pale*, which the owner uses for keeping deer. Parks have a lineage which reaches back beyond the Romans to the landscaped paradises of Achaemenid Persia and, some say, to the Garden of Eden itself.

If there were Roman parks in Britain (for gazelles or fallow deer) they did not outlast the Empire. Our park tradition derives from the Normans' interest in deer-farming. This began a little before Domesday Book, in which 35 parks are recorded. The key to successful deer-farming was the introduction of fallow deer (p. 24), easier to keep in a confined space than native species. Parks thereafter multiplied. In the thirteenth century, Henry III's letter files abound with 'licences to empark', accompanied (if the king was in a good mood) by gifts of live deer from the king's Forests.

Parks were very prominent. In their heyday, about 1300, there were about 3,200 parks in England, covering some 2 per cent of the country. Parks followed Domesday Book woodland. They were thickest on the ground in well-wooded areas, such as Worcestershire, Staffordshire, north-west Warwickshire, and especially Hertfordshire. There were few where woodland was scarce, as in Cambridgeshire or south-east Warwickshire. Something like one-quarter of the woodland of England was within parks; deer, biting the young shoots, would have destroyed woodland. Parks were less common in Scotland, rare in Wales, and almost absent from Ireland.

Parks were status symbols. They belonged to the whole upper class, down to the level of minor gentry, nunneries and colleges. They symbolized a higher status than a moat (p. 177) but lower than one's private gallows. Venison from parks was no ordinary meat, but reserved for feasts and the honouring of guests. It was beyond price – I have not a single record of a sale or valuation – and a haunch was a gift that money could not buy. Certain parks produced specially large timber trees.

Although parks functioned mainly as deer-farms, some at the top of the social scale had an air of romantic landscape – going back, maybe, to the wondrous park of William the Bad, Norman king of Sicily, near

**Tudor Parks**

Few medieval kings were 'passionately fond of the chase', but Tudor and Stuart monarchs were, although their standards of sportsmanship were not high.

Henry VIII, in his later years, was the greatest hunter England had seen, and had a mania for parks. He created the present St James's, Regent's, and Hyde Parks. He confiscated the parks of the headless Duke of Buckingham; he collected the parks of dissolved monasteries; he relieved Cardinal Wolsey of two parks at Hampton Court, and Cranmer of the seven great parks of the Archbishops of Canterbury. In 1539 he created the ultimate park, Hampton Court Chase, whose pale included 10,000 acres of land and four villages.

Henry made a short-lived park in Epping Forest. Here in 1543 he built the structure misnamed 'Queen Elizabeth's Hunting Lodge', the only one of his courtly timber-framed buildings to survive. It is not a hunting lodge (whatever that phrase means) but a standing or observation tower, beneath which a large and gory kill of deer would be enacted. A hunt in a park had a predictable outcome, like a Spanish bullfight.

Queen Elizabeth, the mightiest hunter of all English sovereigns, also hunted in parks, not Forests; she was in the saddle a few months before her death. This sport of kings continued down to Queen Anne, and set a fashion which bridges the gap between medieval and eighteenth-century parks.

*Henry VIII's Great Standing, alias Queen Elizabeth's Hunting Lodge, in Epping Forest. (JB, August 1983)*

**Ongar Great Park (Essex)**
This may well have been the prototype of English parks. It apparently grew out of a 'deerhay' mentioned in a pre-Conquest will, dated 1045. It survived largely intact, though disused, until about 1950. Like many early parks it was very large, about 1,200 acres, and had the typical shape of a rectangle with rounded corners – a compact shape for economy in fencing. The pale at Ongar was set on a mighty bank with a ditch each side. Another early feature is that the parish boundaries are displaced to conform to the shape of the park.

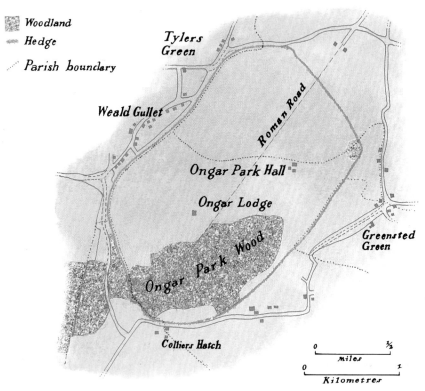

Palermo. Henry I had a palace park at Woodstock (Oxfordshire), as did Henry III at Clarendon (Wiltshire).

Parks were of two kinds. *Uncompartmented* parks were accessible to the deer at all times; the trees were pollarded to protect regrowth, and new trees arose in periods of slack grazing or in the protection of thorns or hollies. Other parks were *compartmented*. A park would be divided into coppices, each of which would be felled like an ordinary wood and then fenced to keep deer out until it had grown sufficiently not to be damaged. Some compartments might be accessible to deer all the time; these were called *launds*, and were grassland with pollard trees. There was a park lodge where the parkers did their business, set so as to command a view of whatever was not hidden by trees.

Not every park was wooded. At Egton, behind Whitby, the turf-built dike of Julian Park sweeps for more than a mile across the High Moor. In Wales the Great Park of Abergavenny included much of the Sugarloaf Mountain.

A park was a troublesome, precarious enterprise. Some owners tried to keep too many deer, which died of starvation and disease. Even in Henry III's well-run park at Havering (Essex), it was necessary to remove 'the bodies of dead beasts and swine which are rotting in the park' and to feed the survivors.

Parks declined in the later Middle Ages. A disused park might revert to being a 'Park Wood', or might become farmland. A park might be moved to another site: the modern park of North Elmham (Norfolk) is not on the site of the medieval park but of the Anglo-Saxon town.

**A Designer Park**
*Humphry Repton's Red Book showing alterations proposed for Langley Park in Kent. A folding panel gives the 'before and after' effect. Writers on landscape designers often suppose that such designs transformed vast tracts of countryside, and marvel that their patrons were content to plant trees the effect of which would not be seen in their lifetimes. In reality they made the most of the existing landscape with the minimum amount of alteration. Part of the tradition was that existing venerable trees should give an air of dignity and continuity to a gentleman's seat. Eighteenth-century designed landscapes are wonderful places for preserving ancient trees and other remains of previous landscapes.
(BAL/RIBA)*

Parks might have died out but for Henry VIII. In the 1520s he revived royal parks as romantic landscape, and introduced a new function as places for ceremonial hunts. Tudor parks could have formal avenues, Wildernesses and Groves of Diana. But it is to Henry that we owe the peculiar English tradition of the 'pseudo-medieval' park inheriting old trees from the previous landscape. Groves were made by dissecting woods; avenues were adapted out of tree-lined lanes; ancient pollards in fields could become features in the new park.

In the eighteenth century there was another revival of parks, especially at the hands of the professional landscape designers William Kent, Charles Bridgeman, Lancelot 'Capability' Brown and Humphry Repton. These masters and their patrons did not 'lay out' landscapes out of nothing. Nor did they plant trees and wait for them to grow; they wanted an 'instant park', with an appearance of respectable antiquity from the start, incorporating whatever trees were already there. Hence many a Capability Brown park, such as Heveningham (Suffolk), contains pollards already old in Brown's time; it is a delight of such places to find their surrealist shapes and improbable bulk unexpectedly amid the formal eighteenth-century plantings.

**Forest Law**

It is essential to distinguish between Forests in the legal and the physical sense. Forest Law (in wooded Forests) covered areas much wider than the wood-pastures where the deer lived. The error of confusing the legal with the physical Forest, multiplied by the confusion of Forest with woodland, is mainly responsible for the myth that medieval England was very wooded.

Deer, landowners, and commoners came under Forest courts. In popular myth these were bloodthirsty courts, cutting off limbs etc. from even minor offenders against Forest Law. In reality the courts were interested in pence, not limbs, and set the fines so as not to be a deterrent. Stealing deer attracted imprisonment or large fines, though offenders were usually given ample chance to escape or be pardoned. Damage to vegetation by 'abuse' of grazing or woodcutting was punished by fines, often no more than the value of the grazing or wood involved.

Forest Law did not stabilize the landscape. Grubbing out private woods or encroaching on commons within a legal Forest was forbidden, but in practice condoned for a small annual payment. The landscape has been rather less stable within the legal bounds of Forests than elsewhere.

## WOODED FORESTS

A Forest in this book means a Royal Forest or its private equivalent, an unfenced area where a great magnate kept deer. I re-emphasize that the word Forest does *not* imply woodland; moor and heath Forests are discussed in other chapters. Forests are a rich field of pseudo-history. People have the notions that they were woodland, belonged to the Crown, covered a third of England, were set aside for the king's personal hunting, and were stringently guarded by terrible laws.

The idea of Forests, and the word, were introduced by William the Conqueror. He was, in effect, declaring, in contrast to Anglo-Saxon kings, 'The kingdom is Ours and all that is in it; and We demonstrate Our supremacy by keeping Our deer on other people's land.' The deer were (in theory) protected by special bye-laws called *Forest Law*. For centuries 'Forest' meant a place of deer rather than of trees.

The Forest system took 150 years to develop in England. The word is first mentioned in Domesday Book, which records about 25 Forests. Afforestment was continued by Henry I (1100-35), who may well have introduced fallow deer; his Forests included Epping and Sherwood. Multiplying the Forests was curtailed by Magna Carta in 1216.

No record survives of declaring a Forest. As with a modern National Park, it would have been necessary to define the boundaries – in effect, to put up notices saying 'This is a Forest' – and to set up a bureaucracy of justiciars, verderers, riding-Foresters, foot-Foresters, etc. The one practical matter would normally have been introducing deer. In 1238 Henry III ordered 120 live fallow to be caged, carted and shipped to Flanders, presumably to start a Forest there.

By 1200 there were about 150 Forests in England. A Forest was the supreme status symbol of kings, earls, and a few princes of the Church. The king had at least twice as many as all his subjects put together. (The word *Chase* is sometimes, though inconsistently, used to distinguish the Forest of a subject.)

Forests were most numerous not in the most wooded areas, but in moderately-wooded counties such as Wiltshire, Somerset, and Shropshire. About half the Forests contained more woodland than the country at large. The sites of Forests were decided not by the terrain but by where the king had lands or palaces. Forests were concentrated in central southern England, where two-thirds of the king's palaces were.

In Wales and Scotland Forests developed independently; they were more numerous but less well-defined than in England, and more often moorland than woodland. Any Welsh marcher lord or petty Scots baron claimed to be as good as the English king by declaring the local mountain to be a Forest.

The king owned the deer in his Forests. In some, such as the Forest of Dean, he also owned the land and trees if any; in others, such as Epping, somebody else was the landowner. Whoever was landowner, physical Forests were also commons and had pre-existing common-rights. The parties in a Forest comprised: the king or other owner of the rights to keep deer, to appoint Forest officials, to hold Forest courts and to pocket the fines; the landowners; the commoners having rights to pasture or woodcutting; and hereditary Forest officials.

Deer in wooded Forests were usually fallow, with small numbers of red and roe. The wild swine, while he lasted, was an honorary deer. These animals were treated with respect, and an inquest was supposed to be held whenever one was found dead. But Forests were not hunting preserves. The ordinary working king had no time to visit 80 Forests, and records of royal hunts are very few. (Scots kings apparently hunted more.)

The king owned trees on about half his Forests. He took timber from Forests for works on castles and palaces, and gave trees to his subjects. For instance:

1243. Order to the constable of St Briavel's that he should let the Friars Preachers of Gloucester have 15 oaks for timber in ... the Forest of Dene ... for the fabric of their church and the construction of their buildings, where they can most conveniently and closely be taken ... in the aforesaid Forest.

Many orders were for small numbers of very big trees. I have measured the very timbers which the Black Friars of Gloucester made from the oaks which Henry III gave them: the trees were about 2 feet 3 inches in diameter at the middle and 50 feet in usable length.

When the king had underwood in a Forest he most often sold it, excluding the timber. Newly-felled areas were ordered to be fenced to protect the regrowth, wherever local custom allowed the king to do this. Some Forests, such as Hatfield (Walk III, pp. 106-111), were divided into compartments corresponding to the coppices and launds of parks.

The produce of the Forests to the king – less than a thousand deer a year, a few hundred big oaks, and some thousands of acres of underwood – was not an intensive use of at least half a million acres of physical Forest. It was not the Crown but commoners and landowners, who preserved few records, who did most of the grazing and woodcutting.

Forests were of more than merely economic value. Medieval kings were poor; their authority depended on making gifts that money could not buy, such as deer and giant oaks. The Forest hierarchy enabled the king to reward faithful service with honorific sinecures. Was not Chaucer honoured by being made under-Forester of an obscure Somerset Forest?

After 1300, the Crown's interests gradually declined, leaving the Forests to landowners and commoners. The destruction of wooded Forests was usually the result, not of neglect, gradual encroachment, or the Tragedy of the Commons, but of outside intervention, such as Charles I's attempts to privatize the Forests.

From the seventeenth century the remaining Crown-owned Forests were encroached upon by plantations, intended to save the Navy Board the future expense of buying oak for shipbuilding. The early

**Henry III and the Forests**
A record of the king's use of the Forests is in the papers of Henry III. He probably never hunted himself. His deer were caught by professionals:

4 Sept. 1251. Order to William Luvel and Henry de Candour, the king's huntsmen, that when they have taken 60 bucks in the king's Forest of Dean, as the king ordered, they should go to the king's New Forest and take another 60 bucks there ... to be salted and transported to London for the forthcoming feast of St Edward [13 October].

The king bestowed deer on favoured subjects at their weddings, graduations, consecrations, pregnancies, and so on; and he ate them at feasts. Some of the King's venison came from far away, as with these orders for Christmas 1251:

25 November. Order to G. de Langeley, justiciar of the Forest, that he shall cause 150 hinds to be taken in the king's Forest of Englewod [Inglewood near Carlisle] for the king's use against the imminent feast of Christmas, and ... shall deliver them to the king's sheriff of Cumberland to be transported to York.

12 December. Order to the sheriff of Noting[ham] that he shall receive ... all the [wild] boars and sows, which the constable of St Briavel shall deliver to him by the king's order, and shall cause them to be transported to York against the imminent feast of Christmas, so that they shall be there at latest on the eve ... And when the king knows the cost, he will cause it to be repaid. [The king had ordered 200 wild swine from the Forest of Dean, 170 miles from York via Nottingham.]

22 December. Order to Picot de Lascelles that he shall come to the king's help with his hounds and nets to take roedeer in the king's Forest of Langwast [ a very long day's ride northwest of York] against the imminent feast of Christmas ...

For this dinner Henry III had 430 red deer, 200 fallow deer, 200 roedeer, 200 wild swine, 1,300 hares, 450 rabbits, 2,100 partridges, 290 pheasants, 395 swans, 115 cranes, 400 tame pigs, 70 pork brawns, 7,000 hens, 120 peafowl, 80 salmon, and unnumbered lampreys.

plantations were failures (the Navy of Nelson's time got more timber from Forests where it had grown naturally), but were made the precedent for later plantations, which ate up nearly half the New Forest and nearly all of Dean.

Forests were hard hit by Enclosure Acts, which empowered landowners to do what they pleased and banished the king's harts and the commoners' geese. Writers of the Enlightenment denounced Forests as the 'nest and conservatory of sloth, idleness and misery'. Enfield Chase (Middlesex), Windsor Forest, and Wychwood Forest (Oxfordshire) successively passed to private owners who, with rare exceptions, instantly destroyed them – often to little purpose, for the land was mostly bad. The destruction of Hainault Forest, by specially invented machines, after 1851 was a public scandal; the modern conservation movement began with efforts to avert a similar fate for Epping Forest.

## WOOD-PASTURES AS THEY ARE NOW

Ancient wood-pastures are favourite places of public resort – Burnham Beeches, Sutton Coldfield Park, Epping Forest – and it is a tragedy that our enlightened predecessors destroyed so many. They can withstand quite severe public use, but their fabric has often deteriorated through disuse. Many park and common authorities now appreciate that cattle and sheep are a normal part of the scene, and are beginning to rediscover the virtues of woodcutting.

The plant life of commons, parks and Forests, and of woodland exposed to browsing, differs from that of ordinary woodland. Cattle, sheep, goats and deer are not indiscriminate destroyers: they have likes and dislikes. They select more effectively than woodmen.

Hayley Wood has been inhabited in recent decades by fallow deer. They devour the regrowth of any coppiced area that is not fenced. Ash, elm and hawthorn, their favourite trees, are easily eliminated; aspen, which tastes horrid, is at the bottom of the menu and survives. In the uncoppiced wood they produce a characteristic *browse-line* by eating the leaves of trees and bushes up to a sharply-defined height; the passer-by, stooping to below the height of a deer's head, can suddenly see a long way through the undergrowth (Walk I, pp. 98-101). The trees would now be very different had Hayley Wood always been exposed to deer.

In general, ash, elm and hazel, palatable trees, are uncommon in wood-pastures unless efficiently compartmented. Oak is an ideal wood-pasture tree: it is a good colonizer of gaps, and takes advantage of temporary lulls in grazing. Beech, hornbeam and aspen do relatively well when exposed to browsing, either because they are left uneaten, or because they recover.

Many wood-pastures had more tree species in the past. Place-names such as *Lyndhurst* attest the former presence of lime in the New Forest, as do *La Tillaie* and *Les Tilles* in the Forêt de Fontainebleau near Paris. Pollen analysis shows that Epping Forest was preceded by a wood largely of lime; not a single tree now survives. Lime, though difficult to kill in any other way, is evidently very sensitive to grazing. In the Avon Gorge, near Bristol, lime is still common in the coppice of Leigh Woods, but in former wood-pasture (Nightingale Valley) it is relegated to inaccessible places on cliffs. Herbaceous plants are even more exposed to grazing. In Hayley Wood fallow deer are very fond of leaves and flowers of oxlip. A large part of the wood is now fenced to protect this rare plant. In Wales and the New Forest sheep, cattle or horse grazing reduces the woodland flora to a monotony of grass and bracken. Ancient woods in the upper valleys of South Wales, now accessible to sheep, are largely restricted to oak and beech. Within and near the woods are cliffs from whose crevices spring many more trees and other plants: for instance, wych-elm, lime, holly and ivy.

## Commons

Wood-pasture commons have a distinctive straggling outline, funnelling out where they are crossed by roads. There are no woodbanks around the perimeter. Lining the margin are boundary houses facing the common pasture and backing on to their private fields.

Pollard trees, not on boundaries but scattered in the interior, distinguish wood-pasture commons from woods (and from commons that have only recently become wooded). An example is Felbrigg Beeches, Norfolk, the remains of Aylmerton Common, preserved for 280 years within a park.

## Parks

The original function of parks still exists; indeed there is a revived fashion for deer-farming. Ancient parks most often survive as

An active wood-pasture common: Binswood, near Selborne, Hampshire. (BG/NI, May 1981)

What sheep have done to an ordinary wood in Wales. This was an oakwood, not a wood-pasture, with coppice stools. The boundary has not been maintained, and sheep have turned it into trees plus grass. (DW/WI, August 1986, Tregowen, Dyfed)

*Starting new pollards in Hatfield Forest, Essex. Maples and ashes, grown up in the protection of thorn scrub, have been pollarded for the first time. This is the last stage in the National Trust's programme of rehabilitating the wood-pasture. (TM, May 1993)*

fragments or place-names ('Old Park', 'Lodge Farm', 'Park Lane', 'Templars' Park') or as the ghost of the outline, subdivided by later field boundaries. If the park is eleventh or twelfth century, the parish boundaries may follow the pale. The perimeter is often marked by a bank with an internal ditch. Actual oaken pales can occasionally still be seen. If a park still has woodland it may have internal woodbanks marking the compartments.

Sometimes a park still has its original trees. Staverton Park (near Woodbridge, Suffolk) is an awesome place of Tolkienesque wonder and beauty. Mighty oaks of unknown age rise out of a sea of bracken, or are mysteriously surrounded by rings of yet mightier hollies. Overshadowed giants moulder half-fallen against other giants. Trees are rooted high in other trees. Staverton was one of the second generation of English parks, created *c.*1200, perhaps out of an existing wood. In 1528 it had its moment of glory when the monks of Butley Priory took the Queen of France 'on a picnic under the oaks with fun and games (*joco et ludo*)'. It has about 4,000 pollard oaks. Much of the 'wildwood' atmosphere results from the trees having fought each

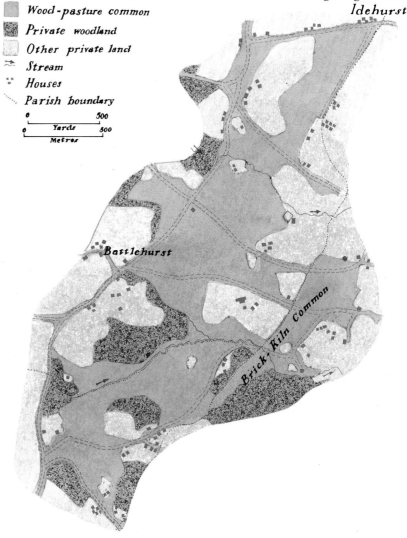

*The Mens, Kirdford, Sussex. A typical wood-pasture common, with a straggling concave outline, crossed by roads, with enclaves of private land and private woodland in the interior: the shape of a piece of land which it is no one person's duty to fence. This may be one of the earliest recorded wood-pastures, the communis silva pascualis attached to Felpham in a charter dated 953. The name Mens means 'common'. It now belongs to Sussex Wildlife Trust.*

*Ancient pollard beeches in Epping Forest. These great trees, though majestic and distinctive, are a symptom of the decline of the Forest since the City of London Corporation terminated the woodcutting rights in 1878. The pollard beeches are overgrown and cast a shade in which nothing will grow. Primroses and polypody ferns have disappeared, crabtree and service are rare, and even hornbeams and oaks have declined; only holly and beech have prospered. The roadside trenches and most of the heathery plains are overgrown, and heather is reduced to a fraction of an acre. (DW/NHPA, 1985)*

other since woodcutting ceased in *c.*1800. (Staverton is private.)

Other parks with ancient trees include the royal park of Henry II at Woodstock, near Oxford, hidden within the vast eighteenth-century park of Blenheim Palace. Sutton Coldfield Park, near Birmingham, is a giant medieval park of the compartmented type, divided into coppices (the Seven Hays) and launds.

Parks with ancient trees are just as likely to be pseudo-medieval, but these are no less important. They give us a window on the ordinary countryside of the seventeenth or sixteenth century. The grandest of all is magnificent Grimsthorpe (Lincolnshire), a designed landscape of the seventeenth century with many older features, perhaps the third largest park there has ever been, and still intact.

### Forests

Wooded Forests cannot easily be preserved in a fragmentary state: even if they are not ruined by planting, the balance of land uses is difficult to maintain on a fraction of the area. On paper, a large fragment of Wychwood Forest (Oxfordshire) survives, but most of its

*Birkland in Sherwood Forest. Sherwood was a vast heath with scattered groves (p. 140), the most famous of which, called Birkland, is now Sherwood Forest County Park. It is a grove of unique and mysterious glamour, owing to its hundreds of tall ancient oaks, all dead at the top long ago. Some, like this one, are completely dead. A huge dead tree is still beautiful, and as good a habitat as a living tree. (DW/WI, October 1992)*

historic features have gone under plantations and sycamore invasion.

Epping Forest preserves a semblance of its appearance in Plantagenet times. Its area and balance were remarkably stable from the twelfth to the eighteenth century. It still has a straggling 'common-shaped' outline surrounded by boundary houses. It was uncompartmented, full of pollard beeches, oaks and hornbeams, with several hundred acres of heath and grassland. It had beech on the upper slopes, hornbeam on the lower ground, and oak between; there were hollies, crabtrees and services. The king had the deer and the fines; the commoners had the grazing and cut pollards; the many landowners had the rest of the woodcutting and any timber.

In the nineteenth century the landowners tried to privatize the Forest, a usurpation resisted by the commoners and those who valued Epping as an open space. In 1878 the landowning rights were transferred to the City of London Corporation by the Epping Forest Act. The Forest was then a complex, balanced system, every acre the product of centuries of peculiar land-uses, a thing of distinction and beauty. The Act required the Conservators of the Forest to 'protect the timber and other trees, pollards, shrubs, underwood, heather, gorse, turf, and herbage growing on the Forest'. Had it been read, all would have been well; but the early Conservators failed to appreciate what made Epping a special Forest. They took a dislike to pollarding, hornbeams and bogs, and failed to prevent trees from overrunning the heather and gorse. They thought they were promoting the 'natural aspect of the Forest', now known to be an illusion, for its natural aspect was a limewood which cannot be recreated. The present Conservators are doing their best to recover the Forest's traditional character, but they have a hard task before them.

### Ancient Trees

Ancient trees, though uncommon, are a speciality of England, especially in wood-pasture. Oaks, limes and other trees live to at least three times the age, about 150 years, at which they are customarily felled as being 'mature'. If pollarded they live longer still, as do ashes, beeches, and other ordinarily less long-lived trees. Europe is a continent of youngish trees, like a human population with compulsory euthanasia at age thirty; one can go from Boulogne to Athens without seeing a tree more than 200 years old. A landscape entirely without old trees lacks two-thirds of the beauty and meaning of trees.

At least since Shakespeare, the English have loved the beauty and mystery of ancient trees. We have written books in their honour; have painted their portraits (p. 25); have invested them with railings and plaques; and have preserved them to give dignity to new parks.

Ancient wood-pasture trees are now better appreciated as a habitat. Old trees, especially pollards, are the home of special plants and animals: hole-nesting birds; bats roosting in their hollow interiors; mistletoe on pollard hawthorns and maples (Walk III, pp. 106-11); peculiar lichens of old dry bark and overhangs; and a host of beetles, spiders, and other invertebrates. Much of the well-known value of oak as a home for wildlife depends on *old* oaks.

Every landscape of old trees has its own *genius loci*. In Birkland, the last remaining wooded part of Sherwood Forest, there are several hundred late-medieval oaks. Their curved and sharp-pointed dead limbs ('his high top bald with drie antiquitie', as Shakespeare put it) form a glamorous, bizarre skyline, typical of this area at least since the eighteenth century. Different are the spreading gnarled pollards of Windsor Forest, the subject of early photographs and royal portraits. Different again are the 'grey, gnarled, low-browed, knock-kneed, bowed, bent, huge, strange, long-armed, deformed, hunchbacked, misshapen oak men' of Moccas Park, Herefordshire (as Francis Kilvert called them in 1876). All these places are famous for insects or lichens or both. In the New Forest, although the old oaks and beeches are seldom of exceptional size, their relative freedom from acid rain makes the Forest the supreme place in Europe for the special lichens of old trees.

England has been given the special duty of preserving old trees. Natural death is seldom the most urgent threat: many have changed little for at least a hundred years. Sometimes they need protection from being overtopped and shaded by younger trees. More often they are threatened by misunderstanding: people regard trees anthropomorphically as 'senile' or 'dying of old age', as if they had a definite lifespan, and do not realize that hollow trunks and dead boughs are a normal part of a tree's development. Ten thousand oaks of 100 years old are not a substitute for one 500-year-old oak.

*The Tea-party Oak, a wonderful pollard, probably about 700 years old, in Ickworth Park, Suffolk (National Trust). Ickworth is a classic pseudo-medieval park. Mighty pollard oaks and other trees give it the air of a Plantagenet deer-park, contrasting with the popular belief that it was 'landscaped by Capability Brown'. But it contains a parish church, which no genuine deer-park ever did, and the great trees stand on faint earthworks and around the platforms of vanished cottages. A survey in 1665 shows no park but hamlets and greens, hedged fields (hence the faint earthworks), groves, and a small open-field – all were swallowed up when the park was made in 1701. Subsequently it was worked on by Brown. The researches of John Phibbs show that the park contains many trees planted both before and after his time. (TM, August 1993)*

# BOUNDARIES AND FIELDS

The story of fields is largely the story of the hedges, fences and walls between them: in Welsh, the word *cae* does duty for both 'hedge' and 'field'. It is possible to have continuous arable land without divisions – there are examples no farther off than Calais – but in Britain and Ireland fixed demarcations are normal.

Hedges, walls and fences have many uses. They confine livestock so that someone does not have to be with them all the time. Hedges are also landmarks to define property boundaries and rights-of-way, a source of wood and sometimes timber, a shelter, an addition to the grazing land, and a source of herbs and fruit. Doubtless they had other functions now forgotten. For the first purpose there has to be a complete circuit; for the others, isolated lengths of hedge will do.

Fields are subject to fashion. Each successive age has updated some of its predecessors' fields, has left others as it found them, and has made new fields where there were not fields before. Just as we have examples, still lived in, of fashions in houses since the Norman Conquest, so there are examples in use of nearly all field-systems since the Bronze Age. As aerial photographs demonstrate, prehistoric fields that still form part of the above-ground landscape are only a small fraction of those that have existed.

Hedges are not specially British: they occur as far away as Peru. All over Europe there is a distinction between lands of hedged fields and lands of open-fields, corresponding to the Ancient Countryside and Planned Countryside of England.

Above: *Various types of rudimentary fence existed in past centuries and can still be seen in other countries.*
Right: *The dry-stone waller's craft is not static. Here is an ingenious modern design making provision for posts and wire. (DC, Grasmere, Westmorland)*

## What Is a Hedge?

Hedges are of many kinds. In Cornwall, a hedge is an earth or stone bank, which may be – but often is not – topped with bushes or trees. In Michigan, a 'fence-row' consists of biggish trees closely set on a low bank of loose stones. Neither of these needs to be kept in being by regular cutting or plashing ('laying') as does the classic English Midland hedge. In sixteenth-century south Essex, a 'hedgerowe' could be a narrow wood.

A hedge is sometimes an artefact, created by someone deliberately planting it. Hedges can also arise naturally, through someone not grubbing out the tree saplings that spring up at the base of a fence or wall and eventually replace it. This was more common in the Middle Ages than in the more tidy-minded modern centuries, but there is a new example at Hayley Wood (p. 100). The United States now has more miles of hedge than Great Britain, despite having no tradition of planting hedges. 'Fence-rows' have been arising by default over the last 250 years in Massachusetts, and over the last 25 years on what used to be the open prairies of Texas. Any hedge develops a life of its own and is colonized by trees, shrubs and herbs which were not there at first.

Hedges also arise as the 'ghosts' of woods that have been grubbed out leaving their edges as field boundaries. The marginal trees, often already forming a hedge to protect the wood's interior, may be left as a hedge. This differs from other hedges, even ancient ones, in having woodland plants (such as small-leaved lime and wood anemone) as well as hedgerow species.

## Prehistoric Fields, Hedges and Walls

In the Land's End Peninsula in Cornwall, there is one of Europe's most impressively ancient farmland landscapes. The Peninsula is a moorland-covered granite dome surrounded by a belt of farmland. The farmland is of tiny irregular pastures separated by great banks, each formed of a row of huge granite boulders topped off level with lesser

### Hedge Management

One extreme of hedge management is to do nothing and allow the hedge to grow into a row of trees, as is usual in the United States. The other extreme is to give the hedge a hurried mechanical trim every year, as is regrettably usual in England. In some areas, such as Essex, there is a long tradition of coppicing hedges as if they were woods.

Plashing hedges (which books call 'hedge-laying') is the practice of not quite severing the stems, bending them over, and securing them in various styles with stakes and ethers (thin interwoven rods). They send up new vertical shoots to make an impenetrable barrier. The process needs to be repeated about every twenty years, otherwise the result will look like the right-hand picture on p. 83.

This craft is widespread, especially in Wales and the English Midlands, but not universal. On the Continent it goes back to Roman times. Here it is being practised on a difficult, irregular, ancient hedge in Oxfordshire. *(GG/NHPA)*

*An Iron Age hamlet, Chysauster, Land's End Peninsula. Around it are small 'Celtic' fields, partly destroyed by modern agriculture. (SBP, June 1993)*

boulders and earth. The banks zigzag and deviate in order to incorporate immovably large boulders or small outcrops. Banks now disused wander down on to the sea-cliffs or up on to the moor. The area is full of prehistoric settlements ('British Villages'), and others may lie unrecognized under the present, medieval, hamlets. Deep lanes meander between the banks and cross streams by clapper-bridges. Within the thickness of one mighty wall is hidden an Iron Age *fogou*, a row of half-underground chambers lit by 'architectural rabbit-holes' among the grass.

Here the whole system is of a piece. The banks, from their construction, are contemporary with the fields. Once formed, they are difficult to alter and cannot be added to. They can be roughly dated by the Bronze Age objects that were buried in the banks. They are among the world's oldest artefacts still in use.

There may be many other prehistoric walls and hedges still extant, but it is not usually so clear that the present field boundaries are the original ones. Land's End fields are irregular, their shapes determined mostly by the practical considerations of getting rid of boulders.

Elsewhere, prehistoric fields express a curious geometrical theory. There is an unmistakably planned pattern of parallel, but not straight, main axes running across country for miles, intersected by cross-walls at irregular intervals. The most famous example are the Dartmoor reaves, low stony banks which represent Bronze Age field boundaries.

### Celtic Fields

Throughout the long history of reaves, 'Celtic Fields' were also being made. This is the traditional name for the small, squarish, irregular or semi-regular fields whose remains, until recently, covered thousands of square miles on chalk downland, moorland, and other terrain that escaped medieval cultivation. They may be surrounded by great banks, the product of immense labour. They can be of any date from Neolithic to Iron Age. The square shape expresses the custom of ploughing in two directions at right angles. Some Celtic fields seem to be fitted into what had originally been reave systems.

### Lynchets

On slopes the action of the plough moves earth downhill, and piles it against the lower field boundary to form a terrace called a *lynchet*. The steeper Celtic Fields tend to be narrow, following the contours to form the flights of terraces marked as 'Strip Lynchets' on maps. Lynchets, positive or negative, can occur against any ancient cross-slope ploughing boundary, including roads and woodbanks; they are not necessarily prehistoric.

*A different type of reave system on Dartmoor from that shown on the opposite page, with lane and hut-circles. Shown in infra-red false-colour. (RCHME, April 1980)*

Lowland examples less often survive; but in 'The Saints', in north-east Suffolk, an area of about 25 square miles is (or was) divided into little fields by cross-hedges between bundles of parallel, not quite straight, main axes. A Roman road and medieval greens and meadows intrude into the semi-regularity.

Reaves tell a story of country planning on a gigantic scale – of an organization able to parcel out tens of square miles as it pleased, whose writ ran in the heights of Dartmoor, and which set its rules of geometry above the practicalities of dealing with gorges and bogs. England has known nothing like this in the last 1,500 years. For a modern parallel we have to go to the land-allotments of Minnesota or Michigan.

This mysterious philosophy of field layout had a life of some 3,000 years. The Céide Fields in County Mayo, Ireland, are a reave-like field system of Neolithic date, preserved under blanket peat. Another planned grid of fields and roads, probably Iron Age, covers about one-quarter of Essex, where it is wholly at variance with the chaotic landownership of historic times.

### Anglo-Saxon Hedges

Old English charters have much to say about hedges. The numerous words for a hedge include compounds like 'hazel-row' and 'thorn-row', which make it clear that a hedge, not a fence, is meant. The earliest written evidence for a hedge is perhaps the 'old hedge' at North Wootton (Somerset) in 816. The earliest record of anyone planting a hedge is 'the hedge row that Ælfric made' at Kington Langley (Wiltshire) in 940. Field-walls, in contrast, are seldom mentioned in what were later to become stone-wall regions.

The charters give the impression of a land already fully hedged, but closer inspection shows that hedges are much more often mentioned in wooded areas (such as most of Worcestershire, northwest Dorset, south Berkshire) than in unwooded areas (such as southeast Worcestershire or the Dorset or Berkshire chalklands). Hedges were not, as a rationalizer might expect, a substitute for woodland. The distribution of hedged and hedgeless areas corresponds roughly to the distinction between Ancient and Planned Countryside today. It looks as if open-field strip-cultivation had already been introduced into some of the areas where it was prevalent in the Middle Ages.

### Open-Field

Quite different from all that had gone before was the practice of strip-cultivation. In its purest form this had seven cardinal features:

**1.** The arable land of a township was divided into a multitude of strips, the strips of each farmer being distributed either regularly or at random around the township.

**2.** The strips were aggregated into furlongs and these into fields. The same crop was grown by all the farmers on each furlong. Each field was left fallow – ploughed but not sown – every second, third, or fourth year.

**3.** The animals of the participants were left free to graze the stubble

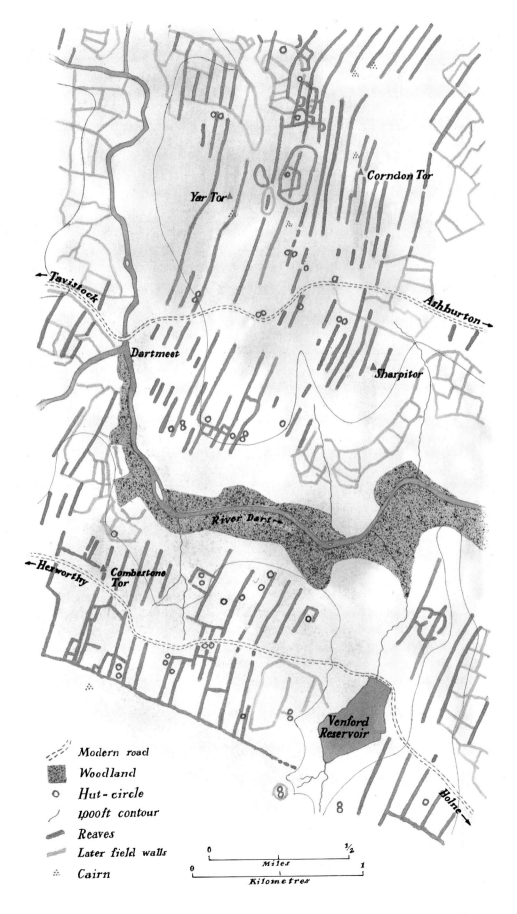

The following labels appear on the map:

Corndon Tor

Yar Tor

←Tavistock

Dartmeet

Ashburton→

Sharpitor

River Dart

←Hexworthy

Combestone Tor

Venford Reservoir

Holne→

Modern road

Woodland

Hut-circle

1,000ft contour

Reaves

Later field walls

Cairn

0      ½

Miles

0      1

Kilometres

**The Reaves of Dartmoor**
This map shows a small part of the Bronze Age reaves of Dartmoor. Prehistoric earthworks and associated cairns and hut-circles are shown in dark lines; pale lines indicate later (presumed medieval) field walls. The main reaves have a general though wobbly sense of direction; the wobbles are not accidental, for they are accurately repeated in all the reaves of a parallel bundle. The reaves jump the great ravine of the River Dart (ending a little above the present edge of the woodland), reappear on the same alignment on the other side, and then are suddenly terminated. Archaeological associations show that reaves were in use in the Bronze Age as the boundaries of arable and pasture fields.

Reaves are best seen by looking north from Combestone Tor on the Holne–Hexworthy road.

*(Redrawn after the original map by E. Gawne and J.V.S. Cox)*

## Roman Fields and Hedges

In Europe and North Africa the Romans indulged in *centuriation*, the planning of land in exact squares of 775 modern yards, oriented exactly north and south (or at 45 degrees to a north-south line), marching on and on heedless of cliffs, rivers or fens. There is no certain example of this in Britain, though Mr Alexander Wheaten has shown me possible Roman field-planning in the woods around Canterbury. Centuriation usually went with founding a colony on vacant land. In Britain, the only big opportunity would have been in the Fens, which instead have the remains of unplanned 'Celtic Fields'. Elsewhere country planning seems to have continued the regular, but not rigid, field grids of the Iron Age.

Archaeologists can recognize field-walls or ditches, but cannot normally tell whether hedges existed. Hedges had a long tradition in Italy: Roman writers knew of several types of hedge, and described sophisticated methods of making a hedge. Julius Caesar encountered a plashed hedge, which he regarded as a deliberately constructed military obstacle, in what is now Belgium.

The earliest physical remains of a hedge in Britain were found in an unlikely place, buried beneath the Roman fort at Bar Hill near Glasgow.

## Anglo-Saxon Strip-Cultivation

The Anglo-Saxons had some open-field cultivation. Old English charters imply its existence or use its technical terms – headland, gore, baulk, etc. This evidence is not from all over England, but is concentrated in areas with few hedges, which later were strongholds of strip-cultivation. There is also archaeological testimony; for example, where ridge-and-furrow is intersected by twelfth-century coal-mines or thirteenth-century moats.

On present evidence, open-field cultivation was invented by the Anglo-Saxons in about the eighth century, possibly in Berkshire or Wiltshire. It spread throughout middle and north-east England and into Scotland. It was taken up by the Welsh, Scottish Highlanders, and Irish. It was exported to the Anglo-Saxon homeland in Germany and all over Europe; and ultimately – but only just – to America.

and weeds of all the strips in common, after every harvest and in the fallow year. (This economized on pasture and conserved fertility.)

**4.** The system was collective; farmers shared some of the labours of cultivating one another's strips.

**5.** Hedges were few and did not form enclosed circuits.

**6.** Strips were ploughed in such a way as to form ridge-and-furrow.

**7.** Regular meetings were held at which the participants agreed on cultivation practices and regulations, and fined dissidents.

Strip-cultivation used to be thought of as a primitive method of subdividing land, superseded by hedged fields. It occurs over most of Europe – at least one-quarter of Germany is covered with strips today. But it is not primitive: it has never been found anywhere in the Roman Empire or before. Nor is it universal: in England it was characteristic of the Midlands (the later Planned Countryside) and north-east, extending into middle Scotland. The rest of the country always had hedged, fenced or walled fields with small-scale pockets of open-field cultivation, including Welsh and Gaelic forms of the practice.

Open-field cultivation seems to us of rococo complexity. In late-medieval Cambridge the arable land in the town's West Fields was divided into about 3,350 *selions*, each nominally half an acre in extent and measuring one furlong by two perches (220 yards long by 11 yards wide). The selions were grouped into 68 furlongs and these into four vast fields which extended away to the town boundary, where they adjoined similar fields in Girton and Coton. Each year an approximate third of the land – one field or the two smaller fields – lay fallow, and the remainder was sown.

Colleges and other landowners had lands scattered in strips through the West Fields. A strip might be one selion, or two or three, or occasionally a block of up to forty selions. One-tenth of the crop was due as tithe to the ecclesiastical tithe-owner of each particular selion. Few owners tilled their strips themselves. Between landowners and the land there intervened a largely unrecorded world of agents, tenants and subtenants. We know little of how selions were grouped by those who actually cultivated them.

Open-field cultivation has left a mark on the landscape in the form of *ridge-and-furrow*: wave-like undulations, typically every 11 yards, in what is now pasture but was once ploughland. Many square miles still exist (though much diminished by modern agriculture) between Oxford and Edinburgh.

The introduction of open-field cultivation was one of the most drastic, though incomplete, reorganizations that this country has seen. It took time. Down to the thirteenth century, documents record open-field in a not fully developed state. In Cambridge it was completed about 1300, and then remained almost unchanged for 500 years. (Cambridge West Fields had, of course, been reorganized out of previous fields. Traces of an Iron Age rectangular planned field system were preserved in the major baulks (see opposite), and are seen today in the rectangular grid of roads which are successors to the baulks.)

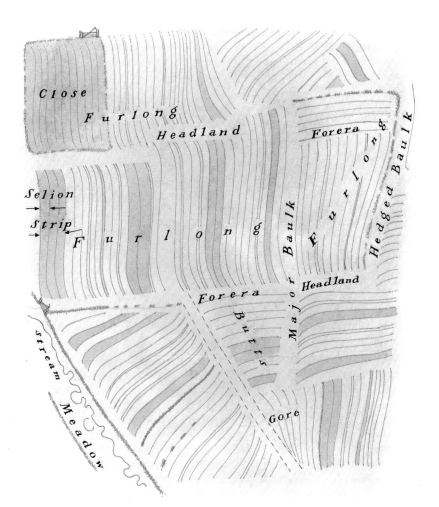

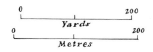

In its heyday, about 1350, open-field cultivation covered nearly one-third of England. From then on, people began to aggregate strips into single ownerships and to privatize them. However, open-field cultivation was far from a dead institution. As late as the seventeenth century, a new open-field system was created in Sudbury (Massachusetts), even though Sudbury (Suffolk) no longer had open-fields.

By 1720 about half the open-field areas, especially in the north, had been privatized by agreement. The remainder – one-seventh of England – was abolished over the next 140 years by a series of Enclosure Acts. Commissioners reorganized each township, replacing the strips (and most of the roads and commons) by a grid of large, straight-edged fields. A few places escaped: the famous open-field parish of Laxton (Nottinghamshire) which is still in working order, and others at Haxey (Lincolnshire), Soham (Cambridgeshire) and Portland (Dorset). So did some of the embryonic open-field systems in Ancient Countryside; for example, at Braunton (Devon). Almost within my lifetime, the Gaels of the remote island of St Kilda reallocated their meagre ridges every year.

Why was open-field made? It came too late to be an inherent consequence of human nature. Scholars have guessed that small farmers combined to contribute oxen to a communal plough-team and

*A hedged landscape overlying ridge-and-furrow. Some of the hedges conform to the ridgework, following the 'reversed-S' curve; these may or may not have existed while it was in use. Others cut across the ridges and are certainly later. Note the headland ridge with an icy pool alongside (left of centre). (SBP, Cleveland, December 1992)*

to share the fruits of their labours; or that land was split up among children and grandchildren; or that peasants ploughed up common pasture and shared it in proportion to the labour invested or the grazing rights lost. But people were doing these things for thousands of years before strip-cultivation appeared. In later centuries ridging was supposed to increase the land area or promote drainage. However, ridging is not confined to soils which particularly required drainage. People made ridge-and-furrow, like many other things, largely because their neighbours did so.

Open-fields are not a pristine cultural landscape; they were made by an agricultural revolution no less definite than that which abolished them. A 'De-Enclosure Movement' flooded like a tide, reaching Ireland, Russia, and almost to Athens. The tide did not reach everywhere; its last ripple touched America long after it had receded in other places. The English Midlands were submerged so widely and for so long that little now remains of what came before. Ancient

Countryside was reached only locally and for short periods, and parts were not reached at all.

Open-field was most successful in highly-cultivated plains, where the farmland had already been made by someone else. Where men had to make their fields before they could till them, they usually remained individualists with scattered dwellings and private fields. Open-field was strongest in districts with little or no woodland; it made the most of existing farmland where there was no room for expansion. Also, it appears to have been part of a social revolution. People took to living in villages instead of the earlier hamlets and farmsteads. Collectivization of agriculture savours to us of tyranny: Stalin and Ceaucescu had the same ideas. But in places like Cambridge, where nobody even knew who was lord of the manor, it grew up by agreement.

## Medieval Hedges

Medieval England was a land of hedges. There was a very obvious difference between Ancient Countryside, with more hedges than ever before, and the less-hedged open-field areas, but even the latter had some hedges. Almost every township had hedges around the paddocks and closes attached to the village, between the pasture and the precious meadow, along the parish boundary, and often bits of hedge among the open-field strips. In northern England, hedges preceded some of the present stone walls.

Most records are of living hedges in the modern sense, but there were also 'dead hedges' for temporary fencing, either stakes interwoven with *ethers* (long flexible rods) or constructed of cut thorns called *trouse*, also used to mend gaps in live hedges. Hedge-mending and cutting of trouse (often in a special thorn-wood called a *spinney*) were supervised by an official called a *hayward*.

All this was part of English culture, and the source of words like hedge-sparrow, hedgehog, and hawthorn (hedge-thorn). Medieval rustics thought of the Man in the Moon as a stupid hedger, as in the thirteenth-century poem 'The Man in the Moon', or like Shakespeare's Moonshine, 'with lanthorn, dog, and bush of thorn'.

## Post-Medieval Fields and Hedges

The planting of hedges gained momentum from the fifteenth century onwards, especially in open-field areas being enclosed. Sometimes it was done with plants dug up in the local woods, sometimes with 'quickset' thorns, bought from nurserymen, which needed protection:

> And lay thy small trouse or thornes, that thou hedgest withall, over thy quick-settes, that shepe do not eate the sprynge nor buddes of thy settes.
>
> John Fitzherbert, *Book of Husbandry*, 1523

Early post-enclosure fields often preserve the shape of the furlongs that preceded them. Occasionally, a whole landscape of strips may be fossilized, for instance on the Derbyshire limestone

## Medieval Ridge-and-Furrow

Ridge-and-furrow comes naturally from the mechanics of driving an asymmetrical mouldboard plough, drawn by eight oxen, within the narrow limits of a half-acre strip. This tends to accumulate soil in the middle of each selion, and also to nudge it towards the ends of the selions, building up a ridge at right angles on the headland. With such an unhandy outfit it is difficult to plough in straight lines: it is better to begin the turn well before reaching the headland. Hence the double curve ('reversed-S') typical of medieval ploughland, familiar in ridge-and-furrow and early maps.

It is sometimes possible to compare ridge-and-furrow with sixteenth- or seventeenth-century maps of open-field cultivation, and to show that the ridges exactly match all the oddities of individual selions. There are, however, open-field areas, such as east Cambridgeshire, which seem never to have had ridge-and-furrow.

Plough-horses came in gradually from the thirteenth century. The change was slow and was not always one-way. The horse is not better than the ox in all respects. Having no horns to serve as towbars, he needs an elaborate collar and harness; and he is not edible on retirement. In many places oxen were still used, or re-used, into the nineteenth or even the twentieth century.

## Later Ridge-and-Furrow

Ridge-and-furrow is not confined to the Middle Ages. For centuries afterwards it was the practice to divide private fields into strips called stetches, and to form embryonic ridge-and-furrow on them. I have a handbook which told the Land-Girls of World War II how to do this.

Late ridge-and-furrow is typically narrower (5 yards or less), longer, set out in straight lines, and weak or inconspicuous. It occurs not in the main arable areas but on moors and downs, and sometimes in parks. Much of it is traditionally ascribed to the great ploughing-up of the Napoleonic Wars, although some is earlier. Ridge-and-furrow can also be produced by cart-ruts (p. 129), irrigation (p. 142), peat-digging (p. 197), and coprolite-digging (p. 175).

*A modern hedge, of hawthorn only, plashed ('laid') to exhibition standard, with stakes and ethers. Such very stylish work is probably possible only with a new hedge. (DW/WI, Buildwas, Shropshire, May 1993)*

### Hedges in Medieval Documents

Expenses ... One man making a certain ditch and planting a live hedge ... 18 perches [99 yards] long and 7ft wide ... 6s. at 4d. the perch.

*Estate accounts,
Gamlingay (Cambs), 1330*

John Sparrow made a trespass ... cutting underwood on a certain earthwork, viz. elm, maple, and bushes.

*Court roll,
Great Canfield (Essex), 1420*

Richard Benhall has 7 perches of hedge overhanging the King's highway with branches and thorns in the lane called Wodnenlane ... penalty 40d.

*Great Canfield, 1512*

Ralph Cheseman cut down and took away thorns growing in the plaintiff's hedges to the value of ½ mark [£0.33, quite a large sum].

*Court roll,
Newton Longville (Bucks), 1283*

James Mede complains that John Palmer senior in the month of March [1443] cut down to the ground, took and carried away divers Trees ... viz. oak, ash, Maples, white thorn & black, lately growing in a certain hedge of the said James between heighfeld and hegfeld, and had been repeating this trespass from time to time for 7 years [previously] ... by which the said James had been wronged and has suffered damage to the value of 20s.

*Court roll,
Hatfield Broad-oak (Essex), 1443*

plateau, where the strips are surrounded by walls of dry-stone specially quarried for the purpose.

From the sixteenth century onwards, many maps and landscape paintings depict hedges, fences and walls – and also rows of trees remaining where hedges had been grubbed out.

Writers drew attention to the difference between fully-hedged counties ('several' or 'woodland') and those still relatively unhedged. Thomas Tusser, being an Essex man, preferred the former: among the many disadvantages of living in champion country was the lack of firewood and the trouble, or 'suit', of fetching fuel from a distance. The term 'Woodland' was used by writers at this time not for woodland in the normal sense, but for land possessing hedgerows which produced wood. The Little Ice Age was drawing on, and hedges were much in demand for fuel. Stealing wood out of hedges was an offence meriting all Sunday in the stocks and a whipping until the offender 'bleed well'.

William Turner, the sixteenth-century father of English botany, began to study hedgerow ecology:

Arum ... Cuckoopintell ... groweth in euery hedge almost in England about townes.

Vitis sylvestris [wild clematis] ... groweth plentuously betwene ware and Barckway [Herts] in the hedges, whiche in summer are in many places al whyte wyth the downe of thys vine.

Alliaria ... Iacke of hedges ... groweth in hedges and diches.

*The names of herbes (1548)*

The Great Enclosures, though not a universal transformation, were a time of more new hedging than ever before or since. The hedges planted between 1750 and 1850 – probably about 200,000 miles – were at least equal to all those planted in the previous 500 years. The same applies to stone walls, in moorland country as well as on former open-field. A thousand million or more hedging plants were necessary, which founded the fortunes of several Midland nursery firms. Nevertheless, the Georgians thought of themselves as destroyers of hedges, owing to agricultural subsidies.

As time went on, hedging became perfunctory. Much of Leicestershire – Quorn and Fitzwilliam fox-hunting country – has strong hedges with plenty of trees, though their straight drawing-board lines, cutting across ridge-and-furrow, cannot be confused with medieval hedges. These, mainly Georgian, enclosures contrast with the Victorian enclosures of many Cambridgeshire parishes, with their flimsy single rows of hawthorn only. At the last Cambridgeshire Enclosure Act – Hildersham in 1883 – few hedges were planted at all.

Even in Ancient Countryside, the pattern of hedges in 1900 was not exactly the same as in 1500. The study of early maps reveals many piecemeal additions and subtractions to the hedge network. At Lawshall (Suffolk), the field size averaged 3.9 acres in 1612 and 8.6 acres in 1922. At Earl's Colne (Essex), fields averaging 5.4 acres in 1598 had been enlarged to 8.2 acres by 1922. Big fields were subdivided and small fields laid together. Hedges added in an early alteration were usually the first to be removed in later alterations. The network remained mainly medieval, but contains many single hedges of all subsequent periods.

New hedging and walling in this period transformed many Scottish, Welsh and Irish landscapes. In Aberdeenshire, a study by Robin Callander shows that the present walls ('stane dykes'), which run in straight lines, are the result of a reorganization between 1770 and 1870 more thorough than in England. There had previously been walls, but almost every single one was demolished and its stones reused. A stane dyke earlier than 1730 is now a rarity, except in remote places where the older fabric was preserved by the retreat of agriculture.

In Ireland it has been supposed that almost all the present hedged and walled countryside results from an enclosure movement beginning in the mid-seventeenth century. This claim seems to be based on the

**A Sixteenth-century Preference for Hedged Country**

A comparison betweene Champion
    countrie and seuerall.

The countrie enclosed I praise,
    the tother delighteth not me,
For nothing the wealth it doth raise,
    to such as inferior be.
There swineherd that keepeth the hog,
            . . . .
there neatherd [cowherd], with
    cur and his horne,    [Champion]
There shepherd with whistle and dog,
    be fence to the medowe and corne.
There horse being tide on a balke,
    is readie with theefe for to walke.
            . . . .
Example (if doubt ye doo make):
    by Suffolke and Essex go take
[in contrast to Norfolk, Cambridge-shire
and Leicestershire]
            . . . .
T'one laieth for turfe and for sedge,
            [Champion]
    and hath it with woonderfull suit:
When tother in euerie hedge
            [Seuerall.]
    hath plentie of fewell and fruit.

T. Tusser *Fiue hundred pointes of good
Husbandrie, as well for the Champion or
open countrie, as also for the woodland,
or Seuerall (1573 edition)*

*Hedges in northeast Wales. The blackthorn hedge in the foreground is likely to be modern; the mixed hedge, prolonged as a lynchet, behind it may be ancient. (DW/WI, Clwyd, May 1990)*

impressionistic kinds of evidence that have proved so unreliable for the history of the English landscape. In reality, hedge systems in Ireland are just as diverse as in England. 'Quickset hedges' are quite often mentioned in seventeenth-century boundary perambulations.

From 1870 until 1945 there was very little change in hedges. Air photographs of 1940 still show an almost complete network of hedges, even in arable areas. Loss of hedges is the most familiar aspect of the destruction of the English countryside between 1950 and 1975. It has affected mainly the eastern counties, where some areas have become as featureless as any desert; but the west did not entirely escape.

### Fields and Hedges As They Are Now

In the twentieth century, hedges were taken for granted and thought to be uninteresting. The different kinds of hedge were not noticed. Although their complex true history was never quite forgotten, people preferred to believe that hedges were all recent and very artificial.

In the 1970s Max Hooper revived the scientific study of hedges. He is responsible for the famous rule that the number of tree and shrub species in a 30-yard length of hedge is equal to the age of the hedge in centuries. This was a correlation derived by counting the species in 227 hedges of known ages from 75 to 1,100 years. Most unexpectedly, age turned out to be a more important determining factor than soil, climate, management, or the whims of those who had planted the hedge.

This rule works in many areas. In Planned Countryside, such as Huntingdonshire or Lincolnshire, hedges are predominantly of one, two or three species, with a minority of pre-enclosure hedges of four, five or six species. In Ancient Countryside, such as Devon and Kent, most hedges are medieval, with at least five species in 30 yards; there are also three- or four-species hedges, resulting from the

rearrangement of existing fields and from post-medieval encroachment on heath or woodland. The richest area of all is Felsham (Suffolk), where (as Ann Hart has shown) hedges of seven or more species predominate: this is a parish of ancient scattered farms, with the remains of what looks like an Iron Age planned field system.

Hooper's Rule may work for three possible reasons:

**1.** A hedge acquires further species as it gets older. Tree and shrub seeds, brought by chance and birds, germinate and occasionally get established.

**2.** In earlier times it was the custom to plant hedges with more species than later. Down to the eighteenth century, hedges were mixed from the start. Enclosure-Act hedges were generally planted with one species only, usually hawthorn. Georgian enclosers usually planted hedgerow trees; after the felling of the original trees the regrowth of the stumps gave the hedge a second species. Victorian enclosers often omitted the trees.

**3.** The older a hedge, the more likely it is to be natural rather than planted, and therefore to be mixed from the start.

Hooper's Rule works as far back as 1,100 years, but not earlier: it does not distinguish Anglo-Saxon from Roman hedges. It usually differentiates between medieval, Tudor or Stuart, and Enclosure-Act hedges. But there are various exceptions. Elm hedges sometimes have too few species for their age. Some kinds of suckering elm invade a mixed hedge, suppress the existing species (as they do in a wood), and turn it into an elm hedge. The pre-Roman field systems of south-east Essex, for instance, have mainly pure elm hedges.

A new hedge established very close to an ancient hedge may acquire species more rapidly than if it were isolated. This often happens where

*Field-walls have a habit of turning into hedges. Here are two near Abergavenny, SE Wales.*
*Above left: A fine example of the 'Atlantic' type of hedge which develops by default in the wet climate of Wales and Ireland: a rainforest-like hedge with great hazel stools, ferns, wall plants like pennywort, woodland plants like dog's-mercury, and many ferns, mosses and liverworts.*
*Above right: An ancient wall with ash trees growing on it. When young these were plashed to add extra height to the wall. A hundred years on, the plashed stems have grown into massive horizontal tree-trunks. (Both pictures: TM, July 1993)*

*A stylish wall in an easy material, millstone grit. The clean, lichen-free appearance indicates acid rain. (DW/WI, Lancashire, October 1988)*

### Field-walls

Almost every stone-bearing district in Europe has its own style of dry-stone or mud-mortared field-wall; indeed mud is sometimes used for walls where stone fails. Styles also evolve with time; some of the most elaborate, for example in Swaledale, appear to be nineteenth century. Stone was seldom brought from a distance, except for churchyard and park walls. Some walls, especially very thick ones, have the function of getting rid of the stones. As with hedges, straight walls tend to be later than about 1700.

A possible method of dating walls, in regions with clean atmospheres, is by measuring the growth of lichens. To work out the growth-rate, one looks at walls of known age, or at the size reached by the same species of lichen on tombstones of the same type of stone.

*Perhaps the most difficult task in walling is to build a dry-stone wall out of granite footballs, as here in the Dee valley, Aberdeenshire. (BG/NI, October 1993)*

the hedges on opposite sides of a road are of different dates. For example, the Broad Way from Cambridge to Grantchester was narrowed at the Enclosure Act of 1802. One of the hedges is now 190 years old, the other much older. The older hedge has an average of 5.2 species per 30-yard length; the post-1802 hedge has an average of 2.8 species, too many for its age. The lengths of new hedge with the most species tend to be opposite the richest lengths of the old hedge.

In the Forest of Neroche, Somerset, there are areas of new hedging resulting from encroachments on the Forest around 1650 and in 1833, surrounded by an area of generally medieval hedges. All three ages have an average of between 6.0 and 6.7 species per 30-yard length. But the species are not the same. Elm and hazel are especially characteristic of the old hedges; furze of those of intermediate age; sallow, privet and oak of the post-1833 hedges. Neroche was a small area of new enclosure remote from the great enclosures of the Midlands. Probably it was not enough to support a nursery firm; the hedge-makers had to make do with plants dug up in the wild. The resulting mixed hedges indicate some degree of selection and are not the same as the ancient hedges.

Hooper's Rule has told us much about the history of hedges from Northumberland and Norfolk to Devon and Kent. It has sometimes been applied uncritically and then, when exceptions are found, has fallen into unjustified disrepute among people who forget that most biological laws have exceptions. To some extent the rule is circumscribed by geography. It should be applied with caution north of Derbyshire, as the number of possible species diminishes northward. Some species may be unable to grow on extreme types of soil.

The anomalies warn us to take archaeological evidence into account. If there are Victorian imitations of medieval churches, why not Victorian imitations of medieval hedges?

Since 1700 most hedges have run in exactly straight lines. They are much less likely than earlier post-enclosure hedges to take account of pre-existing features. The post-1833 hedges of Neroche are instantly distinguishable by straightness from the medieval hedges. A sinuous length in an otherwise straight hedge may indicate that part of a pre-existing hedge has been kept in a reorganization of fields. Conversely, a patch of straight hedges in a landscape of crooked hedges may result from the grubbing of a wood or privatization of a green.

Hedges are associated with many kinds of earthwork. Some have an immediately obvious meaning: a hedge that cuts across ridge-and-furrow cannot have existed while the ridge-and-furrow was in use, nor can a hedge that follows a headland but leaves no room for turning the plough. Others have a significance that can be interpreted only when sufficient records have been amassed: these include the many kinds of banks, walls, revetments and lynchets that accompany hedges.

The structure of a hedge may tell us about its history. A post-1800 hedge usually has its original row of hawthorns still discernible; an ancient hedge often has giant coppice stools or pollard trees.

Particular plants are often more informative than the mere number of species. Two-species hedges commonly consist of hedgerow

*Retreating agriculture on the edge of Dartmoor. Field-walls and banks of all dates since the Bronze Age run out into what is now bracken and moorland, and is slowly turning into hawthorn-wood. (LF, Hound Tor, October 1993)*

hawthorn with ash, oak, briar or blackthorn. Maple and dogwood, which are less good colonizers and are rarely planted, may be the fourth or fifth species in hedges of Tudor age. Hazel and spindle, less good natural colonizers still, are characteristic of medieval hedges which are pre-Tudor and have at least six other species. Hawthorn grows in nearly all non-elm hedges, except for some of the most ancient mixed hedges which lack it. Elder, a good colonizer but shortlived, occurs at random regardless of the age of the hedge.

The dating of field-walls appears to be more difficult to systematize than that of hedges. The megalithic walls of the Land's End Peninsula depend on the abundance of a particular kind of boulder. Others, equally ancient but differently constructed, doubtless remain to be recognized elsewhere. At the other extreme (early nineteenth century), the moors in the Lizard Peninsula have very distinctive straight walls made of sods; the grass has disappeared but the alternating topsoils and subsoils of the turves are visible where the wall has been eroded. The wall was a means of disposing of some of the turf which agriculturalists were in the habit of paring off.

# TREES OF HEDGEROW AND FARMLAND

Hedgerow trees are a distinctive, ancient characteristic of England and probably Wales: their origin goes back beyond record. In Scotland and Ireland they are doubtfully historic. There used also to be trees standing in fields (as in Spain and Portugal today); these rarely survive except where they have been preserved in parks.

Nobody knows how many hedge and field trees there are. Estimates of the number vary widely and erratically: I suspect that this is the kind of quantity, like the length of a coastline or the cost of a motorway, that increases indefinitely as more effort is put into ascertaining it. The best that can be said is that in 1980 there were between 20 and 50 million hedge and field trees in England, covering very roughly 2½ per cent of the land area. (The area under trees is considerably greater than the area of woodland and plantation.)

Non-woodland trees are not the same as those in woods. Oak is almost the universal timber tree in woods; in Britain it is common but not universal in hedges; in Ireland one can travel 50 miles without seeing an oak outside woodland. Hornbeam, native lime and service are very rare hedgerow trees; big willows occur rarely, and black poplar never, in woods; ash and some elms can be in either.

Right: *Hedges and hedgerow trees around the Usk valley south of Abergavenny. Such very large numbers of farmland trees were common in Ancient Countryside in the eighteenth century, but seldom survive today. (TM, July 1993)*

# THE FIVE MAIN GROUPS OF NON-WOODLAND ELMS

**1. Wych elm,** *Ulmus glabra*:
does not sucker but still keeps to sex for reproduction and is not clonal. Widespread in woodland and hedgerow; commonest non-woodland tree of much of north England and south Scotland. A broad-spreading, widely forking tree having big, broad, rough leaves with almost no stalk.

**2. East Anglian group,** *Ulmus minor*:
East Anglia, north Essex, NE Midlands (and widespread in Europe). Bewilderingly variable, sinuous and graceful or short and stubby, often with twiggy bosses on the trunk; leaves narrow, smooth, pale green, long-stalked, very asymmetric. One form, the Boxworth Elm, common around

Huntingdon (and probably nowhere else in the world), is a very rugged tree, like an artist's impression of an oak; it is one of the least susceptible elms to Dutch Elm Disease.

**3. English Elm group,** *Ulmus procera*:
the traditional elms of south and middle England; rare (if known at all) in Europe. Massive, upright trunk, short boughs, heavy masses of dark, almost blackish foliage. Leaves very broad, rough, appearing earlier and staying later than those of other elms. Extremely susceptible to the current Dutch Elm Disease.

**4. Cornish group,** *Ulmus stricta*:
characteristic of Cornwall and west Devon. Stiffly erect trees; very small,

tough, smooth, dark green, long-stalked, nearly symmetrical leaves.

**5. Dutch Elm group,** *Ulmus hollandica*:
usually assumed to be hybrids between East Anglian and wych-elm. Especially in Ireland and west Cornwall. Often combine a wide forking habit and big leaves (like wych-elm) with suckering and narrow leaves (like East Anglian).

*The photograph of English Elm (bottom right) illustrates the mysterious habit which elms have of dropping boughs on hot calm days.*

*Boxworth Elm. (JM, Huntingdon, Cambridgeshire)*

*Dutch Elm. (OR, Arrowan, St Keverne, Cornwall, May 1980)*

*Wych elm. (DW/WI, Lune Valley, Lancashire, May 1989)*

*Cornish Elm. (OR, Bonallack in Constantine, Cornwall, July 1986)*

*One of the few big English Elms left alive. (OR, University of Sussex, August 1980)*

## Elms and Poplars

Elms are the most complex and distinctive hedgerow trees; there are arguably more kinds than of all other British trees put together. Elms have taken to reproducing by suckers rather than seed. Each parent creates a clone of identical elms, each an exact copy of itself, a process that can go on forever.

Suckering elms, being easy to propagate, are planters' trees, closely linked to human affairs. The natural distributions of wild elms (some of which may be ancient introductions from Europe), established by the Middle Ages, have been overlain by successive fashions in plantsmen's elms. In the eighteenth century, English Elm was widely planted outside its ancient limits. In the late nineteenth century, the Huntingdon Elm was a fashionable urban elm; it has a formal shape like an inverted cone, and often escapes Dutch Elm Disease. In the 1930s it was the turn of the Chianti-bottle-shaped Wheatley Elm.

Black poplar, *Populus nigra*, is richly recorded in medieval documents. Its timbers are found in medieval buildings. For centuries it has been largely dependent on people propagating it from cuttings. When other poplars became fashionable it declined.

White poplar or abele, *Populus alba*, is claimed in Gerard's *Herball* (1597) as a contraceptive: 'the same bark is also reputed to make a woman barren, if it be drunke with the kidney of a Mule'. Earlier records mention a non-woodland tree called *abel*, distinct from black poplar. Although white poplar, as a suckering tree, should go on forever, ancient clones are usually of grey poplar, supposed to be a hybrid between white poplar and aspen. What exactly *abel* was, and whether white or grey poplar is native, is still a mystery.

The countryside is a museum of plantsmen's poplars, ranging from the 'Black Italian' of the eighteenth century and the Lombardy poplar of Constable's later paintings to varieties put about by tree geneticists today.

### The Black Poplar

Black poplar is one of the rarest, biggest, and most distinctively English trees, a reminder of the splendour of the medieval countryside. No other native tree can compare with it in rugged grandeur.

Its massive straight but leaning trunk often reaches 100 feet high and 6 feet thick, with heavy branches which arch and sweep downwards. Trunk and boughs are covered with great bosses and very deeply ridged bark. It is a very sexist tree, with at least 50 males to every female. Seedlings are, therefore, extremely rare. It can reproduce by falling down and rooting from the prostrate trunk.

Black poplar is a tree of flood-plains, meadows and hedges; I have only once seen it in a wood, and that wood is younger than the poplar. It is scattered over much of England, perhaps most abundant in fenny valleys in the Breckland and in the Hadleigh area of Suffolk.

These are two of the few black poplars in Wales. *(DW/WI, Clwyd, April 1990)*

# ELM DISEASE

The history of elms is complicated by 'Dutch' Elm Disease. Four organisms are involved: elms, the fungus *Ceratocystis ulmi* which causes the disease, bark beetles which carry it from tree to tree, and (it now seems) viruses which attack the fungus. Interactions between these have created epidemics in Europe (and by introduction in North America) throughout history – most recently and disastrously in England, Ireland, France and Italy. Dutch Elm Disease is the only satisfactory explanation of the well-known sudden decline of elms in the early Neolithic.

Disease is an inseparable part of the ecology of elms. Clones survive and grow again from suckers; suckering may be evolution's answer to the disease. With wych-elm, the big trees are efficiently replaced by seedlings. In most areas elms are now gaining on the disease.

*Mother bark beetles,* Scolytus scolytus, *excavating breeding tunnels under the bark of a freshly-dead elm. (JB/BC)*

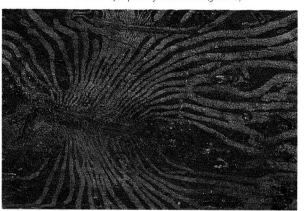

*Bark beetle tunnels under elm bark. The mother beetle laid eggs in the short central tunnel. The grubs tunnelled out sideways, pupated at the ends of the tunnels and turned into beetles. The Elm Disease fungus produced spores inside the tunnels, which stuck to the beetles as they emerged and flew off. The first act of the new beetles is to bite, and maybe infect, a living elm. (PM/Ardea)*

*The current epidemic of Dutch Elm Disease began in Gloucestershire in about 1965. The map shows its progress by 1983, with the proportion of elms killed. By then it had killed every big tree of the common form of English Elm, except in E Sussex. The area of over 85 per cent kill coincides almost exactly with the area where English is the common elm. Progress among other elms is slow and patchy, especially in East Anglian elms, some kinds of which resist the disease.*

less than 10%

10 - 30%

30 - 50%

50 - 70%

70 - 90%

more than 90%

No information or no elms

*'... the perill of συνλεθρισμός or one tree perishing with another, ... ofttimes from the sick effluviums or entanglements of the roots, falling foul with each other. Observable in Elmes set in hedges, where if one dieth the neighbouring Tree prospereth not long after.' Thus Sir Thomas Browne described Elm Disease in 1658. The fungus spreads from tree to tree through the roots of an elm clone, as in this landscape of dead English Elms. (JM/Ardea, Bratton, Wiltshire)*

## The Anglo-Saxon Period

We are not told whether the Romano-Britons had hedgerow, field or settlement trees. There were certainly non-woodland trees in Classical, as in modern, Italy.

Old English names of settlements often mention trees: Thornham, Aston, Sevenoaks, Maplestead, Birch. Usually they have no woodland association and refer to farmstead or village trees. In the middle of Ashwell (Hertfordshire), the river Cam still bursts from the ground in a great spring, to the Anglo-Saxons a 'well', beneath the roots of an ancient ash, successor to the original tree.

In Anglo-Saxon charters about one feature in fourteen is a tree, usually in a hedge or free-standing. Rarely does the context imply woodland, in which trees would not be distinctive landmarks. Early Welsh laws imply hedgerow trees: anybody felling a tree on to the highway forfeited six cows, the tree and the cost of removing it.

Thorn is much more predominant in charters than in place-names: did its small stature and commonness make it less suitable for naming places than as a landmark? It is followed by oak and apple (the context usually implies a wild crab-apple). Other frequent trees in charters are willows and sallows, elder and alder. Beech, birch, aspen and (surprisingly) elm are uncommon. Wild pear was less rare than it is now. There may be one mention of black poplar.

Individual trees were named after somebody (e.g. Coventry, '[Mr] Cofa's Tree') or from some peculiarity. Many trees were *hār*, 'hoar', an adjective used of old men's beards, which may imply beard-like lichens such as *Usnea* and *Ramalina*. Trees were sometimes 'crooked' or 'prostrate'. 'Red-leaved oak' is a record of those rare and striking trees that produce bright scarlet leaves every year: there is such an oak in Hayley Wood (Walk I, pp. 98-101). A 'footy oak' may have been one with a swollen 'elephant's-foot' base.

Sacred trees are few. In the Latin bounds of Taunton is 'an ash which the inexperienced call sacred'. 'Crucifix oaks' recall the crucifixes set on wayside trees in Austria today. An Epistle Oak on the boundary of Ringwood (Hampshire) suggests a liturgical beating of the parish bounds.

Oak, lime, birch, pear, service and beech tended to be in well-wooded areas in Ancient Countryside, although not in woodland themselves. Thorn, blackthorn, apple and elder were abundant on downland or among open-fields. Others – willow (including withy and sallow), ash, alder, maple, elm, hazel, etc. – were the general trees of farmland, hedges and watercourses. To some extent trees in the charters reflect the behaviour of non-woodland trees to this day. Even oak still grows near woodland in modern Ireland, though it has lost that association in England.

## The Middle Ages

No trees are directly mentioned in Domesday Book. In the following century the poem *The Owl and the Nightingale* mentions the earliest hedgerow trees in English literature, an ivy-tod and a lime. From the

### Trees in Place-names

Thorn and ash are the commonest trees in English place-names, followed by willow and oak. Others include hazel, alder, elm, birch and holly. Trees strongly associated with woodland – beech, lime, service – are uncommon. Lime place-names tend to cluster around districts that still have native lime. Birch and alder place-names are commoner in northern England; maple is confined to its present southerly distribution.

Hornbeam is not known in pre-Conquest place-names, but is unsuitable, being a woodland tree and difficult to identify. It is less easy to explain the rarity of elder (a tree of habitations, albeit sometimes thought unlucky) or the apparent absence of yew (with its ancient churchyard tradition) and poplar (a very distinctive non-woodland tree).

Cornish place-names tell a somewhat different story: elder (*scawen*) is frequent, but oak (*dar*) is surprisingly rare, and elms, now typical of Cornwall, are apparently absent from its place-names. Tree-names are common in Welsh (e.g. Llangollen and Derwen, equivalent to English Hazlestow and Oak) and in Gaelic (*giubhas*, pine; *fearn*, alder), but are usually difficult to date.

## Non-woodland Trees in Anglo-Saxon Charters

Oaks, apples and hazels in Ancient Countryside:

> ... To the two oaks that stand into the road; then along the hedge to the east of Lamhyrst; ... to the ivy-tod, ... to the stock that the swing-gate used to hang on; from the stock out through the middle of Hill-lea to the old ash; from the ash south over the road to the apple-tree; from the apple-tree to the white hazel; ... along the hedgerow out to the Limburn ...
>
> *Boundary of Havant (Hants), dated 980*

Thorns and elders in downland and open-field:

> ... Along the stoneway to the long crucifix at Hawk-thorn; then from Hawk-thorn to the long thorn at Icknield way; so to the third thorn at Wirhangra; from the thorn to the fourth thorn standing forth on Wrong Hill; so on to the fifth thorn; to the elder-tree; then west along the little way up to the thorn ... along the old ditch to the place of Æþelstan's tree ... to the red-leaf maple tree ...
>
> *Boundary of Blewbury (Berks), dated 944*

thirteenth century there were hedgerow trees and trees sheltering buildings, lining river-banks, and standing in fields. They gave rise to income, disputes between neighbours or between landlord and tenant, obstructions of the highway, and petty offences. Occasionally their timber can be recognized in ancient buildings through some peculiarity such as pollarding or pruning.

Non-woodland trees existed even in open-field districts. They comprised pollards and timber trees, often larger and more valuable than trees in woods. The species were independent of the local woodland; the commonest non-woodland tree could be oak, ash, elm, poplar, or willow. Apart from the lack of exotics, the most striking difference from the present scene was the abundance of (black) poplar.

Elm, although commoner than in Anglo-Saxon charters, was probably less abundant than today. There are indications of Dutch Elm Disease on the Continent (where St Martin and St Zenobius wrought miracles of bringing dead elms back to life), and occasionally from archaeology in England. However, there was no lack of elm poles for use in fifteenth-century buildings.

People planted hedgerow trees from saplings either bought or dug up in the local woods. However, as in later centuries, most hedgerow trees arose (deliberately or by neglect) from natural saplings in the hedge.

There were some non-woodland trees in Scotland. In the Southern Uplands medieval perambulations, like those of Anglo-Saxon England, mention thorns and trees marked with crosses.

*The Haughley Oak, Suffolk: a non-woodland oak from the medieval countryside, preserved as a garden feature. (TM, Haughley, Suffolk, 1993)*

*Pollard willows along watercourses were a feature of the medieval countryside and of the town fens at Cambridge and Oxford. At Oxford in 1301 an inquest was held on a schoolmaster who fell into the Cherwell from a pollard willow while cutting rods with which to beat his boys. Individual willows are seldom of great age. (AW, Burford, Oxfordshire)*

## The Heyday of Hedgerow Trees

After 1500 hedgerow trees appear in vast numbers in almost all landscape pictures and on early maps. Occasionally the trees themselves are still living. Trees are enumerated in surveys of monastic and Crown lands and private estates, and appear in disputes and tenancy agreements. For example, on a 170-acre farm at Long Melford (Suffolk) in 1546:

> In [a 3-acre grove] and about the scytuacions of the sayde manor & dyverse tenements there & in the lands perteyninge to the same be growynge 200 okes and elmys of 40 and 60 yeres growth parte usually cropped & shredde [variants of pollarding] whereof 160 reseruid for tymber to repayre the houses ... and to maynteyn the hedges & fences about the sayde landes & 40 resydue valued at 6d the tree ...

Oak, ash and elm were far the commonest species, whether timber or pollard trees. Elm increased after the Middle Ages, but willow and poplar declined. Hedgerow timber was preferred for shipbuilding (as yet not a big user).

By the mid-eighteenth century there were more hedgerow trees than ever before or since. On one Suffolk estate there were 39 timber trees and pollards to the acre; they were thicker on that farmland than in most woodland. This was probably exceptional: the owner remarked on the 'Pollard Trees which this Estate is very much incumbered with & if a great deal more was cut down it would be much better for the Land'.

## Vicissitudes since 1750

The latter eighteenth century saw itself as a time of decline in hedges and hedgerow trees, owing to agricultural subsidies, Enclosure Acts, and reorganizing of fields. Pollarding became unfashionable; new pollards ceased to be formed in most areas, except for willows along watercourses.

John Clare was one of the few literary writers to tell us what an

### Non-woodland Trees in Medieval Accounts and Court Rolls

From willows round the pond 19d. From willows at Fokewic 18d.
*Hindolveston (Norfolk) 1265-6*

John House complains that William Bene ... [in 1435] cut off the branches of certain trees of the said John, namely poplars and maples, growing in a certain hedge of his ... and the said William took and carried away the underwood of the branches which he had cut off; and ... the said William again [this year] in the same way cut off the branches of the said trees and took and carried away the branches whereby the said John has ... suffered damage to the value of 10s. [This evidently refers to pollarding.]
*Hatfield Broad-oak (Essex), 1443*

John Petye cut down 1 poplar without permission ...[fined 2s.] Will Gunnild cut down 1 abel and sold it without permission ... worth 2s. 6d.
*Nowton (Suffolk), 1310*

The Lady Countess has one ancient and decayed poplar growing too far over the King's highway [and agrees to let the parish have it for a bonfire].
*Great Canfield (Essex), 1422*

John Gru ... cut off the branches of an ancient oak without permission, amount to 1200 billets worth 6s.
*West Donyland, 1392*

John ... Gybbe cut down one willow in which was a swarm of bees and destroyed the said swarm and took the wax and honey. [Fined 40d.]
*West Donyland, 1391*

*Hedgerow trees made by accident. The characteristic field boundaries of the Breckland are rows of pines with gnarled bases. When Breckland open-fields and commons were enclosed in the early nineteenth century, it was the fashion to make new hedges of pine, not indigenous to the area but thought to suit its arid climate. A few surviving examples prove that it is possible, with an effort, to keep pines in the form of a hedge. Most of these hedges, however, have passed through periods of neglect, which in a few years causes pines to grow up irrevocably into trees. Their character depends on their gnarled bases, relics of a misspent youth. (TM, February 1994)*

Enclosure Act accomplished. He wrote in sorrow and fury at the tidying-up of the medieval landscape of his childhood and the destruction of Langley Bush, Lea Close Oak, and the pollards which had given Helpston (near Peterborough) its individuality:

> when in round oaks narrow lane as the south got black again
> we sought the hollow ash that was shelter from the rain
> with our pockets full of pease we had stolen from the grain
>     . . .        . . .            . . .        . . .
> o words are poor receipts for what time hath stole away
> the ancient pulpit trees and the play            *Remembrances*

Individuality had gone for ever; but loss of numbers was partly offset, especially in Scotland, by trees planted in the hedges of new enclosures. Exotic trees (e.g. sycamore and walnut) appear in small numbers from 1730 onwards, but did not become abundant until the nineteenth century. Hedgerow trees, nevertheless, declined especially in well-tree'd areas, which were levelled down to an average for England of about one tree per acre of farmland. (The Ordnance Survey between 1845 and 1888 tried to map every single non-woodland tree.)

After 1870, hedgerow trees recovered, and at least doubled in the next eighty years. Many Suffolk and Essex views painted by Constable became invisible because trees had grown. Devon and Cornwall ceased to be treeless counties. This increase is linked to recessions in Dutch Elm Disease and in agriculture. It costs money to prevent trees from growing; neglect allowed innumerable saplings to grow into trees. Even a further epidemic of Elm Disease made little difference. The change went unnoticed: in 1951 a report complained of too few young trees – against the evidence of its own statistics.

Recovery was cut short in the 1950s. Unwonted agricultural prosperity coincided with declining markets for free-standing trees as a crop. There was plenty of money to spend on either destroying hedges or excessively maintaining them. Both operations were mechanized. Established trees were regarded as a nuisance and destroyed for various reasons or pretexts, such as that they got in the way of maintaining watercourses. Worse for young trees was the fashion for tidiness. Hedging and trimming formerly done carefully once in five to ten years were now done hastily every year. A man with a tractor, 'brushing' the bank of a ditch, could cut off a thousand saplings in an hour without noticing them.

By 1970 conservationists, including many farmers, realized that hedgerow trees were in bad way, but misunderstood why. It was diplomatic to blame Nature. The present trees were planted – so popular argument ran – in an enclosure movement 150-200 years before, and were then near the end of their life-span. (Rarely did anyone find out how old the trees really were or how long each species lived.)

The result was a fashion for planting rather than conserving trees. Trees were treated as inanimate ornaments without life or meaning of their own. People were encouraged and financed to plant trees as a routine, whether necessary or not. Official trumpets were blown for the planting of tens of thousands of trees, but no voice was raised against the destruction of hundreds of thousands of natural saplings. Meanwhile, Dutch Elm Disease flared up yet again.

## Non-woodland Trees Today

By another reversal of fortune, non-woodland trees are again relatively prosperous. One farmer's land varies from another's; but in general, pressures on land have declined, attempts to educate landowners about trees have at last had some effect, and there is less money to spend on preventing trees from growing. Natural calamities were less destructive than at first appeared. The great storms of 1987 and 1990 destroyed relatively few non-woodland trees: they broke off branches which rejuvenated many trees (by a kind of pollarding) and protected them from subsequent droughts.

Most encouraging is the recovery from Dutch Elm Disease. Many million elm suckers and young wych-elms are reaching flowering size, and the historic elm distribution patterns have survived.

Tree-planting continues to erode differences between regions, between town and country, and between gardens, ancient woods, and the rest of the landscape. Originally a distinction was made between the trees of farmland (still, on the whole, native species) and those of formal parks and gardens. Later it became the practice to plant exotic trees in the countryside at large. Occasionally this created a distinctive local characteristic, such as the Breckland pines. But most Victorian

**Nineteenth-Century Elm Disease**
Elm Disease had been noticed intermittently by scientists since the seventeenth century. From the 1820s onwards it flared up in England, France, Belgium and Holland. These are contemporary descriptions:

> In spring we see the leaves sprout forth from the venerable trunks in all the luxuriance of vegetation, when of a sudden they are blasted as if by lightning, the bark falls from the stem, and long ere into the finest tree perhaps in the park is only fit for fire-wood ... Now every elm is the same degree infected, and every week we may observe that a tree has perished.
> *St James's Park, 1823*

> In an elm a great limb dies all at once from the point right into the trunk, while all the rest keeps green; then another limb goes, and so on until the whole tree is dead within a few weeks...
> *Windsor Great Park, c.1960*

In 1862 the editor of *The Times* was moved to write:

> It is certainly strange that the pathology of trees should have been comparatively neglected in this country ... The elms ... whether insects or impeded exhalation be the cause, these characteristic ornaments of our parks have a sickly look. It has been predicted by a prophet of dendrology that elms will be extinct in England before another century has elapsed. The bare idea of such a calamity should rouse the Woods and Forests – for the functions of that department have not expired with its name – from their lethargy on the subject.

Shortly afterwards the disease subsided. Its cause was not discovered until Dutch scientists worked on it during the next flare-up in the 1920s.

**Pollards**

Pollards still exist in thousands in Essex and Suffolk, but not in every Ancient Countryside county: in Herefordshire, otherwise so like Essex, there are few pollards. In Planned Countryside they are confined to closes around villages and occasional ancient hedges. Enclosure Act hedges are too late for new pollards to have been started in them; if a hedge has pollards it is almost certainly older.

Even pollard willows continue an ancient tradition, and are important for the creatures that live on them. Briars, sizeable ash and holly trees, and other willows grow in their crowns. As with other pollards, lichens grow on their old bark, many insects are specific to their mouldering interiors, and birds and bats roost inside them. Willows are probably the most active branch of pollarding. The city fens of Cambridge, with pollard willows along watercourses, are a medieval survival which sets off the later formal landscape of The Backs.

plantings are an assortment of fashionable trees – horsechestnut, hybrid lime, Turkey- and holm-oaks – the same all over the country. Today the species are native but the uniformity is the same. Conservationists promote oak, maple and cherry as if they need to be kept alive artificially. Service and small-leaved lime , rare trees but not threatened, with a strong and mysterious natural distribution, deserve a better fate than to become an obligatory part of the Standard Broadleaf Mixture.

**Historic Trees**

The biggest assemblages of trees more than 400 years old are in Forests or preserved by chance in parks; but, scattered through the countryside, single vast and bizarre trees (mainly pollard oaks) invite wonder and speculation. Some are well known and loved: there are long lists in Loudon's *Arboretum* (1838). John Clare wrote a sonnet to an

old huge ash dotterel [pollard] wasted to a shell
whose vigorous head still grew and flourished well
where ten might sit upon the battered floor
and still look round discovering room for more.

Ancient trees are almost everyday objects in England, as they are in no European country except Greece. Trees acquire individuality and meaning with age: they tell us of their environment and management when young.

*A 'stag-headed' oak. The dead boughs are the remains of a former, larger, crown of foliage. It used to be thought that stag-head presaged the death of the tree; this is part of the myth that the landscape is full of 'senile' trees, or alternatively that acid rain has taken its toll of trees. In reality it is a normal condition. Most oaks and other free-standing trees go through periods of retrenchment in which the leafage readjusts its balance with the roots. This is very conspicuous with oaks, in which the dead boughs do not rot but remain as evidence for nearly a century, long after the tree has grown a new, smaller, healthy crown. (TM, Bintree, Norfolk, July 1993)*

Most pollards (except willows) are antiquities; even a quite small bolling can be 400 years old. Some giants are older than 600 years; in a few places with a strong tradition new pollards have not been cut for several decades, although this art is happily being revived.

Archaeologists, recording castle earthworks and the holloways of deserted settlements, often fail to appreciate ancient trees as their last living inhabitants. Shrunken villages of the east Midlands have ancient elms marking their streets and hedges.

Other ancient trees are on boundaries. Certain very select trees define parish boundaries on nineteenth-century larger-scale Ordnance maps: 'Oak Pollard', 'Pollard Elm', 'Ancient Yew'. Edges of meadows in flat-bottomed valleys are important early boundaries, often set with giant pollards. Other ancient trees are in hedges of apparently no special significance; they remind us that any ordinary mixed hedge can be more than 500 years old.

Ancient trees occasionally survive in fields. The home close near a medieval farmstead may have half-a-dozen pollard oaks. A characteristic of the edges of the woodless Breckland is a field full of pollard oaks or black poplars. Many can be seen preserved in Ickworth Park (p. 69).

Ancient hawthorns are now to be found chiefly in a few parks and Forests (especially Hatfield Forest, Essex: Walk III, pp. 106-111). One of the boundary thorns of Downing College, Cambridge, stood into the twentieth century beside the Botany School. The Glastonbury Thorn, the most famous sacred tree in England, was apparently burnt as a suspected papist, but grafts had been taken from it and its early-flowering genes live on in cultivation. Ireland still has many sacred thorns.

*Churchyard yews are a mystery: for example the immense yews of Crowhurst (Sussex), Woolland (Dorset) and Tandridge (Surrey). Ancient yews exist in Wales; there are a few in Scotland and Ireland. People believe that yews are very slow-growing and that the big ones are of fabulous antiquity, 2,000 years old or more. They are supposed to have been sacred trees before the churches were built. As far as I know, however, there is nothing to connect yews with any of the pagan religions of Britain, though there may be a connection with early Christianity. The theory that churches were built on pagan sacred sites has received disappointingly little support from excavation. If yews were a feature of early churches, why are there no place-names such as Yewchurch? Yew can grow quite fast when young, and the ages may be exaggerated. A big yew can well be as old as the present church but is unlikely to be older than its Anglo-Saxon predecessor. (Yews were not grown for longbows, which were normally of elm or imported yew.) (OR, Easthope, Shropshire, February 1985)*

98

## WALK I:
### *Hayley Wood, Cambridgeshire*

Grid Reference: TL 290 530

Property of Cambridgeshire, Bedfordshire and
Northamptonshire Wildlife Trust.
Gumboots needed.

Hayley is one of the best known ancient woods.
There is no sign that it has ever been other than
woodland, although parts of it are underlain by
faint earthworks. The area is lacking in known
prehistoric or Roman archaeology. From Anglo-
Saxon times onwards Hayley was one of the
principal woods of the Abbey, later the Bishops, of
Ely. It was confiscated by Queen Elizabeth in 1579
and passed through many private hands before the
Trust acquired it as a nature reserve in 1962.

This is an ash-maple-hazel wood with oaks as
timber trees. It was coppiced from before the
thirteenth century until the early twentieth. The
wood is full of huge ancient coppice stools (pp. 50,
52). Coppicing has been revived since 1964. The

oaks date mostly from between 1780 and 1840, and
are older than most woodland oaks, though
younger than the coppice stools. Being wild trees,
each oak is subtly different in branching angle, time
of leaf-fall, or colour of the young foliage, in
contrast to the relative uniformity of planted oaks.

Coppiced areas in their second or third year of
regrowth have magnificent displays of spring
flowers. The most famous of these is oxlip, *Primula
elatior*. Also abundant are wood anemone, bluebell,
violets, early purple orchid and the succession of
summer flowers of coppiced areas, such as lesser
spearwort and ragged robin. The flowers and the
warm glades between stools attract butterflies and
hoverflies. Birds such as nightingales nest in
underwood of later years' growth.

The wood lies on a flat soggy hilltop and is
particularly wet, especially in spring. Lack of
drainage is a valuable ecological feature which
favours oxlip and other choice plants (or, rather,
disfavours their competitors).

The present state of Hayley is not typical of its
history. The oaks are more numerous, bigger and
more difficult to replace than ever before. About

*Map reproduced from the 1"
Ordnance Survey Map, 1929.*

**Early Records of
Hayley Wood**
The wood is vaguely
mentioned in Domesday
Book. In the *Ely Coucher
Book* of 1251 we find:

> *The Wood.* There is there
> one wood which is called
> Heyle which contains
> fourscore acres. Item, there
> is there one other wood
> which is called Litlelund,
> which contains thirty-two
> acres.

Litlelund (the wood's
name is Viking) lay half a
mile to the west. Other
pages of the *Coucher
Book* refer to coppicing,
the use of underwood for
fuel and hurdle-making,
and the earthwork
around the wood.

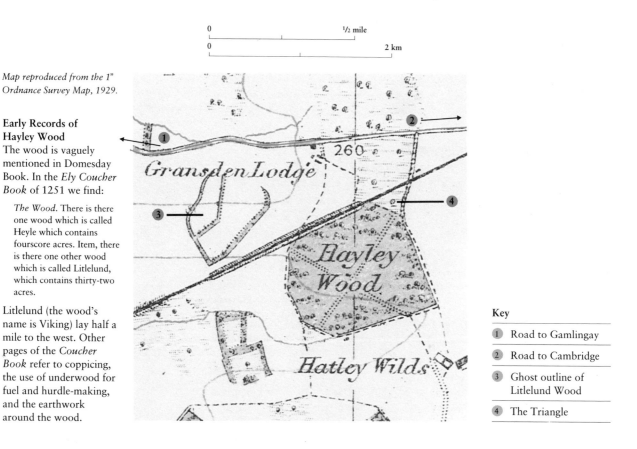

0      ½ mile

0      2 km

**Key**

1. Road to Gamlingay
2. Road to Cambridge
3. Ghost outline of Litlelund Wood
4. The Triangle

## Key

*White line: route of walk*

Air photograph: © Cambridge
University, June 1988

0              500 m

0              500 yards

### Woodbank
The wood is surrounded by a massive
medieval bank with external ditch.
Alongside the Triangle the woodbank
is now in the wood's interior.
Hayley (unlike many woods) has
no internal subdivisions.

### Modern hedge
The Cambridge–Bedford railway
functioned from 1863 to 1969.
The hedge between the railway and
the field sprang up spontaneously
after 1969. Like many natural modern
hedges it is a mixture of many species

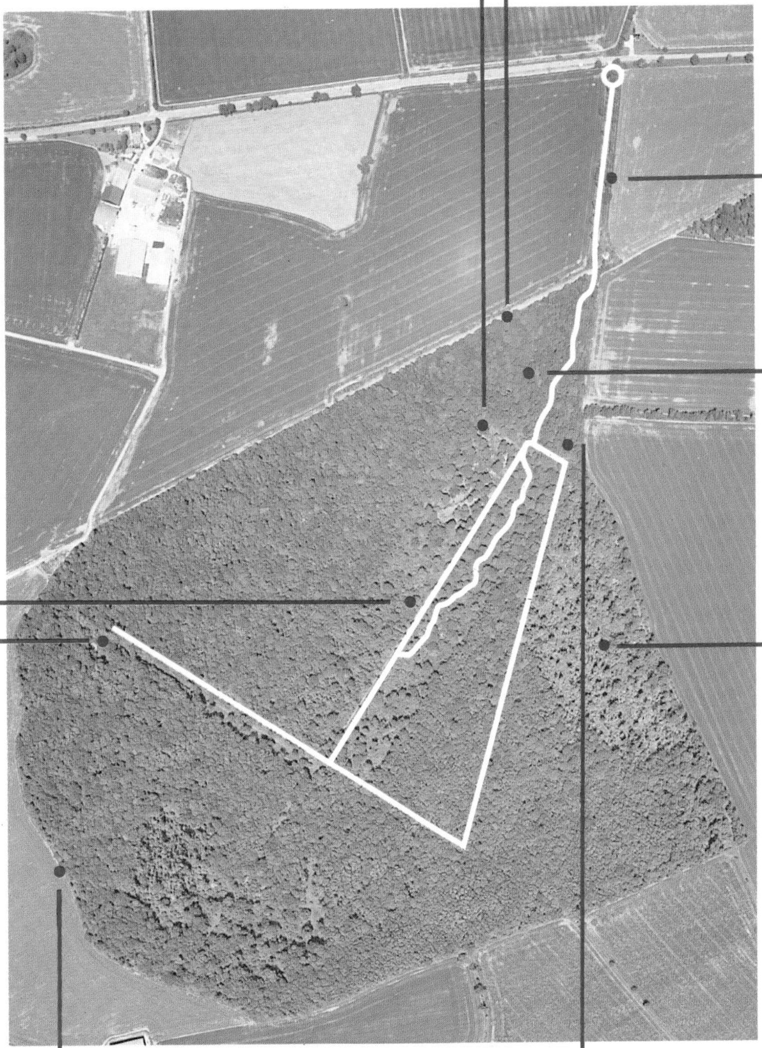

### Ancient hedge
This hedge, probably
medieval, separated
arable land to the east
from a meadow to
the west. It is composed
of a mixture of many
species. The modern
hawthorn hedge
parallel to it was
planted in 1971

### The Triangle
Originally part of the
Bishop's meadow;
then an arable field;
cut off by the making
of the railway; became
woodland in the 1920s

### Coppiced areas
Within the fence is
the best area for
oxlip. Coppicing
has been resumed
in other parts of
the wood since
the date of the
photograph.

### Pond
A mysterious armed
pond, a deliberate
construction
(see photo p.180)

### Elm area
This semicircular
patch is the shape
of an elm clone,
suckering out
from a point on
the eastern boundary
– or rather it is the
ghost of an elm clone,
for the big elms were
killed by the drought
and Elm Disease
and deer have eaten
the suckers

### Shape of the wood
Hayley Wood still keeps its original
sinuous outline, stabilized by the
woodbank, except on the north
where it has been straightened by
the making of the old railway

### Ancient oak
This venerable pollard,
the oldest oak in the wood,
was originally just outside
the wood in the corner
of the meadow

**Woodland Grassland**

Rides, margins and permanent glades within ancient woods have a special type of old grassland. The best examples in Hayley are the verges of the old railway, with woolly thistle, clustered bellflower, crested cow-wheat and the umbellifer *Pimpinella major*, as well as oxlips and wild strawberry remaining from before the making of the railway. The verges have to be strenuously maintained to prevent them from being invaded by trees.

sixty years ago the wood was invaded by fallow deer, most ravenous of woodland beasts. It is also untidy and full of logs and dead trees; this is by intention, since deadwood is an excellent habitat for creatures from liverworts to woodpeckers. (Hayley is particularly rich in mosses and fungi.) In woodland as elsewhere, conservationists should respect decay and detest tidiness.

Hayley is an excellent place to study the effects of deer. The visitor should compare the trees and herbaceous plants inside and outside the various deer-fences. (Crouch down and see what the wood looks like from a deer's point of view.) The fences exclude fallow deer, but muntjac, which have different tastes, are small enough to get through them. Areas which have been coppiced in the presence of fallow deer are grassy and poor in oxlip; the original coppice stools have often been replaced by thickets of aspen, a clonal, suckering tree which fallow detest.

The lane up to the wood was once a through road. It leads to the first part of the wood, called the Triangle, which is a recent addition; it was growing corn almost within living memory and it illustrates what happens to a field left alone for seventy years. There are many more oaks than in the old wood, and almost no hazel. Except near the old wood, it lacks oxlip, dog's-mercury, and wood-anemone, plants of ancient woodland. The Triangle is on ridge-and-furrow, not the medieval kind (p. 79) but a seventeenth-century imitation.

Above: *Valerian, a woodland-grassland plant abundant on the Hayley railway.*

*(All photographs: TM, October 1993)*

Right: *A modern, natural, mixed hedge along the old railway.*

*Old oaks alongside the Triangle. These grew up as hedgerow trees when the Triangle was a field. They had plenty of space, hence the spreading boughs which have been overtopped by younger trees growing in the Triangle. The triple oak grew from the stump of a predecessor which is older than any oak in the wood proper.*

*A corner of a deer-fence. The fence was set up in 1972, and the areas inside and outside have been twice felled since. Inside the regrowth is normal; outside it has been ravaged by deer. Deer are the biggest problem in woodland management today.*

Above: Pholiota mutabilis, *one of the many fungi that grow on dead stumps.*

Left: *Experimental pollarding. In the 1970s hundreds of new pollard ashes and maples were started in order to prevent the deer from eating the young shoots. These maples have made one year's growth in the second cycle of pollarding. Pollarding does not, of course, protect oxlips and other herbaceous plants.*

# WALK II:
## Glen Tanar, Aberdeen

Grid Reference: NO 480 965 (near Aboyne)

Property of Glen Tanar Charitable Trust, whose directions must be followed by anyone wishing to leave the main tracks.

Caledonian pinewoods are not the remnants of an imaginary Great Wood of Caledon a hundred miles across. Although pinewoods have been characteristic of the eastern Highlands since wildwood times, wildwood largely disappeared by the Iron Age.

Each pinewood has its own history, but not like that of English ancient woodland. A pine tree burns, dies when cut down, and easily grows from seed; the woods do not have permanent edges, nor many specifically woodland plants.

Glen Tanar woods are known since the seventeenth century. A description in 1725 shows them not very different in extent or appearance from today, except for a big trade in timber floated down the river.

There are four main generations of pines, from great round-topped trees of the eighteenth century to the youngest of about 1980. Any one area has only one or two generations. Trees older than 1850 tend to be more spreading; there was then much goat-grazing and the woods may have been more open, in the nature of wood-pasture.

Pines advance and retreat into moorland, though blanket peat discourages them. Occasional trees spring up on slumps and disturbed areas. When these pioneer trees produce seed, the spaces between them are filled with crowded young trees. Burning heather probably limits the spread of pines into moorland; on this estate, where browsing and burning are discouraged, pines are increasing. Established pinewoods have had occasional catastrophic fires, probably an essential part of the ecology of pine.

Roads and settlements have changed out of recognition since the Middle Ages. The main Firmounth and Mounth Roads came from the south, over the mountains; it may have brought, among others, Edward I of England in his wrath. Up to the eighteenth century there was a village of Braeloine with shops, an inn, a mill and arable land. The house and chapel are modern.

### Key

*Green line: Mounth Road (route of walk)*
*Black line: Firmounth Road*

1 Etnach deserted farm

2 Halfway Hut

3 St Lesmo's Chapel and deserted village of Braeloine

4 Firmounth Road

P Areas of pine increase

*This map shows much less Caledonian pinewood than there is today. Pinewoods have increased in the areas marked with P. (Reproduced from the 1" Ordnance Survey Map, 1929.)*

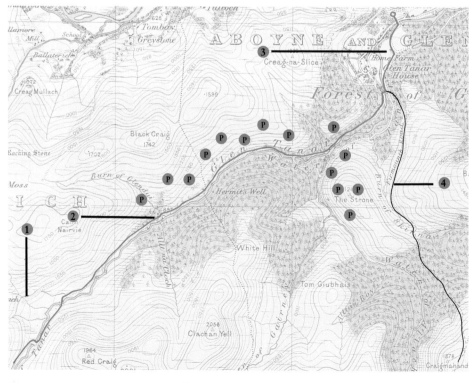

0 ——— 2 miles

0 ——— 4 km

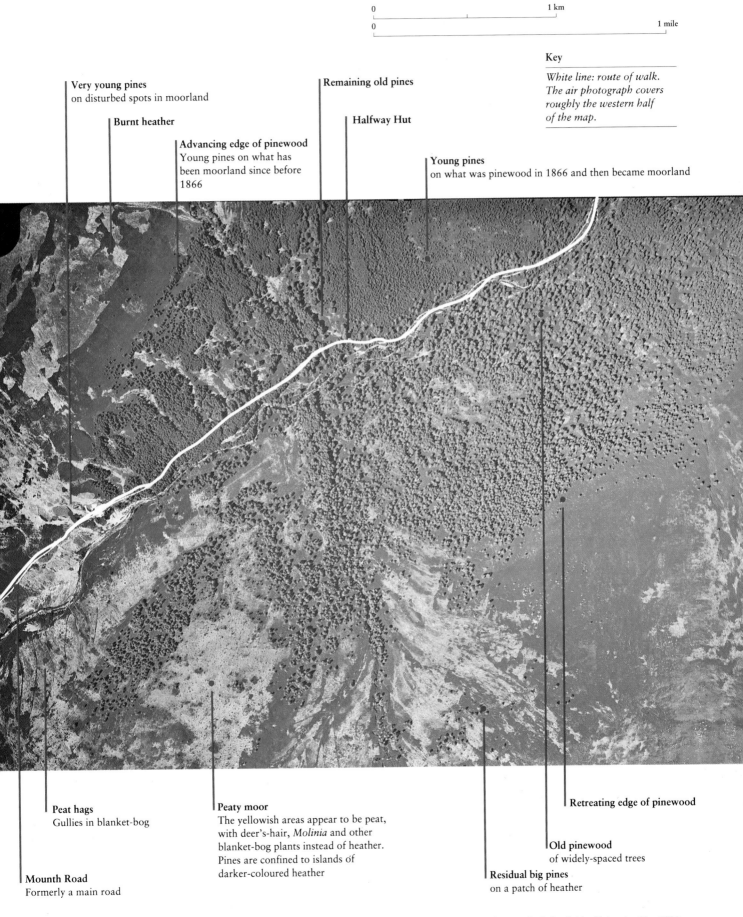

0            1 km

0            1 mile

**Key**

*White line: route of walk.*
*The air photograph covers*
*roughly the western half*
*of the map.*

**Very young pines**
on disturbed spots in moorland

**Burnt heather**

**Advancing edge of pinewood**
Young pines on what has
been moorland since before
1866

**Remaining old pines**

**Halfway Hut**

**Young pines**
on what was pinewood in 1866 and then became moorland

**Peat hags**
Gullies in blanket-bog

**Peaty moor**
The yellowish areas appear to be peat,
with deer's-hair, *Molinia* and other
blanket-bog plants instead of heather.
Pines are confined to islands of
darker-coloured heather

**Retreating edge of pinewood**

**Old pinewood**
of widely-spaced trees

**Residual big pines**
on a patch of heather

**Mounth Road**
Formerly a main road

*Air photograph: © Cambridge University, May 1990*

Above: *The Caledonian Pine is a subspecies peculiar to Scotland, with short needles. When free-standing it long remains pyramidal in shape and then becomes a massive rounded tree. Its thick rough bark is distinctive; in this unpolluted atmosphere it is clothed in lichens.*

*(All photographs: TM, October 1993)*

Right: *An old (though still living) pine on a rock outcrop; originally free-standing, it is now hemmed in by its children.*

*The chapel of St Lesmo, a nineteenth-century building on the site of the deserted village.*

*An area of two ages of pines. Most of the trees are probably of the mid-nineteenth century; they have grown up between scattered older individuals.*

Above: A *view down Glen Tanar from above. On the right are scattered old trees, some of them dead, marking a retreat of pinewood to moorland. On the left, young trees are advancing into the moor, which has not been wooded in recent centuries.*

*Old pines, widely spaced, in an area at the upper end of the valley which is difficult for pines to colonize.*

*Etnach, at 1,250 feet one of the highest farms in Scotland. It must always have been precarious, but was evidently still used into the 1960s.*

# WALK III:
## *Hatfield Forest, Essex*

Grid Reference: TL 540 200
(near Bishop's Stortford)

Property of the National Trust.
Gumboots needed except in dry summers.

Hatfield is the last wooded royal Forest in England in which all components survive: deer, cattle, coppice-woods, pollards, scrub, timber trees, grassland and fen. It is the only place where one can step back into the Middle Ages to see, with a small effort of imagination, what a Forest looked like in use.

Hatfield is a microcosm of English history. Its owners have included King Harold, Robert the Bruce, the accident-prone Dukes of Buckingham, Sir Richard Rich (the wickedest Englishman who ever lived), a Royalist villain and a Parliamentary hero. Five owners forfeited it for high treason.

*Right: This map is the last edition of the Ordnance Survey (1929) to make the correct distinction between coppices (green) and scrubs. The Doodle Oak was a famous ancient tree which last bore leaves in 1858.*

Hatfield was declared a Forest probably by Henry I about 1100. He presumably introduced the fallow deer whose descendants are still there. It was then the south end of the largest wooded area in Essex, but was not wildwood. The Forest and its surroundings have a prehistoric dimension, and had been less wooded in Roman times. Around the Forest is an Ancient Countryside of fields, roads, hedges and scattered farms, many of them little altered since a perambulation in 1298.

The king owned the deer; he took about 11 head a year, which suggests that there were fewer deer than there are now. At first he owned the land as well, but in 1238 he gave it to Robert's great-

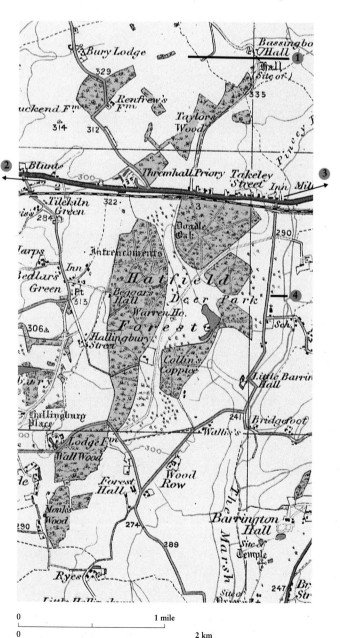

Key

*Green line: route of walk*

① Stansted Airport

② To Bishop's Stortford and M11

③ A120 to Braintree

④ Entrance

*Above: Map of Hatfield Forest by Hollingworth and Lander, 1757, showing coppices (dark) and plains with scattered trees. (Essex Record Office)*

0            1 mile

0            2 km

**Portingbury Rings**
Possibly an Iron Age farmstead with small fields attached, now embedded in the middle of a medieval coppice. There are several Roman and prehistoric sites within the Forest, and many on the site of Stansted Airport to the north

**Coppicing**
Coppicing goes back at least to the fourteenth century. It lapsed in the early National Trust years, but was revived in 1974. The Trust now has a big coppicing programme

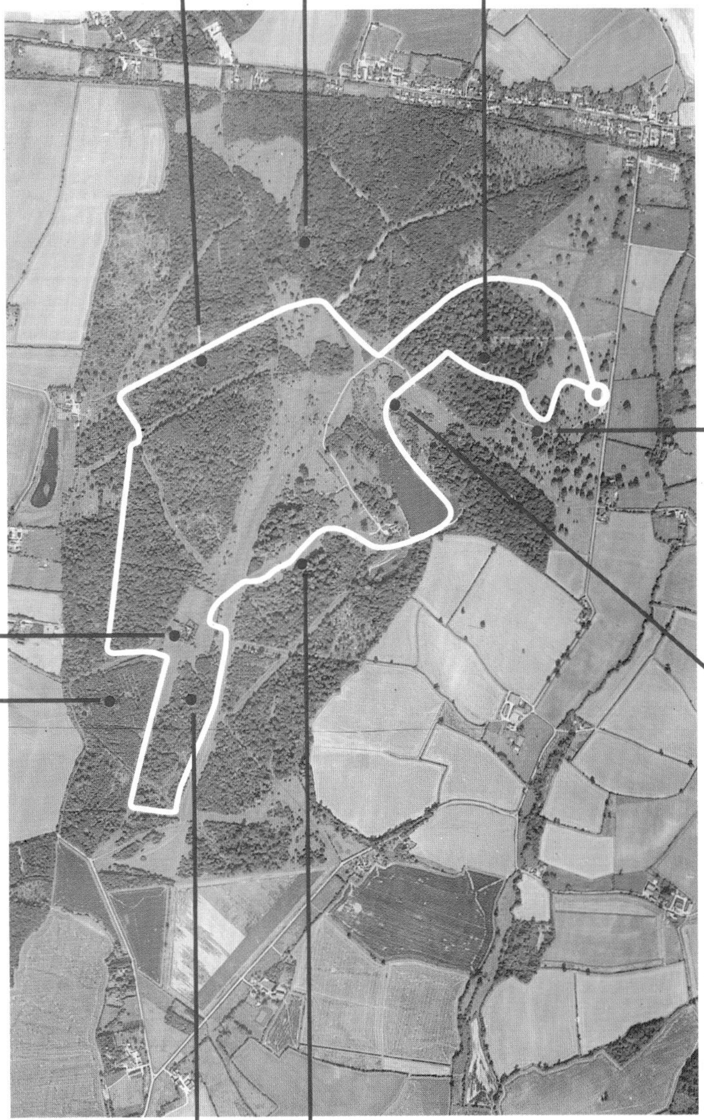

0                     1 km

0                   ¹/₂ mile

*Air photograph: Geonex*
*(© Stansted Airport), September 1986*

**Key**

*White line: route of walk*

**Forest Lodge**
Now a private house, this was the lodge in which Forest officials did their business, kept their equipment, and kept an eye on the Forest. It is the only surviving medieval Forest lodge; it was adapted to its present shape *c.*1590

**Pollards**
The plains in the Forest are set with pollard hawthorns, hornbeams, maples, oaks, ashes, and a few beeches, elms and crabtrees. Many of these are magnificent ancient trees

**Emlin's Coppice**
This ancient wood was grubbed out and replanted with oak and larch in the 1960s, in accordance with the 'conservation' fashions of the time – although even then this crude treatment was controversial

**Pollard hawthorns**
A particular speciality of Hatfield Forest are some 270 ancient hawthorns, at least 300 years old, mostly collapsed but very much alive. Like other ancient trees they are a wonderful habitat. Hatfield is the chief stronghold in England of mistletoe, which grows mainly on pollard thorns and pollard maples

**New pollards**
The Trust has set about reversing some of the encroachment of scrub on grassland. Every time this is done, old pollards are preserved and new pollards started to become the ancient trees of the future

**The Warren**
A prehistoric earthwork converted into a chain of pillow-mounds for rabbits to burrow into. Originally this area was almost treeless. The great horsechestnuts and other exotic trees were planted in the 1850s by the Hublon family

*A coppice at three years' growth, with a crabtree in bloom. Underwood grows slowly because of the depredations of deer. This, however, is a normal consequence of being a Forest, in contrast to ordinary woods such as Hayley which did not have deer. Attempts to fence deer out of newly-coppiced compartments can never have been entirely successful, and there were frequent complaints that cattle were getting in and eating the young shoots. Even a badly-grown coppice is an excellent habitat for small birds.*

*(All photographs: TM, April-May 1993)*

*A pollard hornbeam at about ten years' growth. The National Trust, on taking over Hatfield Forest, ceased cutting the pollards, but resumed in 1977, since ancient hornbeams collapse if not cut. Pollarding is an essential part of maintaining old trees as a habitat for rare and specialized animals. To its great credit, the Trust has always kept up the grazing.*

grandmother. The parties in the Forest comprised the king, the landowner, the lord of the manor, the commoners and the hereditary woodward. In their squabbles down the centuries, the commoners generally came out on top, through playing off one lord against another.

After 1729 the Forest owed its survival to newcomers, the Houblons, a London business family, who loved and appreciated it. In their hands it even lived through an Enclosure Act in 1857. However, it did not survive quite intact: on the east and south sides it lost its Forest shape and is now bounded by straight lines, and in the middle it acquired the paraphernalia of eighteenth- and nineteenth-century landscaping.

Hatfield is the classic example of a compartmented wood-pasture. It is divided into coppices and plains. Coppices were supposed to be cut on a regular cycle and fenced to protect the regrowth. Plains were always accessible to livestock – deer, cattle, sheep, horses, donkeys, pigs, goats and geese – and the trees in them were pollarded, not coppiced. The plains also contained scrubs, thorny thickets in the protection of which new generations of trees arose.

The National Trust acquired the Forest in 1924. The vicissitudes of a historic landscape do not suddenly end when it passes into the hands of even the most eminent conservation body. For a long time Hatfield's significance as the last remaining Forest in working order was not appreciated. Fortunately the grazing was kept up, but the coppices and pollards were no longer regularly cut; in a moment of weakness in the 1950s the Trust failed to resist the fashion for 'improving' grasslands; in the 1960s a bulldozer was making 'vistas' at random through the coppices; dead or 'unsightly' trees were summarily burnt; and there was inappropriate planting.

Times have changed and Hatfield is now being managed with an attention to detail worthy of the Trust's reputation for conserving historic buildings. In 1994 sheep grazed for the first time in many years. Hatfield vividly illustrates deer *versus* trees, but (unusually) this conflict is part of its ancient character. The Forest has lived with Stansted Airport for half a century without suffering much harm; but conflicts may come (air pollution, pressure of visitors, etc.) if use of the airport increases.

Grasslands are a special feature. They have not fully recovered in forty years after 'improvement'. Certain areas escaped, especially the colourful fens along the Shermore Brook and the old gravel-pits in the middle. A sign of unimproved grassland is anthills.

The woods are mainly ash, maple and hazel in various proportions, with areas of hornbeam and alder. The Forest is one of the world's best localities for the common maple, with some immense trees. There is some oxlip – surprisingly, considering the history of deer.

The ancient pollards are the home of rare insects, which often have very precise requirements: e.g. a beetle which goes with spiders' webs under loose bark and feeds on the spiders' leavings. Only specialists can fully understand the elaborate ecosystem which each ancient tree constitutes; but every visitor admires their wonderful shapes, bizarre colours and improbable bulk, and notices the mysterious golden boughs of mistletoe which add to the romance of this extraordinary place.

*One of the northern coppices being cut. In 1924 there was a great felling of timber throughout the Forest. This coppice was subsequently cut about 1930, after which a new crop of oaks and ashes sprang up abundantly. Coppicing was abandoned shortly after, but has now been resumed. Some of the 1930 oaks and ashes are now being cut for timber, along with the cutting of the underwood. The coppice has been fenced against cattle, but it is difficult to exclude deer.*

*The lake and Shell House. The Forest survived the Age of Enlightenment by being treated as an extension of the park of Great Hallingbury to the west. The lake was made in c.1750 by damming the Shermore Brook as the beginning of a scheme of formal landscaping. Beside it was built the Shell House, a delightful Baroque grotesquerie, the scene of genial picnics and hunting parties. For the next hundred years many exotic trees were planted in the area – horsechestnuts, cedars, planes, black walnuts etc. – which are somewhat discordant in a medieval Forest. The delta of the Shermore Brook, where it enters the lake, has become a remarkable wetland, a breeding-ground for snipe and warblers and the home of rare moths and aquatic mosses.*

*A hornbeam-wood east of the lake. For some reason the owners decided to reduce the size of this coppice in the 1850s. This, the part excluded by the new woodbank, illustrates what happens to a wood not cut for 150 years.*

*Below: A pillow-mound, adapted out of a prehistoric earthwork in the seventeenth century in order that rabbits might burrow into it. The area is known as The Warren. Rabbits were one of many pretexts for the commoners oppressing the landowner. Nearby is the warrener's cottage, a very stylish brick house of c.1690.*

*The second biggest oak in the Forest today, and the third biggest that there has ever been in historic times. It is not a pollard. It dates probably from the 1680s, and was originally one of the timber trees of a defunct coppice. In the Middle Ages, when trees were smaller, this oak would have been almost unbelievable. Even in 1819 the felling of an oak in the Forest, less than half as big as this one, attracted a crowd of 300 people.*

*Hornbeams on a woodbank. The coppices in Hatfield Forest are regular woods with banks and ditches round them. Each coppice was supposed to be felled every eighteen years. After felling it was fenced to keep out deer and the commoners' livestock. After six years deer-leaps were made 'for the deare ... only to leape in and out'. Nine years after felling the fences were removed so that all the animals could get in and eat whatever coppicing vegetation remained. The system did not always work very well.*

*A pollard oak near Forest Lodge. The Lodge, probably originally built in the fifteenth century, was very carefully sited so that the Foresters could keep an eye on as much of the Forest as possible between the coppices. Trees have so much increased in the plains since that it is difficult to appreciate the lines of sight.*

*An oak coppice stool, with the author as scale object. This is an anomaly in eastern England, where oak as a coppice tree is rare and confined to specially poor soils. The many high oak stools in the western coppices of Hatfield in some way reflect its turbulent history as a Forest. Oak gets on quite well with browsing animals, which eat its competitors.*

# WALK IV:
## Upper Swaledale, N.W. Yorkshire

Grid Reference: SD 910 980 (village of Muker)

The western part of this walk (Pennine Way), over high and very rough ground, should not be attempted in bad weather or without good boots.

Swaledale is a remote, somewhat independent place, known through the researches of Andrew Fleming and T. Gledhill (to whom I am indebted for my knowledge of it). Remains of successive cultures – Iron Age, Roman, Anglo-Saxon, Viking, monastic and a big lead-mining industry from the seventeenth to the nineteenth century – overlie each other and are excellently preserved as earthworks (pp. 8-9). This part of the dale is now a quiet roadless gorge.

The environment is dramatic. Alternating limestones and acid rocks produce cliffs ('scars'), screes, gorges, waterfalls ('forces') and hundreds of mysterious 'shake-holes', depressions formed by one rock dissolving another. The Swale is a fierce river,

liable to tremendous spates; it is one of the few English rivers still to have a braided course and a wide gravel bed. The moors between the dales are burnt to encourage young growth of heather on which sheep and grouse feed.

The Vikings, industrious with spade and mattock, contributed much to Swaledale in place-names and dialect words (for example 'force'); but there appear to be both earlier and later English settlements. Some early settlements were remarkably high; a few of these, such as Kisdon at well over 1,000 feet, are still inhabited.

The obvious landscape of field-walls and hay-barns dates partly from the nineteenth century, when cattle had replaced the mixed farming of earlier times. The later dry-stone masonry is particularly stylish; even field-walls are embellished with courses of projecting stones. Many houses and walls are much older, and there are remnants of an earlier hedged landscape. Early masonry tends to be more workaday, of natural boulders. The heavy tilestone roofs are distinctive; sometimes the gables show traces of an earlier, steeper, thatched roof. The dale is now largely used for sheep; it is very

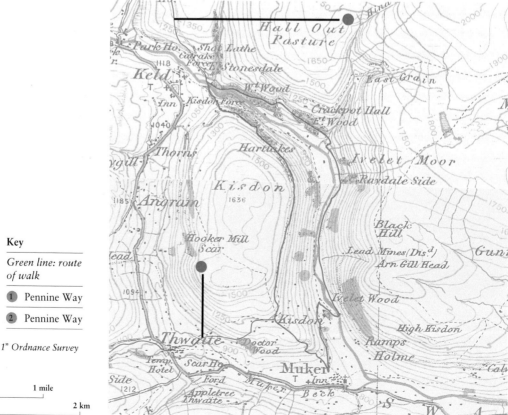

**Key**

*Green line: route of walk*

① Pennine Way

② Pennine Way

*Map reproduced from the 1" Ordnance Survey Map, 1929.*

0            1 mile

0            2 km

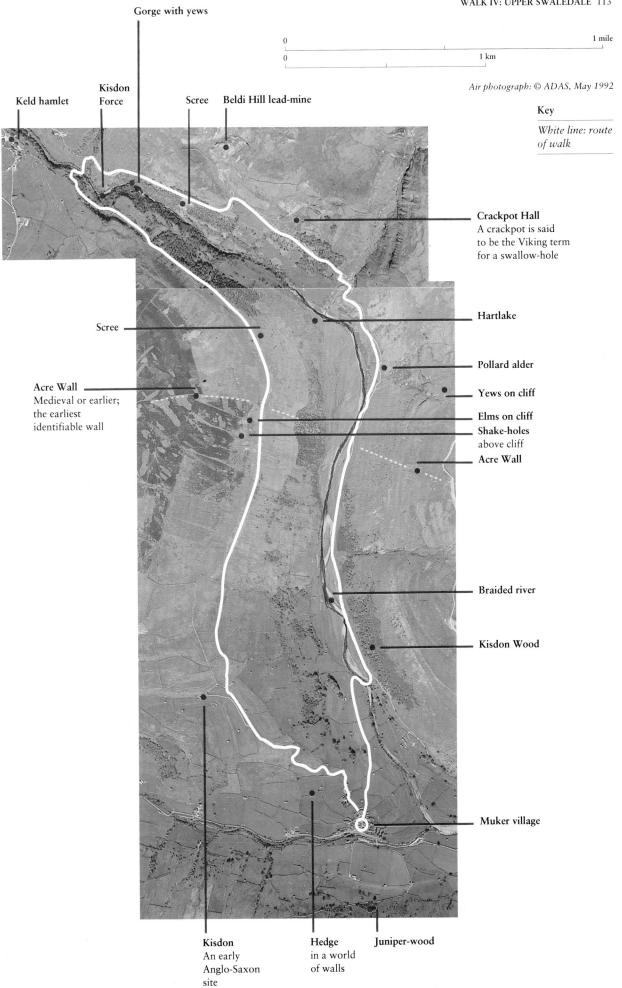

Gorge with yews

Kisdon Force

Keld hamlet

Scree

Beldi Hill lead-mine

0    1 mile
0    1 km

*Air photograph: © ADAS, May 1992*

**Key**

*White line: route of walk*

**Crackpot Hall**
A crackpot is said to be the Viking term for a swallow-hole

**Hartlake**

**Pollard alder**

**Yews on cliff**

Scree

**Acre Wall**
Medieval or earlier; the earliest identifiable wall

**Elms on cliff**

**Shake-holes** above cliff

**Acre Wall**

**Braided river**

**Kisdon Wood**

**Muker village**

**Kisdon**
An early Anglo-Saxon site

**Hedge** in a world of walls

**Juniper-wood**

*Ivelet Wood. In much-grazed country, woods often survive on scree or bare rock, areas with soil being grassland or moor. The old parts of the wood are hazel, growing on mossy boulders. The fringes of the wood are hawthorn.*

*(All photographs: TM, February 1994)*

depopulated and full of deserted houses and barns.

Swaledale, although never very wooded in historic times, has been more wooded than it is now, with wood-pastures such as Ivelet Wood. The wood-pastures were converted to charcoal-making in industrial times. Subsequently they were no longer protected from grazing and shrank within their boundaries, leaving the charcoal-hearth platforms in moorland. Ivelet Wood has since expanded, presumably at a time of slack browsing.

As in most of these Walks, there are now more trees in the landscape than for at least 300 years. The trees of Swaledale are odd, principally ash, birch and hazel in the woods, hawthorn and birch in extensions to woods, and yew, elm and ash on cliffs where they escape browsing. There are ancient hollies (probably cut for iron rations for sheep) and woods of juniper. Most woodland flowers are confined to cliffs. A great mystery is the absence of oak: there seems not to be a single oak in Swaledale except near the mouth. Timber tends to be either elm or imported.

The lead industry replaced earlier sources of lead in Derbyshire and the Mendips. It departed leaving hundreds of bell-pits and drifts, mounds of spoil, 'hushes' (gullies in which erosion had been encouraged to expose ore), and factories and flues for processing the ore. A century ago this would have been like the worst industrial dereliction today; but time and Nature have rendered it romantic. How banal modern landscape restorers would have made it!

*A pollard alder. Alder is rarely seen as a pollard tree. Such venerable alders, richly mantled in mosses, are a feature of Swaledale.*

*Yews on cliffs. Yew, although poisonous, is much eaten by animals, and like other palatable trees survives on cliffs. Any accessible yew is bitten down to a bush.*

Left: *Flats of the River Swale. The river here once had a braided course, as it still does elsewhere. Overlying the old courses of the river are the walled fields of three deserted farms. One of these, Hartlake, may go back to the Anglo-Saxon settlement. Its name is appropriate: 'hart' + 'lake', from Old English* lace, *a backwater. The ghost of the backwater can still be seen. Trees and woods are confined to the steep valley sides.*

Above: *Wych-elm stools on cliff. Elm has been one of the principal trees of the Pennines since wildwood times. Like ash and yew, is a very palatable tree, and in Swaledale grows mainly on cliffs. Wych-elm does not sucker but forms huge ancient stools. Men have climbed down the cliff to coppice them.*

Left: *A hedge in a world of walls. Although Swaledale has always had some field-walls, many of them are nineteenth-century and replace earlier hedges. Here is a hedge that escaped being replaced.*

# HIGHWAYS

> By far the greater part of modern roads go back at least to the Saxon age, and many thousands of miles of them, the ridgeways, have had a continuous existence going back into times long before history began.

G.B. Grundy wrote this in 1933, and later research has amply confirmed it. Britain has always had efficient and wide-reaching communications for people and goods. Even in the Neolithic period, stone tools were transported from East Anglia to the Lake District and *vice versa*. By 1066, King Harold, starting from London, fought the Danes near York and the Normans at Hastings all in three weeks – a speed of action that few modern armies could improve on. Wagons brought hundreds of thousands of tons of stone to build cathedrals, churches and castles in stoneless areas.

'Highways' include roads, buildings and footpaths. Some of these are mere rights-of-way across field or moorland, but most are *lanes* – ribbons of public territory with hedges and ditches separating them from the adjacent private lands. Britain has had vehicles for 2,500 years, and has a tradition of roads as structures, with boundaries and surfaces, and bridges or paved fords at river crossings.

Highways are older than mankind: deer and badgers make paths too. Evidence of specific highways is of two kinds. Boundaries or structures of disused lanes or tracks are revealed by excavation or aerial photography. There are also long-distance routes, conventionally called 'prehistoric tracks' although some were probably lanes, many of which are still highways; these rarely involve actual prehistoric remains, and the evidence for the identification is mainly circumstantial. The second kind tend to be the trunk roads of prehistory and the first kind the minor roads and footpaths.

*Right: A trackway along the North Downs in Surrey. It is of unknown age and was once quite an important road; it has probably never had boundaries. Highways, for obvious reasons, tend to be better fertilized than surrounding roughland; this probably explains why wild parsnip (which demands greater fertility) grows alongside the track but not on the rest of the down. (TM, August 1993)*

### Prehistoric Highways

The banks or crop-marks of disused 'Celtic' or other prehistoric field-systems often reveal lanes as well as fields. Most settlements and farmsteads were reached by at least one lane. In prehistory, as later, not every field adjoined a lane, and many could be reached only across other fields.

Where prehistoric field-systems are still in use it is likely that the lanes that go with them are prehistoric too. This is almost certainly true of many of the lanes of Cornwall. It is very possible, though difficult to prove, that much of our minor road system, at least in Ancient Countryside, is really prehistoric. Many lanes in Hampshire, Essex, north-west Dorset etc. are certainly of Anglo-Saxon antiquity, but as yet we have little evidence of how much older they may be.

Long-distance roads such as the Icknield Way, the various Ridgeways and the Pilgrims' Way in Surrey are usually regarded as prehistoric main highways. This is based partly on tradition, but there was an argument which ran as follows. Neolithic, Bronze and Iron Age people lived on high ground where their settlements, barrows and field-systems are still obvious on downland or moorland. These habitable areas were islands in a sea of uncultivable and impassable wildwood on heavy lowland soils. Main routes followed the populated ridges and avoided the inhospitable lowlands. This notion has been disproved by discoveries in the last 40 years, which show that ancient settlements were in fact more abundant in the lowlands, although their remains are less well preserved. Nevertheless, the traditional 'prehistoric tracks' are probably genuine, at least in their general direction. Their exact courses, if not their boundaries, are sometimes proved by Anglo-Saxon records and parish boundaries to be well over 1,000 years old. Many are ridgeways, but there may be other routes. The traveller along the Chilterns, for instance, could choose between the 'Upper Icknield Way', following the chalk escarpment above the spring-line, and the 'Lower Icknield Way' over the claylands at the foot of the scarp. The upper would have been an all-weather road, but steep and circuitous; the lower saved time and effort, but its many fords and sloughs would have made it a summer and autumn route.

It can no longer be asserted that the recognized prehistoric tracks are the whole, or even the most important, of those that existed. There were presumably others, on low ground, which can now rarely be distinguished from other roads.

### Roman Roads

The uncompromising red lines of Roman roads stare out of almost every page of the motoring atlas. By tradition, they were laid out by military engineers to link towns and fortresses across trackless and houseless wildwood. However, most Romano-British villages, villas and the like are not on recognized Roman roads, yet they must have had access. The roads that we recognize as Roman are merely the trunk roads among a network of lesser roads, partly pre-Roman, which can scarcely have been less dense than it is today.

*The fabric of prehistoric highways is beautifully preserved in the wooden 'trackways', of Neolithic to Iron Age date, across the peat of the Somerset Levels. Here a Neolithic trackway is being excavated by the Somerset Levels Project. These specialized highways have left no mark on the visible landscape. (SLP/JC).*

We notice Roman roads by their straightness. Roman surveyors took the most direct way between two points, not the easiest, quickest or most easily defended way. The route was influenced only by the more formidable natural obstacles. Gradients, fens, wet hilltops, perils of ambush and any protests of people whose land lay in the way were apparently ignored.

Whoever set out the Foss Way evidently knew in which direction Lincoln lay from Exeter, to within a fraction of a degree. Between deviations forced by the Somerset Levels and multiple river crossings in Nottinghamshire, the middle 150 miles of the Foss never depart by more than $6^{1}/_{2}$ miles from the direct line. The departures are due to the method of setting out the road on the ground in detail after its general alignment had been determined. This was done by sighting from hilltop to hilltop; the road changes direction slightly every few miles, nearly always on high ground.

In contrast Stane Street, the road west from Colchester, looks amateurish with its frequent changes of direction, rarely more than two miles straight at a stretch. There are two kinds of 'Roman' road: those like the Foss Way and Fincham Drove with rare, sometimes rather abrupt, re-alignments; and those like Stane Street and the road from London to Colchester with frequent slight zigzags (map, p. 121).

The Foss Way was probably made in the heat of war, surveyed hastily through hostile territory to join the military bases of Exeter and Lincoln. Its planners, having all the manpower of the Roman army to do the hard work, did not avoid minor obstacles; they could reduce the aligning of the road to a mere problem in navigation. Roads of the Stane Street type generally have a civilian function. Stane Street itself linked Colchester with lesser towns at Braintree and Braughing. Such

*A milestone from the Roman road one mile east of Chesterholme, Northumberland. Inscriptions on milestones supplement what writers like Siculus Flaccus tell us of how Roman roads were organised in Europe. The making and maintenance of roads was shared among many individuals and organisations, from the emperor to individual landowners – a system more complex than highway authorities in Britain today. Varying standards may explain the apparently haphazard way in which some roads survive and others do not.(JB/AA&A)*

roads are met by the straighter type of road in such a way as often to suggest that the straighter roads are later. Sometimes they conform to field patterns and sometimes not. Stane Street itself cuts across an earlier hedgerow pattern around Braintree.

The distinction between Roman and prehistoric roads is not very clear. One 'Roman' road, Wool Street near Cambridge, is known to be of Iron Age origin. Stane Street and many other less straight 'Roman' roads may well be pre-Roman too. Among minor roads the distinction is even more difficult. We can rarely be sure of distinguishing minor Roman from prehistoric roads; who can say how many existing country lanes date from either period?

### Anglo-Saxon Highways

By the later Anglo-Saxon period big heavy things like millstones, timber, salt, iron and bells and fragile items like pots were being transported to the remotest parts of England. Travellers thought little of going overland to Italy.

It is sometimes supposed that the Roman roads went out of use and were later partly restored. In practice roads survive through continuous use. A neglected gravel road gets overgrown with blackthorn; after ten years it becomes a thicket more impenetrable than if it had never been a road. Survival of roads demonstrates continuity of communication and settlement from the Roman to the Anglo-Saxon period. Roman roads that survive in bits and pieces are more eloquent than those that are still through routes.

Highways form one in six of the features mentioned in Old English Charter boundaries. The many Anglo-Saxon words indicate some thought of classification. Important highways were called *stræt*, 'street'. These were vehicle roads, often Roman; many are still main roads today. There are references to Watling Street, the Foss Way, the Berkshire Icknield Street, Ermine Street and 'Buggilde *stræt*' (now called Ryknild Street, a Roman road in Worcestershire).

The term *herepad*, 'army path', is commonly taken to signify a road made for military purposes. On the map, however, *herepads* usually turn out to be ordinary roads. The idea is apparently that of a highway wide enough for an army; in practice it meant a B-class road in contrast to the *stræt*, which was an A-class road. *Herepads* rarely had names.

The charters' commonest term for a highway is *weg*, 'way'. It can mean something less important than a *herepad*, but it may also have been vague as in later centuries: the same road may be called Icknield Street and Icknield Way. Most *wegs* are now minor roads. Whether they were all vehicular in Anglo-Saxon times is uncertain: once a 'wheel-way' is specified. *Pad* and *stig* ('path') correspond to modern bridleways and footpaths (occasionally a 'horsepath' is specified).

The word 'road' itself is not uncommon; its exact meaning cannot be inferred. Nor can we tell whether 'lane' had exactly its modern meaning.

The charters mention greenways, stone-streets, broadways, smallways, sandy-ways, roughways, port-streets (leading to a market

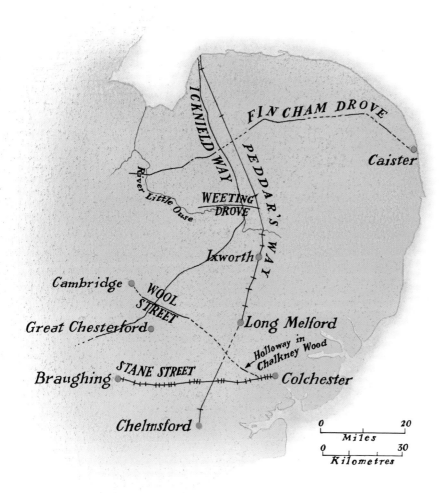

Left: *A few of the Roman roads of eastern England. Peddar's Way is a Roman road of the very straight type, with few changes of alignment. Fincham Drove is also a Roman main road, leading less directly from the Midlands across the Fens to the port of Caister. Wool Street has been shown by excavation to be a pre-Roman road, later than the Icknield Way which it crosses, which was partially Romanized at the Cambridge end; in its Iron Age state it can be seen in Chalkney Wood, Earl's Colne. Stane Street, with its frequent changes of direction, looks like a road laid out in the Iron Age by someone who knew of Roman surveying methods.*

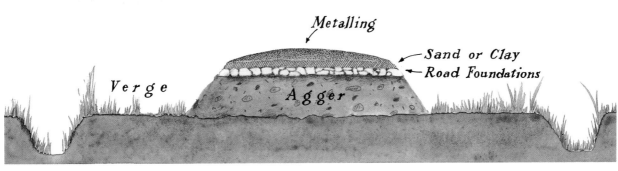

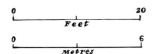

### The Construction of a Roman Road

A Roman road typically had two side ditches, between which was a raised embankment (Latin *agger*) with a surface metalled with gravel, stone or ironworks slag. The ditches might be 80 feet apart, the *agger* 40 feet wide and 3 feet high, and the metalling 20 feet wide. Not all main roads had ditches and *agger*, and the dimensions varied. Roads had bridges, paved fords and, in difficult terrain, causeways and cuttings.

Right: *A rare example of what are said to be the actual flagstones of a Roman road, at Blackstone Edge, Ripponden, west Yorkshire. Most Roman roads, however, did not have big paving-slabs. (RH)*

*Peddar's Way at Little Massingham, Norfolk. This Roman road is very precisely aligned, to within half a degree over 42 miles. It runs from nowhere to nowhere. It is probably a military road, built to hold down the Iceni tribe of East Anglia after Boadicea's revolt in AD61, and never had a destination. The first twenty years of Roman Britain were bloody and precarious. Boadicea's revolt horrified even the Roman world: two of her three massacres would have been averted had the legions got there in time. (TM, August 1993)*

### Holloways

These are the lanes mysteriously sunk in ravines which protect them from sun and the blasts of winter, lined with great trees whose roots overhang far above, their cavernous shade the home of delicate plants like hart's-tongue, shining cranesbill and moschatel. Holloways are the result of centuries of erosion as feet, hooves and wheels loosened the unpaved surface and allowed heavy rain to wash it away. Many are already mentioned as such in Anglo-Saxon charters.

Holloways occur in Ancient Countryside wherever the geology favours erosion. Those down to Flatford Mill (E. Bergholt, Suffolk) are formed in an accumulation of loess washed down from elsewhere in prehistory. Upper Greensand forms dark and intricate rock-sided holloways around Midhurst in the Sussex Weald. Lower Greensand forms many in Wiltshire and Dorset. (See photograph, p. 128.)

town), church-paths, etc. The term 'saltstreet' or 'saltroad' occurs around the great inland salt deposits of Worcestershire. The term 'ridgeway' is common all over England. All classes of highway are often described as 'old' or 'hollow'.

River and stream crossings are mentioned 666 times in English charters, one-sixth being bridges and the rest fords. Their distribution depends on the character of the rivers. Devon, with its countless small streams, has many fords and very few bridges. In the Fens, with their deep and muddy watercourses, half the crossings are bridges.

Place-names tell a different story. About 520 settlements in Domesday are named after crossings; of these only some 40 mention bridges, the rest being fords or wades. Evidently the place-names date on average from a time when bridges were less common than in the period of the charters. Towns named after bridges (Borough*bridge*, *Bridg*north) have a habit of not being mentioned in Domesday.

We know nothing of how major fords were arranged. The mind boggles at the thought of main roads crossing the unbridged Thames at Ox*ford* or Walling*ford*. The frequent place-name Stan*ford* suggests a constructed ford of stone like those which still exist on minor roads. Each of the dozen places called Stratford tells of a Roman bridge allowed to rot away. The charters, however, occasionally mention 'stone bridge', suggesting a Roman bridge still in use, as Roman bridges still are in Spain.

During the Anglo-Saxon period most of the important bridges were reinstated. From at least the eighth century bridge-work or pontage, the repair cost of a bridge, was spread among the townships at some distance on either side. Rochester Bridge – a timber bridge of ten spans across the deep and fiercely tidal Medway – was a surprising engineering achievement for the Anglo-Saxons. The landowners of dozens of named places were made responsible for the upkeep of individual piers and spans.

Another remarkable Anglo-Saxon bridge must have joined North and South Fambridge (Essex), connecting the field grids of the Rochford and Dengie peninsulas across the wide, tidal Crouch estuary. Later generations were unable to maintain this bridge, or Hullbridge above it; the lowest bridge today is five miles upstream.

### Medieval Roads

In the Middle Ages the road system of England was rather denser than it is now. In Ancient Countryside almost all the modern lanes already existed, together with others that have disappeared. Most of them had names. Every wood, meadow, house and barn and most fields and furlongs had vehicle access, and there were also footpath rights-of-way across fields. Moors and heaths were crisscrossed with tracks linking hamlets and farms. In open-field areas only the through roads have survived to the present; the countless ways leading to the strips have mostly been swept away by enclosure.

Less has been written on medieval than on Roman roads, but there can be no doubt of their importance; what of the Canterbury Tales or

Bideford Bridge, Devon, one of the great medieval long bridges across a tidal estuary, still in daily use. Great bridges had a spiritual and not merely a utilitarian significance: they were works of charity and piety, the gift of benefactors or subscribed by the public through indulgences. Many of them had chapels or even resident hermits.

These major bridges were maintained in various ways by lords, corporations, monasteries and local authorities, sometimes out of philanthropy, sometimes for the income from tolls.

Bridges are a neglected aspect of medieval architecture and still offer scope for the thrills of discovery. Medieval bridges tend have pointed arches with parallel stone ribs under them, and parapets with triangular 'refuges' for pedestrians. (BB)

the ceaseless journeys of King John? Monasteries depended on pilgrims and on their distant estates. The East Anglian cloth industry was not located near its raw material or its markets. Any town presupposes arrangements for moving thousands of tons of stuff, from wine to tiles and from firewood to the contents of cesspits. Water transport (where available) cost about one-fifth as much per ton-mile as roads, but there were few canals or navigable rivers, and the sea was dangerous.

The medievals were not great builders of new roads, except perhaps in the Fens or in connection with new towns. Roads were usually taken for granted as established features of the landscape. Any through road, even between two villages, is dignified as 'the King's way'; lesser highways are called 'common way', 'lane', 'vennel' (still the Scots word for a lane), 'church way' and so on. Medieval petty courts were as much concerned with road offences as their modern successors. The commonest transgression was allowing ditches (or worse) to flood the highway:

> William Barbor junior built a latrine on his holding which runs into the King's way to the nuisance of passers-by.
>
> *Court roll, Hatfield Broad-oak (Essex), 1443*

The going rate for fines was typically 1d. per perch (5½ yards) of offending ditch. Barbor did nothing about his latrine and was fined at every subsequent court for at least four years. Almost as common were fines for leaving timber, wood, earth, muckheaps or dead horses on the highway, for digging pits in it, or for allowing hedges and trees to obstruct it. Farmers were expected to maintain bridges and culverts where water from their land ran on to the highway. Little positive attention seems to have been given to surfacing roads, but this mattered less than it would now: wheels were designed for soft ground and many roads were wide enough to pick a way round sloughs.

Except for certain minor private lanes, and for unfenced footpaths across fields, highways were part of the common land of the manor. They had definite boundaries (hedges or ditches) and did not belong to the adjacent farmers. Much business in manorial courts was concerned

*A ford still in use at Eynesford, Kent. It has the typical arrangement of a paved way for vehicles through the river, with a bridge for pedestrians (and animals at times of high water) beside it. (DB/C, July 1993)*

*The famous clapper-bridge across the River Dart at Postbridge, Devon. Clapper-bridges, made of great stone slabs, are often said to be of prehistoric antiquity, though there is no means of proving this. They are fairly numerous in Devon and Cornwall; some still carry main roads. Here a later arched bridge stands beside the ancient one. (DW/WI, October 1992)*

with encroachments on common land, called purprestures.

Purprestures could occur on any common-land, but they most often took the form of narrowing a road, either by a neighbouring farmer pushing out his frontage or by a third party setting up a smallholding within the road itself. Manorial courts often condoned purprestures on payment of an annual fine to the lord of the manor. Major diversions of roads were rare and required the king's permission.

We know something of which were the main roads from the famous Gough Map, made *c.*1360, and also from the routes taken by wandering kings. Many medieval roads are still trunk roads, but there are important differences of detail. The main road into Cornwall did not march across Bodmin Moor and Gossmoor as does the present A30 but went by devious ways. At the time of the Peasants' Revolt (1381) the main road from London to Norwich crossed the River Lark at Icklingham where there is now but a Breckland cart track. The present A1 – the Roman road known from Anglo-Saxon times as Ermine Street – was not the only medieval main road from London through Huntingdonshire: there were two other parallel routes which are now no longer main roads. The state of the road surface and bridges doubtless determined which would be used at any one time. This is why many an obscure lane is now called Old London Road.

Among the greatest achievements of medieval engineering are the long stone bridges, built between 1150 and 1530. The earliest was perhaps at Exeter: $6^1/_2$ of its round Norman arches survive. From the

thirteenth century there was the great bridge of Huntingdon, which now withstands 15 times the load that its builders would have anticipated. London Bridge, alas, is no more, but we still have the great tidal bridges of Barnstaple (Devon) and Wadebridge (Cornwall); the town bridges of Durham (two), Wakefield, Monmouth, Abergavenny and Stratford-on-Avon; the east Midland bridges of St Ives and Great Barford; three bridges on the lower Tamar; the Auld Brig o'Ayr, the Auld Brig o'Balgownie (Aberdeen) and the bridge of Carrick-on-Suir (Ireland) – the list could be extended to more than a page.

Timber-framed bridges in the Rochester manner have disappeared leaving no mark on the landscape – although the last main-road bridge in this tradition, at Selby (Yorkshire), was demolished only in the 1970s. Something is known of the carpentry of the lesser bridges, whose timbers come to light when moats are drained.

Ordinary bridges were usually maintained by individuals as a manorial custom:

> John Dowe ought to make a bridge, called a fotebregge, in the King's way leading from Dunmowe to Hatfeld brodok ... on pain of losing 4s.
>
> *Great Canfield, Essex, 1510*

## Post-medieval Roads

The dissolution of the monasteries in the 1530s destroyed the most powerful corporate bodies with responsibilities for long-distance transport. The principle of road and bridge maintenance as an

### Highwaymen

Medieval England, like modern Detroit, was dangerous; the traveller could expect to be mugged. Although heathland was the preferred habitat of the top highwaymen from Robin Hood to Dick Turpin, travellers had a strong and persistent fear of woods and wood-pastures. Even today it is remarkable how seldom one sees ancient woodland from a main road. Where contact with woodland was unavoidable it was the practice to make *trenches*, linear clearings each side of the road, to give travellers the appearance of security. Around St Alban's Abbey in the Chilterns this was begun before the Conquest. Many trenches were cut in the thirteenth century. In 1285, following a murder on Ermine Street south of Huntingdon, a statute was enacted requiring

> that the high roads from merchant towns ... be widened, where there are woods, or hedges, or ditches, so that there be no ditch, underwood, or bushes, where a man may lurk to do evil near the road, for two hundred feet on one side and for two hundred feet on the other side.

The place of the Ermine Street murder is still instantly recognizable today. The road runs narrow between Bourn Wood and Longstowe Wood, as in 1285 the only woods on the long stretch from Huntingdon to Royston. The woods have been allowed to grow up to the road again, but now within the woods are the thirteenth-century woodbanks made to define the edges of the trenches.

obligation of landowning was crumbling; new owners of monastic land took up their rights more often then their duties. Traffic appears to have increased. Very few new bridges were built. The cost of transporting goods rose 2½-fold (in real terms) between 1540 and 1690, even though carters' wages fell. Next came the growth of public transport for persons and goods, and the development of the habit of thought that regards time spent in travelling as wasted. From the mid-sixteenth century belated attempts were made to reconstitute local arrangements for maintaining roads, but the problem of assigning responsibility for main roads was not easily solved.

One of the chief duties of Parliament in the eighteenth century was to pass Acts for making or improving particular roads, often through turnpike trusts. Military roads, attributed to General Wade, were built across Scotland and northern England to prevent a repetition of the rebellions of 1715 and 1745. Some of them were taken over for civilian use and are still main roads; many others fell into decay. The bridges have lasted better than the roads themselves. In the Scottish Highlands, roads were often reorganized to follow valleys. Older roads still survive in their ancient state as tracks across moorland, often passing unnecessarily high over the mountains.

Much more numerous are Enclosure-Act roads. At the parliamentary enclosure of open-fields, the ways leading to furlongs were often replaced by a planned, greatly reduced set of parish roads. Some of these were old roads, altered or not; others were new. The new roads run in the straight lines fashionable at the time, but, as C.C. Taylor points out, the commissioners of one parish often forgot to join their minor roads to those of the next, resulting in kinks or zigzags at parish boundaries. Other piecemeal changes in roads are diversions around eighteenth-century parks.

The turnpike movement destroyed highways; by improving some roads it caused many parallel unimproved roads (including two of the three Great North Roads) to fall into disuse. Again in the twentieth century the building of new main roads has been more than balanced by the disappearance of lesser highways, especially in the 1930s when minor roads were tarred; roads not favoured with tar often become disused. This could happen even with main roads, such as the old Cambridge-Oxford road via Croydon (Cambridgeshire). Many thousands of minor roads were demoted to bridleways and footpaths.

### Ancient Highways As They Are Now

The survival of an ancient road can mean many things. Occasionally one can walk on what are said to be the very flagstones of a Roman road (see photograph, p. 121, below right). At the other extreme, the motorist on a dual carriageway or the walker threading featureless ploughland may follow the exact line of an ancient highway of which nothing is visible. The course and the boundaries of a road may be of very different dates.

Ancient highways are best preserved on plateaux or up and down slopes. On cross-slopes they easily disappear through the continual creep of soil from above. Roads get displaced at river crossings: where a Roman bridge fell down, the road has often been diverted to a ford a mile away, and diverted again when a bridge was built. Roads following valleys are difficult to distinguish from later roads also constrained to follow the same valleys.

Ancient roads should be sought on the last edition of the 1-inch Ordnance Survey, which records both parish boundaries and public footpaths. Maps display alignments – straight or curving – that are not easily visible on the ground. The Roman or Iron Age layout of south-east Essex is obvious on the 2½-inch map.

Alignments are dangerous evidence and need corroboration. Enclosure-Act roads as well as Roman roads are straight; a straight stretch of road in a medieval landscape often results from the enclosure of a small common. The whole pseudo-science of ley-lines grew out of the accidental, uncorroborated lining-up of miscellaneous objects on maps. A genuine ancient long-distance road is nearly always a parish boundary in places. Where there is an apparent gap the route often continues as a public footpath or hedge. Traces of the road structure should be sought in aerial photographs as soil-marks or crop-marks. Ancient woods across an alignment preserve features elsewhere destroyed by ploughing.

Ancient roads, Roman or otherwise, usually have a course consisting of a series of small wobbles, as if indeed 'the rolling English drunkard made the rolling English road'. Over the centuries, travellers

## Turnpike Trusts

In the eighteenth century much of the responsibility for main roads was taken over by quangos called turnpike trusts. They had powers to make new roads and to levy tolls. 'Turnpiking' and other planned improvements included surfacing, rounding of bends, and making cuttings and embankments to spare horses and brakes on steep hills. The turnpike into Cornwall continued to use the medieval New Bridge over the river Tamar, but lessened the breakneck medieval descent to the bridge by inserting four hairpin bends. Many completely new main roads were built in Ireland. Examples in England include Acle New Road across the marshes to Great Yarmouth, and the road which disastrously splits Epping Forest along its length; both are of c.1830.

## Drove Roads

Many long-distance minor roads run across country in great curves. Their names – Drove Road, Bullock Road and the like – recall their eighteenth- and nineteenth-century use for driving cattle on the hoof from distant pastures to markets in England. Most drove roads, however, are probably older than this trade.

*Examining a cart-track on the Goonhilly Downs. The Lizard Peninsula has many cart-rut plants, including the tiny rush* Juncus mutabilis, *the water fern* Pilularia globulifera *and several aquatic buttercups. In the foreground is the special heath* Erica vagans, *one of the commonest plants on the Lizard and one of the rarest outside it. (TM, July 1993)*

*This holloway, sunk in Old Red Sandstone at Llanellen near Abergavenny, is overhung with ancient coppiced beech-trees (native in this area). Few plants grow under their dense shade. The holloway, though tarred, continues to expand sideways under the beech roots: a counter-example to the popular theory that trees universally protect against erosion. (TM, July 1993)*

have gone round fallen trees, sloughs, holes, muckheaps, purprestures, and dead horses; they have continued to go round after the obstruction has disappeared. Roman roads rarely have the long views ahead which the Ordnance map, on which widths are exaggerated, leads one to expect. Medieval and earlier roads are very variable in width, and have boundaries which are even more sinuous than the road itself. Post-medieval roads usually have accurately parallel hedges. Where one hedge is straight and the other sinuous this may indicate that a farmer has seized one side of the highway. In Ancient Countryside the highway often narrows suddenly where a cottage in a long narrow garden has been built in it. Such 'squatter' houses and gardens, sometimes of some antiquity, may go on one after another for miles within the original width of the road.

A highway, being part of the common land of the manor, is not usually demarcated from any commons which it crosses. Roads widen into funnels ('horns') as they pass into greens, heaths or wood-pasture. In Cornwall a lane from each farmstead funnels out between fields on to the moorland.

People crossing unfenced land make new tracks alongside old ones which get rutted. Bundles of parallel tracks can often be seen marking ancient routes across heath or moorland.

Although the statute regarding trenches (p. 126) was not everywhere obeyed, any long parallel-sided gap between a wood and a road is strong evidence that both the wood and the road date from before 1300 (there are examples along the roads through the ancient woods that ring Canterbury, and on the A1). Evidence for trenches has often been destroyed or hidden by enlargement of woods, road-widening and the fashion for 'planting up odd corners'.

## Conservation

There are many threats to the course, structure and vegetation of historic highways. Ploughing and obstruction of rights-of-way across fields is a familiar, age-old offence:

> William atteWater senior ploughed the church-way in a field called Warmelee to the grave nuisance ... [fined 1d.]
>
> *Court roll, Hatfield Broad-oak, 1444*

A modern version of purpresture begins with a householder mowing the adjacent verge outside his garden, continues with boulders placed to prevent people from driving on it, and ends with the ditch filled in and the verge absorbed into the garden. Farmers have grubbed out hedges and ditches to cultivate the highway up to the edge of the asphalt. This too is an ancient abuse:

> The Abbot of Sibton ploughed up a certain Royal way in Thorington [Suffolk] in width 3 feet and in length 20 perches.
>
> *Hundred Rolls, 1272*

Until recently local authorities were curiously reluctant to prevent public land from thus slipping *gratis* into private hands. They often evaded this duty on the false pretext that the soil of highways belongs to adjacent landowners.

Roadside verges have been neglected and abused: dug up, buried, or sprayed with weedkillers in the childlike belief that this would prevent weeds from growing on them (weedkillers, alas, kill cowslips more effectively than they kill weeds). Verges, once mown too often, are now mown too seldom: they turn into tussocky grassland and then into woodland. (Anyone wishing to see what roadside verges ought to be like should go to Sardinia.)

Much effort and research went into landscaping the new vegetation of motorway verges, but little into the deteriorating plant cover of existing highways. This neglect has partly been remedied: county Wildlife Trusts mark specially important lanes and verges and report them to highway authorities so that destructive treatment can be avoided.

## Highway Vegetation

Verges of highways are old grassland of a peculiar kind, traditionally grazed and fertilized by passing beasts and by washings from the road surface (see photograph, p. 116). In much of England, road and railway verges are now the chief home of such general grassland plants as cowslip, knapweed, rockrose and hay-rattle. More specific verge plants include oat-grass (*Arrhenatherum elatius*), kex or cow parsley, hedge-garlic (*Alliaria petiolata*), wild parsnip (*Pastinaca sativa*) and black horehound (*Ballota nigra*). Chalkland verges have great knapweed and its broomrape parasite (*Orobanche elatior*). A specially rich kind of verge is often to be found where an ancient road approaches an ancient wood.

Tracks and earthen road surfaces themselves support certain plants that withstand being stood on. These include the plantains whose pollen marks the beginning of civilization in the Neolithic period. Little-used tracks and paths and the trodden ground around pasture gates have a specialized flora. Most of these plants require seasonal moisture. Species of muddy tracks are probably the most severely threatened class of the British flora apart from cornfield weeds. Most of them appear to stay in one place rather than to colonize new sites; they are lost partly because traffic is concentrated on fewer tracks and partly through people's love of drainage. Mousetail (*Myosurus minimus*) lives in cattle-trodden gateways on Fenland pastures. A specialized plant of permanent water trickles in Cornish holloways is the delicate Cornish moneywort.

# GRASSLAND AND HEATH

Grassland and heath are the classic 'semi-natural' vegetation. They are natural, composed entirely of wild plants, yet they would hardly exist without past and continuing human activities. They were once wildwood, and if not grazed or mown they would become woodland again in a few decades.

There are two very different kinds of grassland: meadow, which is mown for hay, and pasture, which is grazed by farm animals. Mowing and grazing happen at different times of year; animals pick and choose what they bite, but the scythe does not; and so they encourage different plants. Meadowsweet, sorrel, oxeye, and salad burnet are easily destroyed by grazing but withstand mowing; yarrow, picnic-thistle and some buttercups tolerate grazing but not mowing. Mowing at specific times of year can favour one set of plants over another. Other grasslands, each with its own management regime, are road and railway verges, the lawns of colleges and great houses, churchyards, and the ribbons of grassland along the tops of sea-cliffs.

Heathland, as its name implies, includes the group of plants called heaths, the most common of which is the plant called heather by Scots and ling by English. It differs from moorland in not having a peaty soil. It resembles the sunny garigue of southern Europe, whereas moorland is a southern extension of the soggy tundra of the far north. Heaths are plants that have a finite life-span. They are flammable, and burning (if not left too late) rejuvenates them.

Right: *Heath at Rhinefield, New Forest. This heath, like many, is now at risk of turning into pinewood; but traditionally heaths were not under-used land. Heather was grazed or cut for various purposes. Even bracken had its place in the economy, and practices were sometimes designed to conserve it. Heath could be more valuable than arable land.*

Heath and grassland are exceedingly diverse. Even the sorry remnants that are left are almost as varied as woodland. Grasslands vary according to soil, terrain, season of mowing or grazing, and management history. There are grass-heaths, bracken-heaths, lichen-heaths, and the special grasslands and lichenlands of mountaintops.

Most of what looks like grassland in Britain and Ireland is really an arable crop, sown with varieties of ryegrass, timothy, clover, etc., and ploughed up and sown again every ten years or so. This chapter is concerned exclusively with old grassland as a permanent feature of the landscape.

Old grassland and heath often appear to be underused land, but this is a recent anomaly. In southern Europe, farmers rejoice in flowery meadows with rampion and oxeye, scabious, cranesbill and orchids. They regard hay from sown grassland as unfit for bovine consumption; so it was in Britain until a century and a half ago.

## Beginnings of Grassland and Heath

At our geographical latitude, around most of the world, trees are the natural vegetation. Grassland is the common alternative in places that are too dry or too high for trees, or grazed too much by wild beasts. The prairies of North America were partly the result of land management by American Indians to encourage and control the herds of buffalo on which they fed. The first consequence of intervention by European settlers was often an increase of trees.

The British and Irish climate is much too wet for grassland without plenty of grazing. We had no beasts on the majestic scale of the American buffalo herds. Our pre-Neolithic folk did not have the advantage of inflammable trees and grasses, which enabled American Indians to burn their landscape. Natural grassland would have been confined to high altitudes, the far north, and occasional locations where wild cattle and deer congregated.

Towards the end of the last glaciation, much of the country had

*A Dorset heath: Godlington Heath in Purbeck. The slopes are covered with heather; bracken grows on the better-drained soils at the foot of the slope; there is a bog in the valley.*
*(BG/NI, August 1992)*

been covered with semi-arctic grassland. When trees took over, from about 10,000 to 4,000BC, grassland became very rare. When Neolithic people arrived, the pollen record shows the sudden reappearance of grasses (as well as cereals) and grassland herbs. Grassland is a product of the transformation of the landscape that began in 4,000BC and continued into Roman times.

Where did grassland plants come from? Surprisingly few were introduced by Neolithic men. Some, such as white clover, may be newly-created species (p. 27); others, such as meadowsweet, grow in woodland as well as grassland. Most reappeared from fragments of late-glacial grassland surviving on high mountains, in the far north, or on sea-cliffs. This includes meadow plants such as meadow-rue, bird's-foot trefoil, meadow saxifrage, sorrel, and oxeye, and also pasture plants such as sainfoin, wild parsnip, marjoram, and lesser stitchwort. Meadows and pastures – now well-defined plant communities – have put themselves together mainly from a selection of plants that once grew in places too high or too far north for wildwood.

A few grassland plants did survive at low altitudes. Occasional pollen grains or fruits show that ragged robin, self-heal, bugle and devil's-bit persisted through the wildwood period. These are now associated with 'woodland grassland' – woodland rides and margins – which evidently had some counterpart in wildwood.

Pollen studies show that before 6,000BC the traditional heathland areas were covered by limewoods, hazelwoods or oakwoods.

*Grassland on cliffs near Dollar Ogo, on the east coast of the Lizard Peninsula, Cornwall. Natural grassland may have survived through wildwood times in such very wind-exposed places: exposure to wind would not prevent trees from growing, but might stunt them so that animals could browse their tops.*

*Clifftop plants such as oxeye often bloom in profusion after a furze fire, much as do the flowers of woodland after coppicing. (TM, July 1993)*

**Wet Grassland**
Old wet grassland is one of the most precious and beautiful habitats. Once it was common. Most medieval Forests contained areas of damp pasture; most rivers were bordered by damp meadow. Little remains after 150 years of destruction and neglect.

Above: *Marsh orchid in Hatfield Forest, Essex. (TM, May 1993)*
Below: *Meadow thistle (Cirsium dissectum) in Wendlebury Meads, Oxfordshire. (BG/NI, June 1981)*

Heathland, however, goes back in a small way before the beginnings of agriculture. The modest clearings made by Mesolithic men sometimes lasted long enough to develop into heath. Although woodland will not burn, the heather or bracken that replace it will: fire can be used to maintain heathland once formed.

Heaths were created on a much larger scale in Neolithic times and in the Bronze Age. Many of the barrows and other structures upon them were sited so as to be seen from a distance. They often have heathland soils buried beneath them, which proves that the heath came before the earthwork. Many of the great traditional grasslands, likewise, have barrows and henges, and therefore lost their trees no later than the Bronze Age. Neolithic and Bronze Age men created much of the downland of the chalk, and also made grassland at previously wooded altitudes in the mountains. Some areas later to be arable, such as south Norfolk, passed through a period as pasture in the Iron Age. Conversely, 'Celtic fields' and other remains show that vast areas of chalk downland were once under the plough.

### Heath, Meadow and Pasture in Anglo-Saxon Times

Heathland was much more prominent in Anglo-Saxon England than it is today. This is shown by direct mentions of heaths in charters and also by place-names. There are at least 14 places called Hatfield, Heathfield or Hadfield ('field' being Old English *feld*, an open space), at least 15 called Hadley or Headley ('heath-clearing'), and others called Hatton ('heath-town'). More than a hundred place-names allude to broom (Brampton, Bramley, Bromley) and 26 to gorse (or furze or whin). Bracken, a Norse word, occurs in such place-names as Brackenthwaite, but is less common than its Old English equivalent *fearn* of which *Farn*ham is a derivative. These show that heathland occurred all over Anglo-Saxon England and lowland Scotland. It was commoner in Ancient Countryside than in areas which had a strong open-field tradition.

Charters and place-names reveal an association of heath with woodland and wood-pasture. Heaths were common among the great woods of the Weald; the beginnings of Wealden heathland (for example Ashdown, a heathland Forest) can be traced back before the Norman Conquest. They occurred in most other big concentrations of woodland. King Harold's foundation charter of Waltham Abbey in 1062, the earliest document to mention what was later to become Epping Forest (Essex), says:

> First at Tippaburne; from the burn [that is, the stream] up to the heath; and from the heath to the boundary of Thecdene [Theyden Bois] with Æffan hecce [probably Abridge] ...

Epping Forest contained many heaths down the centuries; a shrunken remnant of this one, encroached upon by trees, is the present Sunshine Plain in the Forest.

Heath, then as now, could turn into woodland. The boundary of Ditchampton on the Grovely Ridge (Wiltshire), dated about 1045,

mentions a 'heathfield', successor to Iron Age pasture, which by the Middle Ages had become woodland and is now Heath Wood.

The division of grassland into meadow and pasture is related to feeding animals round the year. Before tractors, almost every farm had both ploughland and livestock. The livestock could feed on pasture (including heath) for much of the year, but from January to April there was a lean period when grass was not growing. Horses and oxen that pulled the ploughs were working hard at this time and had to be fed well, hence the need for hay. Hay had to be cut rapidly and laboriously by hand, and risked spoiling in bad weather. The best grassland, on which the crop grew thickest, was reserved for hay. In theory, every farm should have had access to a minimum of meadow and pasture to keep the beasts of plough. In practice, although hay had presumably existed since the scythe was invented in the Iron Age, meadow was rather slow to become widespread.

The first evidence of grassland management is in a grant by King Hlothere of Kent, dated 670, of an estate in Thanet with meadows (Latin *prata*) and pastures (*pascua*). Many Anglo-Saxon charters

*Stonehenge and the monuments round it were constructed in the midst of wildwood. Until this century Stonehenge was surrounded by a great tract of chalk grassland, part of which had existed for at least 5,000 years.*

*Even Stonehenge has its biological aspects. The faces of the stones are covered with ancient lichen communities, except for the buried surfaces of stones that fell and were later re-erected, and for places where graffiti were scrubbed off in the 1960s. (TM, July 1986)*

**Domesday Book: the Example of Dorset**
Dorset is very well recorded in Domesday Book. Pasture adds up to about 28 per cent of the land area. Arable works out at 44 per cent of Dorset, woodland at 13 per cent, meadow at 1 per cent. All the land-uses together account for 86 per cent of Dorset, a reasonable fit given the roughness of the data and of the arithmetic. Dorset in the eleventh century was roughly half arable, three-eighths grassland and heath, and one-eighth woodland. One-quarter of the pasture, in the southeast of the country, represented the Dorset heaths. Most of the remainder represented the chalk downs, which covered nearly half of middle Dorset. There was a thin scatter of pasture in the more highly cultivated north and west.

mention pasture as part of the land being conveyed; meadow is often specially mentioned as an unusual, valuable kind of land, sometimes detached from the rest of an estate as at Harwell and Sunningwell (Berkshire). There are five other words for grassland, the meaning of which is rarely straightforward. Pasture is seldom recorded in boundaries, probably it was too commonplace to be distinctive. When beating the bounds across a chalk down, the thorns, dells, stones, 'heathen burials' etc., were noted; the downland itself was not noteworthy.

## Domesday Book

In Domesday there are well over 10,000 entries of 'x acres of meadow', but they add up to only some 30,000 acres – about 1.2 per cent of the land area – less than arable, pasture, wood, moor or heath. It was very widely scattered. Eight settlements out of ten had meadow, though only five out of ten had wood. Wiltshire was typical: of 335 settlements, 283 possessed meadows, but usually of only 20 acres or less. All the meadows in Wiltshire amounted to 8,000 acres, less than 1 per cent of the county's total area.

Meadow was most common in Lincolnshire and the East Midlands. It was more thinly scattered in areas of ancient enclosure. It was conspicuously rare in the big concentrations of woodland such as the Weald and Chilterns, and in southwest England.

Pasture is mentioned sporadically throughout Domesday England, but only in the descriptions of the southwest and perhaps Oxfordshire is there an attempt at a complete record. 'Pasture' evidently included heath and sometimes moorland as well as grassland.

England as a whole, as covered in 1086, had 81,000 ploughs,

*A rare survival of old grassland on neutral soil (neither acid nor alkaline). Green-winged orchids and cowslips, near Yeovil (Somerset). (BG/NI, 1989)*

theoretically drawn by 648,000 oxen, which with cows, calves and bulls implies at least a million cattle. There can hardly have been fewer than 2 million sheep, even if one sheep sufficed to clothe each person. At 5 acres per beast and 1 acre per sheep, grassland or heath would have had to cover one-quarter of the country. This is probably an underestimate, for we have yet to make provision for dairy cattle or the unnumbered beasts of towns, transport, religion and war.

The evidence, though incomplete, suggests that by 1086 most of the big downlands already existed. There was pasture scattered in greens, commons and fields throughout the country. Some places specialized in pasture; others must have had difficulty in feeding even the oxen that drew the ploughs. Meadow was far from fully developed: it had spread to every part of England, but many places had only an acre or two. It developed more rapidly among the communal-enterprise villages and the open-field farming of the Planned Countryside. In the 'do-it-yourself' landscape of what is now Ancient Countryside, meadow was hardly beyond the experimental stage by 1086. Lack of meadow in the southwest can perhaps be explained by the long growing season, which made hay less necessary.

### The Middle Ages

From 1250 onwards, land surveys often contain precise lists of meadows, pastures and heaths, both private and common. The *Ely Coucher Book* of 1251 says of Little Gransden (Cambridgeshire):

> Mowing meadow, viz. In Weldis under Heyle wood thirteen acres.
> Private pasture, viz. What is called Grauis [Groves], twenty-five acres, where the plough-oxen of the parson of Grantesdene can feed with the Bishop's oxen.
> Item, there is a certain pasture which is called Langelund, and it is common to all the village.

Langland Common is forgotten, but the similar one on the Bishop's estate at Barking (Suffolk), listed as 'Berkingetye', still exists.

England in 1250 was more crowded than in 1086; grassland was scarcer and more fully used. Meadow had increased all over the country, and was very valuable land. Arable land was typically valued at 6d. per acre per annum, private pasture at 12d., and meadow at 24d.

Hay was needed not only for local consumption. Many farms grew it for cash. Although root crops, later a staple winter fodder, were not grown before 1650, there were alternatives to hay. Straw, stubble and weeds on fallow land might not have been very nutritious, but there was plenty of them: at least a quarter of the arable land of medieval England was fallow, used as pasturage, at any one time. There was some sustenance in brambles and suchlike within wood-pasture. And it was not unknown to feed oxen on corn.

Meadow took up all the land suitable for it, and some that was unsuitable. The best was land liable to flooding. By the thirteenth century, most flood-plains were meadows. This is why ancient woods never adjoin rivers unless the banks are too steep for meadow. At Little Gransden, lacking a flood-plain, the meadow was in 'the Wilds

Left photograph: *Halvergate Marshes, Norfolk. This was a great estuary in Roman times. When sea-level fell, the salt-marsh became valuable grazing land and was parcelled out among many parishes, some of them ten miles and more away. When sea-level rose again, the pasture was retained by embanking the rivers and installing windmill pumps. Many square miles still remain, although the grassland is partly spoilt by 'improvement' and the ditches (some of which began as salt-marsh creeks) are polluted. In the 1980s there was a classic controversy over a*

*proposal to destroy the marshes and replace them with arable land, which was narrowly and incompletely defeated. (TM, July 1993)*

Right photograph: *Glen Tanar, Aberdeenshire. Until recently, sheep would seldom have been honoured by being put out to grass; the grassland itself, up to 200 years ago, was probably arable fields belonging to a village of which only the church remains. (TM, October 1993)*

### Grassland and Fertility

A less obvious function of pasture and meadow was to fertilize arable land. The soil slowly lost fertility – as it now does more rapidly – as minerals leached out by rain or were transferred, via crops and the human body, to middens, gardens and churchyards. Before fertilizers were imported, these minerals were replaced from the dung of animals that had fed on grassland. Sheep, especially, could be fed on pasture during the day and folded on arable at night, which saved the trouble of handling the dung. Later it was often said, at least in books, that the dung of sheep was more valuable than wool or meat.

under Hayley Wood', a much less suitable location. Here, as usual, the tenants were required to make the lord's hay as a labour service.

Common pastures varied from thousands of acres of downland to the 90 acres of Barking Tye, and the acre or so of innumerable hamlet greens. A grassland common was regulated by the manorial courts just like a wood-pasture common.

There were common as well as private meadows. A few are still extant, such as Port Holme near Huntingdon (Cambridgeshire) and the great meads around Oxford and Cricklade (Wiltshire). Common meads were divided into strips called doles, the lord and each commoner having the hay on one or more doles. After the hay was cut, the meadow was usually grazed as common pasture for the rest of the season. Doles were often reallocated each year, as is still done in Pixey Mead near Oxford by drawing wooden balls. Strip-systems in meadow were more widespread than in arable.

Heathland shrank through assarting, the encroachment of farmland. Heath, however, was a valued resource, worth not much less than arable. In the twelfth century, the Colchester Cartulary mentions at Sandy (Bedfordshire) 'all the heath which was anciently fenced and a warren'; this is Sandy Warren, once the home of rabbits, now the home of the Royal Society for the Protection of Birds, where scraps of heath still linger among Victorian plantations.

At the same time, the age-old gain of heath from wood-pasture, probably by too much grazing, reappears. Dedham (Essex) in the fourteenth century had a large common, part of which was wooded. In the sixteenth century the manorial bye-laws included special clauses protecting the 'Lynde Trees upon Dedham heath', which might be pollarded 'so that they kille not', but which might not be felled 'by the grounde'. Lime trees could only be relics of an ancient wood. (Conservation was successful, for the limes survived even the destruction of the heath, and Mr D. Chesterfield tells me that they are still there in hedges.) Change from wood to heath is not always noticed in the documents. Middlesex, in Domesday Book a very wooded county, had by the eighteenth century become a very heathy county. Woodcutting rights originally attached to trees might easily be transferred to furze or ling.

Heaths were used for many purposes, not all compatible with each other. There was some tendency for commons to be used more for grazing and private heaths to be used for fuel. Furze produced a quick hot blaze for heating ovens, getting up a fire in the morning, or burning heretics; furze was a common fuel until the nineteenth century. Ling was used as fuel and as low-grade thatch. In north Norfolk it was cut regularly, like a coppice-wood.

A special use of heathland was for rabbits. A landowner could put rabbits on a common without infringing the grazing rights of the commoners. They shared the grazing with the commoners' sheep and cattle, and enabled the landowner – often a religious house – to get a good return from land on which he had few other rights. Heathland warrens existed all over England and the Scottish Lowlands. The biggest concentration was in the Breckland, where a dozen or more adjoined each other for mile after mile.

Heath fires occurred down the centuries (for instance in Hainault Forest [Essex] in 1372, and in Sherwood Forest in 1624). They were legislated against:

Item, to inquire who may have caused waste or destruction of the ling or fern in the Forest or may have burnt them to get better pasture for his animals, because they are the chief refuge for the Lord King's beasts.
*Sherwood Forest Book, 1251*

By a statute of 1692, persons burning heaths between Candlemas and Midsummer were whipped and sent to the house of correction. But, as Gilbert White complained a century later, even so robust a deterrent could not prevent conflagrations in 'large old furze' which consumed 'the very ground; so that for hundreds of acres ... the whole circuit around [looked] like the cinders of a volcano'.

Not all heaths were burnt. People rarely set fire to their own or each other's crops. Many heaths were so closely grazed as to be difficult to burn, and those that were not grazed were being kept up to be cut for other purposes. Fire in a heath, as in a wheatfield, was a rare accident which most people did their best to prevent. Heathland plants and animals now endangered by fires could not otherwise have survived to the present.

### Bracken as a Useful Plant

Bracken's general uses included fuel, litter for livestock, and thatch; its minor functions, as L. Rymer has shown, ranged from rain-making to contraception. The Japanese eat it, although it is carcinogenic.

The Roman settlers of Vindolanda (Northumberland), who lived like pigs, used bracken as litter for men as well as beasts. Sales of bracken are commonplace in estate accounts. Heathland fuels are mentioned in a lease at Hevingham (Norfolk) in 1609: the tenant of the park was required to 'brewe and bake with furres lyinge and brakes [furze, ling (heather) and bracken]', not with wood. At Petworth (Sussex) in 1349-50 men were paid three weeks' wages to cut bracken for 'composting the lord's land'. In many places bye-laws forbade cutting bracken before late summer, presumably to avoid weakening the plant.

In the nineteenth century bracken was an industrial crop. It was burnt to produce potash; the ashes were used in glassmaking, soapmaking, and as a detergent. Bracken was important to brickmaking as well as a popular domestic fuel. Attempts were made to use it as fodder for beasts.

Most conservationists believe that bracken has increased; this may be due partly to it no longer being harvested. The removal of dead fronds exposes the underground stems to frost.

*Lakenheath Warren, Suffolk, the scene of researches by Mrs G. Crompton and Dr J. Sheail. (TM, August 1993)*

### A Breckland Rabbit Warren

The Bishop of Ely set up Lakenheath Warren probably in the twelfth century. It produced rabbits commercially until World War II. It comprised 2,226 acres of heathland, on which there were also common-rights of grazing sheep and cutting bracken.

The rabbits were confined (more or less) by a great bank and ditch, more than ten miles long, topped with furze. Because Lakenheath adjoined other warrens on both sides, leakage of rabbits probably did not matter much. Most of the perimeter bank still stands; on the north side it is double or even triple, for the adjacent Wangford Warren had its own bank. Rabbit management was highly organized and included growing hay in Lakenheath Fen to feed the coneys in winter.

The warren lodge has been replaced by a Victorian building, but its fellow on Thetford Warren, six miles away, still stands as a mighty ruin, almost a castle, to remind us of the importance of rabbits to the ecclesiastical economy and of security risks in storing valuable rabbit-skins and salt rabbits. At the warren lodge of Brandon (Suffolk), in the 1380s, no expense was spared in hiring masons and carpenters and in bringing stone from Northamptonshire and timber from Norfolk.

There are also lengths of bank, probably for encouraging rabbits to burrow, marl-pits dug to improve the pasture for the rabbits, and in places faint ridge-and-furrow marks from ancient ploughing. The two World Wars added many other features, including chalk figures cut as targets for bombing practice, and craters from letting off unwanted ammunition.

The vegetation includes (besides heather and grassland) areas dominated by lichens growing on the ground, characteristic of the dry Breckland.

### Heathland Forests

Many medieval Forests were predominantly heathland. Sherwood Forest was not a vast wood (as popular imagination supposes), but a vast heath encompassing a number of woods and parks, about 65,000 acres in all. In Domesday Book at most one-third of this area was recorded as woodland. It is first described as a Forest in 1154.

The *Sherwood Forest Book* of 1251 has much to say about heathland management in relation to Forest Law. Henry III frequently ordered deer from Sherwood; great oaks given by him are still holding up the roofs of Lincoln Cathedral. No more than one-quarter of the Forest was woodland at this time. The Forest continued in existence as heath until the eighteenth century, woodland (including the famous Birkland and Bilhagh woods, p. 68) having shrunk to about one-tenth of the area.

The Forest of Wolmer (Hampshire) in Gilbert White's day (*c.*1750) consisted 'entirely of sand covered with heath and fern ... without having one standing tree in the whole extent'. This was probably nearly so five centuries earlier: Henry III's letters often refer to deer from Wolmer and timber from the twin Forest of Alice-Holt.

Even among wooded Forests, which were mostly on acid soils, there were few that entirely lacked heathland. In 1199 the monks of Stratford Langthorne were allowed to send 960 sheep into a heath, the present Wanstead and Leyton Flats in the south of Epping Forest. Nearly one-sixth of medieval Epping Forest was heath; the heath and the tree-land, although not demarcated in any way, were very stable until the changes in management of the last hundred years.

The most wooded large Forest was probably the Forest of Dean, but even this had small heathy 'greens'; some of these survived until the era of the Forestry Commission.

Fallow deer did well in heathland: most heathy Forests produced them, though not as abundantly for their area as wooded Forests. Heathland Forests afforded the local inhabitants the usual opportunities of contributing to the Exchequer through fines for being caught breaking the Forest Law.

## Later Changes

After the Black Death in 1349 pressure on land diminished; the shrunken population could not use all the arable land. At Little Gransden the villagers gradually took over all the Bishop's arable and meadow, adding them to their own common pasture and arable. Queen Elizabeth confiscated and sold the manor. The new owner, having found 'one old booke called the Byshopps Cowcher', discovered what the demesne lands had been in 1251 and tried to get them back, which involved fifty years of litigation. The villagers retaliated both in the courts and on occasion 'with Gunns, pistolls, halberts, pikes, swords, pitchforks, great Clubbs and some of the women with stones in their Aprons'. In 1607 the evidence was called

*Ponies grazing under common-rights on a New Forest heath. The New Forest (Hampshire) is largely heathland. Several of these heaths go back to the Bronze Age. In recent centuries, native woodland has covered about a quarter of the Forest; the pattern of heath and woodland has been nearly stable, and the place-names indicate that many of the isolated woods have been apart at least since the Middle Ages. Even in William the Conqueror's time, more than half of the Forest was probably heathland.*

*This heath was invaded by birch trees some decades ago; since then grazing has increased and has prevented younger birches from coming in. (DW/WI, May 1990)*

*A formerly irrigated water-meadow.
Water was led off from the river at a
weir into channels called* carriages,
*which distributed it over the meadow.
Overflowing the carriages, the water
then flowed over the surface to be caught
in channels called* drawns, *which
returned it to a lower point on the river.
In the 'catchwork' system the water
flowed from carriage to drawn by the
natural slope of the ground. On
absolutely level meadows, as here, there
was a system called floating, whereby the
water flowed down the sides of a kind of
ridge-and-furrow.
(SBP, Wiltshire, September 1991)*

of Christopher Meade, an archaeologist, as to the distribution of ridge-and-furrow, which proved where ploughland had been.

Little Gransden is a picturesque example of the change from arable to pasture, or even heath, that happened all over England in the later Middle Ages. Not all pasture on Midland ridge-and-furrow is of the 1350s; some may be as late as the eighteenth century. But the change was well advanced by 1500. Sometimes the lord got rid of the tenants, and sometimes the tenants got rid of the lord. An important influence (though not at Gransden) was the growth of the wool and cloth trades: sheep were more valuable than corn. Lawyers and men of substance bought up estates and ranched sheep where there had been open fields.

After 1500 there came that supreme technical achievement of English farming, the irrigated water-meadow. The earliest allusion in England is in 1523:

> ... yf there be any rynning water or lande flode that may be sette or brought to ronne ouer the medowes from the tyme that they be mowen vnto the begynning of May and they will be moche the bettr and it shall kylle drowne & driue awaye the moldywarpes [moles] and fyll vp the lowe places with sande & make the grounde euyn and good to mowe. All manner of waters be good so that they stande nat styll vpon the grounde. But specially that water that cometh out of a towne from euery mannes mydding [midden] or donghyll is best and will make the medowes moost rankest. And fro the begynning of May tyll ye medowes be mowen and the hay goten in the waters wolde be set by and ron another way.

J. Fizherbert, *The boke of surveying and improvments*

Irrigated water-meadows became fashionable, and by 1630 were widespread in south and west England. They were engineered and maintained by professional drowners with an elaborate system of channels for river water, levelled to within a fraction of an inch.

Floating a meadow increased the crop of hay at least fourfold. It also advanced the growing season during the hungry early spring. A usual downland practice was to irrigate the meadows in winter; to turn off the water in March and let the sheep pasture the young grass; to take the sheep off in late April and let the grass grow up to hay for two months. In summer, the meadow might either be used as pasture or be irrigated again for more crops of hay. The main purpose of irrigation was not to prevent drought. The water fertilized the grass with calcium out of chalk springs; it brought nitrate and phosphate from the leachings of arable land, the dung of roads and farmyards, and even the sewage of Winchester. And it was supposed to warm the grass, for the river would normally be warmer in winter than the air.

### Heath and Grassland Unfashionable

From the end of the seventeenth century, the Agricultural Revolution worked against heathland. New farming technology made it possible to cultivate all but the most difficult soils, which put an end to much private heathland. Bracken, ling and rabbits fell under general disapproval. Multiple land-uses were despised; land ownership began to be regarded as conferring an absolute right to do what one pleased with one's property; and the common-land status of the larger heaths was attacked by agricultural writers. Heaths were described as 'dreary and desolate wastes' – maybe they were, to those who saw more of them than we can – and as 'useless' and 'barren deserts', the resort of highwaymen. Forests were supposed to encourage immorality, and heathland Forests were more immoral than other kinds.

Enclosure Acts were a legal technique for suppressing commons as well as open-fields. Most commons survived late enough in England to be recorded in large-scale county maps. Norfolk was the supreme county for agricultural improvement, and it is instructive and melancholy to compare Faden's map of 1792-4 with the Ordnance Survey of 1838. By 1793 most of the open-fields (and the medieval woods) had gone, but the county was still pervaded with a cobweb of ramifying heaths and commons. Heaths may have been spared because of technical difficulties in cultivating them, or legal difficulties in securing the agreement of interested parties. Or landowners may have had scruples against usurping rights of the poor which could not adequately be compensated. In a few years, however, the difficulties and scruples were overcome, and the heaths vanished as if by magic. Mousehold Heath northeast of Norwich, which had covered 6,000 acres, was reduced to 180 acres by 1801. Even so, it was almost the largest heath left outside the Breckland.

The same happened at different times elsewhere. The heaths of Essex, once quite extensive, almost disappeared outside Epping Forest. Those of Sherwood Forest were swept away mainly in the 1790s, and

*A Surrey heath showing (very unusually) a pine that has died without leaving children; but the heath is not spared, for birches are growing up instead. Nearly one-sixth of the whole of Surrey has turned spontaneously into woodland, mainly in the mid-nineteenth century. In the 1790s Surrey had been about 20 per cent heath and 4 per cent woodland; according to the Ordnance Survey, it is now 3.2 per cent heath and 15.6 per cent woodland and plantation.*

*The machinery of justice: Caxton Gibbet, Cambridgeshire. Crime was popularly associated with heathland Forests and other heaths. Trouble over poaching in Windsor Forest led to the Black Act in 1723, which created fifty new capital crimes. (OR, June 1972)*

of Windsor Forest in 1857.

In southern England, heaths met another fate. For centuries trees and bushes had grown intermittently on commons, and had been included among their fuel resources. From the early nineteenth century onwards, on hundreds of commons from Hertfordshire southwards, grazing and cutting declined below the minimum necessary to keep trees from invading.

Destruction of heath was resumed in the twentieth century with agricultural 'reclamation' in World War II. Little of the heath sacrificed to the war effort was regained in peacetime. More important still was tree-planting. Trees had been planted on heaths in the nineteenth century, and self-sown descendants of introduced Scots pines hastened the decline of the Surrey heaths. Afforestation of heath became an official policy when the Forestry Commission was founded in 1919. About half the three largest remaining heathland areas – Breckland, Sandlings, and the Dorset heaths – thus disappeared. Natural growth of trees destroyed the heaths of Epping Forest and Burnham Beeches. There is almost no heath left in Leicestershire, Lincolnshire, or non-Breckland Norfolk. The remaining 180 acres of Mousehold Heath, although acquired by Norwich Corporation in 1880 as a place of public resort, lost their grazing and turned into oakwood.

The growth of trees was encouraged by the massacre of rabbits through myxomatosis in 1954. Other changes followed. In Breckland many of the rabbits' favourite plants, such as the catchfly *Silene otites* and the curious fern *Botrychium lunaria*, which had long survived in a bitten-down state, suddenly flourished, only to be smothered later by the competition of taller tussocky grasses. Ling and furze, not rejuvenated by browsing, grew up tall and even-aged; when a drought or frost carried them off, they were replaced by grass or bracken.

In the darkest days of ericophobia, the voices of Gilbert White, John Clare, George Borrow and Thomas Hardy were public reminders of the glory and mystery and freedom of the heath. But few listened: people do not value heathland until they have lost nine-tenths of it. As late as 1937, W. G. Clarke, the great Breckland scholar, wrote of the passing of the heaths with only lukewarm disapproval.

Was the destruction of the heaths necessary? The extra farmland, although of poor quality, made an appreciable difference to the nation's resources, and we would now have the greatest difficulty in maintaining all the heath that there was in the eighteenth century. I can hardly speculate on what might have happened had thought been given to using heathland more efficiently instead of turning it into ordinary farmland.

The decline of old grassland was quite as disastrous. By 1700 grass and clover seeds had become articles of commerce, so that pasture could be treated as merely another arable crop. Enclosure Acts abolished many grassland commons and brought the turf under the whim of private ownership. Sown grass slowly become fully acceptable as a substitute for old grassland.

In the early nineteenth century, the northern half of the English chalk downland – 170 miles of it, from Royston to Flamborough Head – was almost annihilated, and the southern half much reduced. By 1860, C.C. Babington, Cambridge Professor of Botany, was moved to write:

> Until recently (within 60 years) most of the chalk district was open and covered with a beautiful coating of turf, profusely decorated with ... interesting plants. It is now converted into arable land, and its peculiar plants mostly confined to small waste spots ... pits, and the very few banks which are too steep for the plough. ... Even the ... entrenchments, and other interesting works of the ancient inhabitants have seldom escaped the rapacity of the modern agriculturist, who too frequently looks upon the native plants of the country as weeds, and its antiquities as deformities.

Some of the chalkland was a failure as arable land, but never recovered the full grassland flora. Destruction was resumed in the mid-nineteenth century, and again, after a lull, more thoroughly than ever following World War II.

Meadows fared worse still. Irrigated meadows are too sophisticated and require too much attention to detail to be successful in the twentieth century. Other meadows mostly survived until 1945, but nearly all by now have been drained and ploughed, planted with poplars, or at best have become pasture. Arable and livestock farming have become segregated into different parts of the country, so that each no longer uses the other's byproducts and unsuitable land.

Grassland does not disappear by plough and poison alone: it turns into woodland. Detached fragments of grassland are difficult to maintain. Some, as on the Devil's Ditch near Newmarket (Cambridgeshire), were kept going for a time by rabbits, but after myxomatosis struck, hawthorns strode in. Acidic grasslands have been overrun by bracken. Disused grassland, at best, becomes tussocky and loses its smaller and more precious plants.

Grassland can be spoilt by quite small changes of management:

**The Fate of Dorset Heath and Chalk Grassland**

In 1086 heath and chalk grassland covered about one-quarter of Dorset, possibly slightly more in the early nineteenth century. The heaths declined from some 75,500 acres (one-eighth of Dorset) in 1811 to some 15,000 acres today. The destruction was most active between 1934 and 1960. Losses were mostly to agriculture and forestry, but also to urbanization: Poole Heath, the biggest, was eaten up by the nineteenth-century new town of Bournemouth.

Heaths have fared unusually well in that only four-fifths have been lost. Their literary fame (thanks to Thomas Hardy) may have saved them from a still worse fate. More than half the chalk grassland went in the early nineteenth century, and most of the remainder in the twentieth. Dorset has less than one-twelfth of the chalk grassland that it had in 1800. It also has some notable examples of old grassland on other soils, as at Kingcombe in Toller Porcorum.

**'Improved' Meadow and Pasture**

Even where a meadow or pasture appears to survive, it has usually been 'improved' with fertilizer and weedkiller, and is now little different from sown grassland. Chemical fertilizers, like weedkillers, encourage one or two strong-growing plants to get the upper hand and suppress the others. The rich mixture of plant species is converted into the sward of coarse grasses, with clovers and perhaps a few buttercups and thistles, that in Britain is called 'improved' grassland.

Until the early 1980s, people were still destroying old grassland, and thinking of clever ways to get at the last scraps on steep slopes. Unexpected people did this. The Ministry of Works set a bad example by over-tidying the surroundings of historic ruins. The pastures of Wimpole (Cambridgeshire) received less 'improvement' from the last private owner than when the National Trust took over the estate.

mowing instead of grazing, or mowing at a different time, or cattle instead of sheep. Gang-mowers, used in municipal parks, are pernicious: the mowings are not used but are left to rot, which in the long term has much the same effect as a dose of fertilizer.

Old grassland in private lawns is still hated by gardening writers. Despite the precedents of the flowery lawns of Chatsworth House, and the more old-fashioned Cambridge colleges with their harebells and rare clovers, it is taken for granted that lawns should imitate plastic grass. Readers are urged to soak their gardens in fertilizer ('feeding the lawn') and weedkiller – but those readers will then complain when the grass needs frequent cutting and watering as a result. Even the humble daisy is despised, and I have known people try to destroy fairy-rings, despite the curse on doing so.

**Heaths As They Are Now**

Heathland is an ancient and beautiful part of our heritage. It is a symbol of liberty: most heaths are *de facto* open to the public, and their destruction curtailed the Englishman's already meagre right to explore his own country. It is the habitat of nightjar, stone-curlew, Dartford warbler, smooth snake, and many other celebrated animals and plants. It is full of antiquities, and of complex and fascinating soil and vegetation patterns. It is a special responsibility of England: the Dutch, Danes and Swedes have been even more single-minded in destroying their heaths, and most of what is left in Europe is ours.

Rarely does a heath survive in full use: the best examples are probably in the New Forest. Most remaining heaths are small ones, or fragments of large ones. Grazing is seldom, and fuel-cutting very

*Chalk grassland with marjoram, dropwort and scabious, on the south-facing slope of the North Downs. (TM, Newlands Corner, Surrey, August 1994)*

*Chalk grassland being invaded by trees at Rowridge Down, Isle of Wight. A major cause of destruction of old pasture was the introduction of myxomatosis in 1954, which killed the rabbits and allowed trees to take over unhindered. (BG/NI, June 1980)*

rarely, kept up. Even where woodland has not developed, the original short and varied vegetation has often been replaced by monotonous bracken, tussocky grasses, or tall furze or ling.

The survival of heathland is precarious. On most heaths (except in the New Forest) there is not enough grazing to keep down oak and birch. Many heaths are in danger because they are fragmented. A collection of small heaths has a longer edge, across which trees can encroach, than one big heath, and is also less attractive to birds like the Dartford warbler. Pines planted on part of a heath may produce seedlings which destroy the remainder. The conservation of most heaths is an endless struggle against trees. (And yet people have even *planted* trees on heaths in the name of conservation!)

Most surviving heaths are commons, and have the characteristic shape of commons, with concave outlines, crossed by roads which enter the common by funnels (p. 65). A heath-common proclaims itself as the piece of land left over after all the private land has been hedged. The boundary is lined with houses, which are usually fewer than with other types of common.

Straight edges to heaths are usually the result of partial destruction. A vanished heath may leave 'ghosts' in the form of boundary-houses now stranded among fields.

Patterns in heathland vegetation result from soil-forming processes, the intrinsic behaviour of plants, and various human and animal activities. The Breckland is the scene of classic studies, extending back nearly a hundred years, of all these interactions. Many of the patterns can be seen by the public in places such as Thetford Heath, Cavenham Heath, and Grime's Graves.

Breckland 'heaths' vary from almost typical chalk grassland, bright with summer flowers where enough rabbits have returned to keep down the tall grasses, to the most acid soils with either pure ling or a bizarre and colourful mixture of different lichens. Often these are juxtaposed in wonderful patterns known as stripes and

### Chalk-heath

Heaths occupy acid soils, but are not only in parts of the country that have acid rocks. Some heaths are excellent dispellers of the myth that soils are necessarily formed by the weathering of the underlying rock. Much heathland is over solid geology of chalk or limestones. A few inches of acid soil are sufficient for ling and many other heath plants. The resulting mixture of chalkland species with those of acid soils has long fascinated naturalists.

Newmarket racecourse lies on, and preserves, an area of chalk grassland with the seemingly incongruous name of Newmarket Heath. Careful search by D.E. Coombe and others has revealed that there really is a heath, with ling and other plants on patches of acidic surface deposits. Mowing the turf prevents ling and other acid-loving plants from flowering, but probably immortalizes them by resetting the ageing process.

Arable fields outside the Heath now have typical thin chalk soils, but this was not always so. The great earthwork called the Devil's Ditch, sectioned by the making of the Newmarket bypass, was found to have beneath it a deep, originally non-chalky soil overlying the chalk. When the Ditch was made, in the late Roman or early Anglo-Saxon period, the area was evidently chalk-heath, a memory of which remains in the names Burwell Heath and Swaffham Heath for the adjacent fields.

Chalk-heath has now mostly been destroyed by cultivation. Ploughing effaces the acid soil and removes all evidence that there had ever been a heath. Surviving examples are widely scattered on chalk and limestone; the *locus classicus* is Lullington Heath National Nature Reserve near Beachy Head (Sussex).

*Inland sand-dunes, a curiosity of the Breckland. In about 1570 the dunes on Lakenheath Warren 'broke prison'. Over the next hundred years, loose wind-blown sand slowly crept northeast, burying buildings and fields and even blocking the Little Ouse river. Soon after, the sand went to sleep as mysteriously as it had awoken.*

*A few Breckland plants are adapted to being gradually buried by advancing sand, as is marram – grass on coastal dunes. There are still a few active blowouts; this one, with its surrounding lichen-heaths, is maintained by Suffolk Wildlife Trust. Like most heaths it is menaced by encroaching trees.*
*(DW/WI, Wangford Warren, Suffolk, August 1981)*

*Stripes and polygons in the Breckland. In roughland they are visible as contrasting types of natural vegetation; in arable land they appear as soil- or crop-marks; in plantations they sometimes cause differences of windblow among the trees.*

polygons. These are so sharp, repetitive and regular that it is hard to believe that they are not artificial; they are in reality a natural relic of the last Ice Age (see photograph opposite, below).

Stripes and polygons are a regular alternation of two different types of vegetation; for instance, heather *versus* chalk grassland. On a gentle slope there is a pattern of alternating stripes, usually of 10 to 15 yards between repetitions, running up and down hill. On a level plateau the pattern reorganizes itself into a regular network of meshes of heath enclosing polygons of chalk grassland. This results from an alternation of chalky and sandy soils, extending at least 6 feet below the surface. This geological pattern was created when the Breckland was tundra, some 12,000 years ago. It was then covered with several feet of a water-sodden slurry of frost-shattered chalk overlying a permanently-frozen subsoil. Every winter the slurry expanded as it froze, generating great squeezing pressures which produced patterns in the subsoil whose fossilized remains control the vegetation today.

Overlying the stripes and polygons are patterns produced by the intrinsic behaviour of plants. Bracken grows in ever-widening circles. It has a creeping, branching underground stem from which fronds arise year by year. New plants very rarely begin from spores, but once started they spread to cover many acres. Some Breckland bracken plants may well be six centuries old. Bracken advances at the edge and dies away in the middle, forming a circle with a hollow centre. In sandy parts of the Breckland, the sedge *Carex arenaria* grows in circular, clonal patches for a similar reason.

Other patterns result from millennia of heathland activities. At Grime's Graves (Norfolk), hundreds of hills and holes, with special plant communities, mark the shafts of Neolithic flint-mines.

Ling in heathland, as in moorland, has often been replaced by grass or bracken. In some places (such as locally as in Dorset), its disappearance is attributed to too much grazing. In Epping Forest and on many small heaths, its disappearance goes with lack of grazing. Probably ling needs to be maintained by a particular degree of grazing, or by cutting or burning, before it gets too old to rejuvenate.

Few of the recent changes in heath in any way compensate for the loss of its *genius loci*. Mousehole has lost its distinction as a heath without gaining distinction as a wood. Wiser men than I have spent many years on the problems without finding an easy answer. The only adequate solution is some revival or modification of traditional management.

## Grasslands As They Are Now

Historic grassland survives by the square mile in some highland areas such as Teesdale, and in three areas protected by the military: Salisbury Plain and Porton Down (Wiltshire) and the Stanford Battle Area (Norfolk). Up and down the country there are thousands of fragments. Some are on difficult terrain: my native River Waveney has resisted being tamed and still has the 25 miles of meadow of my childhood. Some are protected – for one lifetime – by an old-fashioned

### Heath Fires

Heath fires have multiplied. This is usually attributed to ever-increasing public carelessness with matches, but is more plausibly yet another result of lack of management. The longer old furze, dead bracken, and suchlike, are allowed to go uncut, the more combustible they become – and the hotter the resulting fire. Many heathland animals cannot run away, and some plants are killed by a single burning. Fires threaten smooth snake, sand lizard, natterjack toad, silver-studded blue butterfly, adder, and ground-nesting birds. They have probably eliminated juniper, the broom-like *Genista pilosa*, and the clubmoss *Lycopodium selago* from most heaths. It is vain to hope that fires will prevent trees from invading. An oak or birch only a few years old survives most fires: it is killed to ground level but promptly coppices. Burnt areas are especially attractive to birch seedlings, which come up in abundance and prevent heath vegetation from returning.

*Porton Down, Wiltshire. The Porton military ranges are one of the largest remaining areas of chalk downland. Although very rich in plant and animal life, they illustrate (as Terry Wells and others have shown) that ancient grassland is specially important and cannot be re-created. Most of Porton was ploughed in the Middle Ages, and partly again about 200 years ago. Some typical plants are rare at Porton and are largely confined to areas that escaped these ploughings.*

*Many of the largest and best heaths and chalk grasslands are in the hands of the military, who have an excellent record of caring for them. In civilian hands they would hardly have survived at all. Their future, in an apparently non-militant age, is a cause for concern. (JM/Ardea, June 1971)*

or public-spirited owner. Grassland survives on commons and greens through being no one person's property. It exists precariously on golf-courses, race-courses, playing-fields, road and railway verges, cliff-edges, prehistoric earthworks and old quarries.

Commons, and their smaller sisters (greens and tyes), are a precious survival of old grassland on neutral or acid soils. Most of them are in Ancient Countryside. Typical of East Anglia is the green up to half a mile wide, grazed by horses and cattle, its long grass brilliant with cowslip, meadow saxifrage, hay-rattle, cuckoo-flower, and green-winged orchids; scattered around its edges are ancient houses half-hidden in trees. Such are Barking Tye (of the *Ely Coucher Book*), Chippenhall Green, Burgate Great and Little Greens, and Mellis Green in Suffolk, or Morningthorpe Green and Fritton Common in south Norfolk. This already ancient type of settlement was taken to America and made the pattern of New England villages. Roadside verges are an extension of the common.

Most greens existed in the early Middle Ages. Often they are older than the towns and villages in which they are now embedded. In mid-Norfolk the greens came before the houses bordering them: during the twelfth century, people forsook the villages in which they had been living and moved to the edges of the greens. In contrast, Long Melford (Suffolk) has a green but was a Roman town.

Old grasslands have special plants such as juniper. A century ago many chalk downs were dotted with juniper bushes, as they still are in France. Juniper can be the first stage towards woodland: other trees spring up protected by the juniper prickles, and eventually a wood is formed. The junipers cannot survive in a wood, though their dead remains can last for a century. Chalkland juniper has thus been the

victim of its own way of life, but has been much more reduced by ploughing and burning. Juniper has a good historical and prehistoric record; it is one of the grassland plants that came out of the tundra. It survives on chalk downs because these are among the few well-drained, unshaded lowland habitats which are not now burnt.

Old grasslands have indicator plants in much the same way as old woods. (A few plants are indicators of both: adder's-tongue, pignut and autumn crocus grow in ancient grassland and ancient woodland but have little power to colonize in either.) Many of them appear not to grow easily from seed; plants do have an opportunity to start from seed where the surface is broken by molehills, rabbit-scratchings, and anthills, all of which have distinctive floras.

Anthills are characteristic of grasslands of respectable age. Many butterflies require old grassland because their caterpillars feed on specific plants: the most famous is the Large Blue, whose remarkable life-cycle calls for ants and wild thyme.

The dark-green fairy-rings of old grassland are produced by fungi which start at a point and gradually spread outwards. Big rings of puffballs or *Marasmius oreades* can be centuries old.

Can old grassland be re-created? It might be thought so: downland ploughed long ago is often not strikingly different from ancient unploughed areas, though it seldom has the more exacting indicator plants. An excellent tract of old grassland is the Hills and Holes at Barnack near Peterborough (Northamptonshire), the quarries from which came the matchless Barnack building stone, exhausted in the late fifteenth century. A meadow or pasture rich in native plant life can be made in about 150 years – less time than it takes to make a good wood, but impracticably long in terms of human whims and setbacks.

It is possible (at a price) to buy 'wildflower' seed mixtures which claim to imitate such grassland. These claims should be treated with caution. A recent large-scale attempt to re-create chalk downland near Cambridge had a most interesting, but unexpected, outcome. Although the seed came from a very reputable source, what came up was an

Right photograph: *Fritillary, a famous plant of a few old meadows, where it may grow by thousands. It has diminished in the last fifty years more than almost any other British plant. Some survivals are in large flood-plain meadows, some of which are still dole-meadows. It also occurs in very different, but also ancient, upland meadows in Suffolk, where it may grow with anemone, creeping jenny, and other woodland plants. (DW/WI, North Meadow, Cricklade, Wiltshire, May 1990)*

Left photograph: *Pasque-flower, the most famous and beautiful rare plant of ancient chalk and limestone grassland. It is quite robust – it survives picnicking and lack of grazing – but it is instantly destroyed by ploughing, and never returns. It has steadily declined as one after another of its sites has been cultivated. (DW/WI, Therfield Heath, Hertfordshire)*

amazing mixture of plants, some of them from southern Europe and the Near East.

Old grassland, once damaged, can take a very long time to restore. The grasslands of Hatfield Forest have taken forty years to recover after improvement in the 1950s; some areas eluded the improver's tractor, and their orchids and sedges survive but have spread very slowly. The Cambridge city commons still bear the marks of a weedkilling twenty-five years ago (from which the weeds quickly recovered).

A meadow or pasture rich in native plant life can be made in about 150 years – less time than it takes to make a good wood, but impracticably long in terms of human whims and setbacks.

But what of the outstanding grasslands? Many typical chalk grassland species are unexpectedly rare or missing on the Porton military ranges. Dr Terry Wells and others attribute many of these absences to the ploughing of the area during the Middle Ages or in the late eighteenth and nineteenth centuries. They have no difficulty in recognizing grasslands of varying ages up to 130 years since last ploughing. Such plants as horseshoe vetch (*Hippocrepis comosa*), bastard toadflax (*Thesium humifusum*), the gentian *Gentianella amarella*, and milkwort (*Polygala calcarea* and *P. vulgaris*), which used to be quite common in chalk grassland, are largely restricted to centuries-old turf. These plants have little power to spread, although they get on to ancient earthworks.

*A fine churchyard with old grassland. Rickinghall Inferior, Suffolk. (TM, June 1993)*

Churchyards are very special. They extend into areas from which all other wild vegetation has long ago been banished. The tiny, beautiful churchyard of Little St Mary's brings wildness (and a rare plant) into the middle of Cambridge; others preserve wildness where there is nothing but fields. Churchyards, alas, are not exempt from the idolatry of tidiness and the plastic-grass mentality. Parochial church councillors who destroy the gravestones of their ancestors, in order to mow the grass more often, can have the same lack of respect for the beauties given them by their Maker. But a small majority of churchyards are still treated as God's Acre, loved and appreciated for what they are, and not as municipal gardens.

A churchyard is usually at least as old as the oldest fragment of the church; many are well over a thousand years old. It will often have been grazed as well as mown – the herbage being the parson's perquisite – and have been periodically disturbed by gravedigging. A moment's reflective calculation suggests that the average English country churchyard contains at least 10,000 bodies.

No two churchyards, unless over-tidied, are alike. Each one usually has areas mown several times a year or only once, shaded areas, damp areas on the north side of the church, and similar features – at least half-a-dozen kinds of grassland. A characteristic churchyard plant is meadow saxifrage (*Saxifraga granulata*), which grows on my grandfather's grave and will one day, I hope, adorn mine. (The other lowland saxifrage, *S. tridactylites*, is equally typical of churchyard walls.) Some churchyards tend to a chalk grassland flora, with oxeye, calamint, quaking-grass, and occasional rarities like man orchid. Others imitate woodland, with primroses and anemones. The nettles and cow-parsley are a *memento mori*, for in them is recycled, while awaiting the Last Trump, part of the phosphate of 10,000 skeletons.

Churchyards and churches are crowded with other wildlife: reptiles and amphibians (especially the slow-worm), bats, ferns and the various lichens on different building-stones and tombstones and even, occasionally, on ancient windows.

# MOORLAND

Britain and Ireland, in the eyes of other nations, are the world's great moorland countries. Ours are the lands of peat fires, of the 'bonnie, bonnie banks o'Loch Lomond', of Ilkley Moor, of the Hound of the Baskervilles. Moors run from Killarney and Land's End to Cape Wrath and the Shetlands. Scotland is the only accessible country that is more than half moorland, and visitors come from all over the world to see it.

The most famous moors are heather moors, but there are others dominated by bog myrtle and crowberry, by cotton grass and bog asphodel, by grasses (especially on the high tops), by sphagnum and other mosses, and by lichens. What distinguishes moorland from heath is the presence of peat, which is the accumulated remains of centuries of past plants.

Moors exist because of climate. Where the ground is forever wet, plant remains do not rot but compress and blacken into a layer of peat over the mineral soil. High rainfall also leaches minerals out of the soil and encourages those plants that favour very infertile soils, such as heather and sphagnum which are rot-resistant. In the rainy west, where the moors perpetually run with water, peat (here called *blanket-peat*) is many feet thick and covers even steep slopes. In drier eastern Scotland peat is only a few inches thick, and moors grade into heath.

Literary writers have often regarded moorland as primaeval wilderness. More recently, the idea has got about that moors (for all their beauty and variety) are 'wet deserts', the result of 'environmental degradation', and ought to be doing something useful like growing sheep or trees, although attempts to bring this about are often short-lived.

Right: *One of the last great wildernesses of Europe: the bogs of the Flow Country, Caithness. (DW/NHPA, November 1991)*

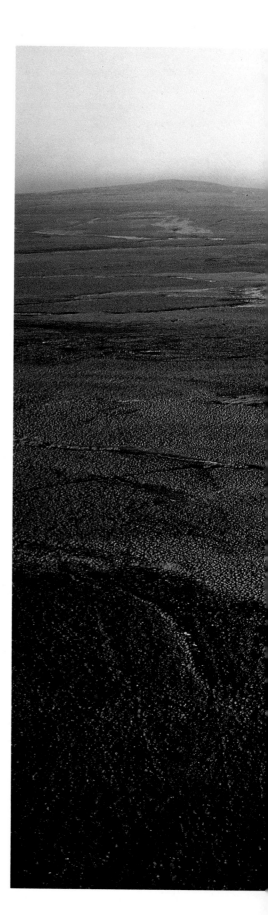

*Hundreds of barrows and stone circles, from Cornwall to Caithness, are witnesses that wide areas, now moorland, had ceased to be wooded by the middle Bronze Age at the latest. They were meant to be seen from a distance, and many of them had astronomical relationships demanding a clear horizon. The Nine Stanes, sited prominently on a ridge behind Stonehaven in east Scotland, are now hidden by planted trees. (TM, October 1993)*

## How Did Moors Arise? How Far Are They Natural?

The answer is not simple. For centuries people have dug tree-trunks out of moorland peat for fuel and timber, and have inferred that the hills were once wooded. Often the logs appeared as if charred, or axe-cut, or made into dugout boats. These finds may have given rise to the 'legends' (never documented) of great woods in Scotland being burnt to deny cover to wolves or Vikings. In fact, most of these trees were thousands of years older and fell down through natural agency; the hollowing, blackening and cracking were mainly due to natural decay.

The fact that trees grew on what is now moorland before significant human activity does not prove that moorland would still be wildwood if that activity had never occurred. Moors, especially of the more peaty kind, are not easily colonized by trees. (Foresters coerce trees to grow on blanket peat by ploughing, draining and fertilizing, but this technology has nothing to do with native vegetation.) Peat takes on a life of its own and gradually expands over the centuries. Trees are losing the battle with peat in some western Caledonian pinewoods today. The old trees live out their lives, but peat creeps under them, and their successors cannot take root.

Moorland may be wholly natural or artificial in origin, or a mixture of both. Leaching and peat formation would by now have turned large areas of wildwood to moorland; felling, pasturage and cultivation have speeded the change. In high-rainfall areas and in the far north, wildwood was always precarious and moorland is mainly natural. Even here, however, peat has probably grown faster where would-be farmers later destroyed the trees. Eastern Britain is less

favourable to peat; most of the drier, less peaty moorland, like heathland, would still be wildwood but for human intervention.

*Moorland has spread out from a nucleus of natural tundra in the far north. This is the vast peaty wilderness on the River Strathay in Caithness. (DW/WI, November 1991).*

### Early Human Activity

From the Neolithic period onwards, human activity began to predominate, as witness countless barrows, standing stones and stone circles. But moors were not used solely for funerals and astrology. Much of what is now moorland was once cultivated and populated. Such cultivation did not last long: soils became leached, the land became pasture and eventually blanket-bog, and the settlements moved downhill.

The time-scale of these events varied, and there was not always an arable stage. On Dartmoor, the heyday of settlement was the Bronze Age; depression set in by the Iron Age. In other areas the peak of settlement tends to be the Iron Age. In Derbyshire cultivation persists today at well over 1,000 feet altitude, but the soils here are unusually fertile and have resisted leaching.

The retreat of wildwood and later of agriculture encouraged the spread of the shade-intolerant plants now abundant in moorland – heather, cotton-grass and bog-myrtle – and of juniper and clubmosses, which have recently diminished again through burning.

By the end of the Iron Age all the large moors existed, though not all as extensive as they are now. The retreat of agriculture from the edges of moorland has been intermittent. When farming has prospered, neighbours of moorland have tried to add to their acres by intakes, and little farms have been set up, though not for long, in the midst of the moor. Edges of moors are an archaeological

*Grimspound on Dartmoor, a Bronze Age farming settlement much higher than settlement and farming extend today. (BN/AA&A)*

palimpsest of superimposed field systems, a record of centuries of endeavour and failure.

### Medieval Moorland

Most moors, except in Devon and Cornwall, are in poorly-documented parts of the country. Anglo-Saxon charters for Devon mention Dartmoor tors. Charters for Cornwall refer to barrows and small rock outcrops on the moors of Goonhilly Downs, some of which can be seen today (Walk V, pp. 210-213). The extent of the moors in the tenth century AD cannot have been very different from what it is now.

In most of England, Domesday Book records moors merely as gaps in the pattern of settlements. The Lake District and northern Pennines are not recorded at all. Recorded settlement in 1066 usually stops abruptly at about 750 feet altitude; in Exmoor it rises to 900 feet, but in the North York Moors few settlements are named above 500 feet. These altitudes are usually some 250 feet lower than the highest modern farmsteads, but probably do not represent the actual upper limit of eleventh-century habitation. Small farms at high altitudes often originated as summer pastures – the 'shields' of England or the *hafodau* of Wales – for settlements lower down. The real upper limit of settlement was probably little if any lower in the eleventh century than it is now.

In Somerset, Devon and Cornwall, Domesday attempts to record moorland along with other pasture. For the moors of the Lizard, Bodmin and Exmoor we are given dimensions which agree remarkably well with the actual acreage of the moors. Dartmoor is under-recorded.

Moorland in the north of England ought to have expanded mightily after the 'Harrying of the North' in the winter of 1069-70. The wrath of William the Conqueror, enraged by an insurrection, exploded with the force of many atomic bombs. Or so Domesday seems to say: 15 years later, some 300 settlements bordering the moors from Derbyshire to the Tees were enrolled as 'waste'. However, surprisingly few of these were permanently deserted, and there is little evidence that either moorland or woodland did in fact increase as a result.

Soon after, pressure on land pushed cultivation again up into the moors. A famous but typical example is Fernacre, a lonely farm at nearly 1,000 feet on Bodmin Moor. Many such little farmsteads, and some villages, appeared round the edges of moorland in the Pennines and elsewhere. Their dates (where they can be dated) point to the twelfth and thirteenth centuries, a time when new lands were also being won from fen and woodland. Some of the land was arable at altitudes where there is now only rough pasture.

The Forest movement came to moorland. At least 39 moors in the Pennines and Lake District were designated as Forests, including Peak Forest (Derbyshire), Bowland (west Yorkshire), and Rossendale (Lancashire). Others included Dartmoor Forest and Exmoor Forest, Stiperstones and Clee (Shropshire), and Pickering (North York Moors). There was at least as much moorland as woodland in the physical Forests of medieval England.

The Scots took moorland Forests very seriously. Well-known examples in the south include the Forests of Ettrick, Jedburgh and the Pentland Hills. The earliest known in the Highlands is the fourteenth-century Forest of Ross, on Beinn Eighe. New Forests continued to be created in Scotland all through the Middle Ages and long after.

Red deer flourished on moorland in the Middle Ages. Most of those eaten by Henry III came from the moorland Forests of the Pennines and the Lake District, occasionally from Exmoor. The haughty Bishops of Durham had a Forest in Weardale, out of which they slew and ate great herds of harts and hinds. (Red deer come also from heathland Forests, but relatively few from woodland.) In Scotland, the kings drew red deer from various moorland Forests; Edward I helped himself to them when invading Scotland. Like other Forests, those of moorland provided revenue from poaching fines and grazing rents.

In Wales, too, there were regular moorland Forests like Radnor Forest and Ffores Fawr (Brecon). But every little marcher lord was ambitious to declare the local mountain to be a Forest. Most Welsh mountains, such as Blorenge (Walk VI, pp. 214-19) have thus been petty Forests.

Dartmoor was not much of a Forest: hart and hind rarely came before its courts. Instead the Forest administration had the complex task of administering the common-land grazing of the Forest, levying small 'fines' on adjacent parishes whose livestock strayed into the Forest from the commons, and collecting somewhat larger fees for animals sent into the Forest from non-adjacent parishes. Licences were also issued to *carbonarii,* 'coal-men', presumably makers of peat charcoal used for smelting tin.

Cattle and goats were grazers of moorland as well as sheep and deer. Goats were of particular importance in Wales; escaped animals

**The Cistercians**
Use of moorland is traditionally associated with the Cistercian order of monks, who reached Britain in 1128. By their Rule, Cistercians were required to inhabit solitary places and to be farmers. They were able and energetic, and scholars have credited them, often on slender evidence, with many transformations in the landscape. They found solitude more difficult to come by in crowded England than in their native France.

Their most important houses were close to moorland and had large moorland estates. They also penetrated Wales (e.g. Strata Florida) and Scotland (e.g. Sweetheart Abbey), and even the Scottish Highlands at Ardchattan on Loch Etive.

The Cistercians were indeed farmers, sometimes agribusinessmen, who won land from moorland and pushed up the frontier of tillage, and increased the grazing of the remaining moorland. However, monkish sheep typically numbered thousands rather than tens of thousands, and it is an exaggeration to credit them with changing whole landscapes.

*Rievaulx Abbey. Rievaulx, Fountains, Jervaulx, Byland and Kirkstall Abbeys in Yorkshire derived much of their wealth from wool and attached great value to moorland pastures (such as Fountains Fell in Malham, 26 miles from Fountains Abbey). (CM, June 1980)*

were doubtless the ancestors of the 'wild goats' now found in North Wales and elsewhere, many of which preserve the characteristics of medieval breeds.

Moors were important sources of fuel – peat, furze and heather – and of bracken (p.139).

## Post-medieval Moorland

Moors (of which Exmoor is the best documented) were grazed by cattle, sheep and horses, with cattle as the predominant livestock on many moors. In the old-time Scottish Highlands the principal cash crop was black cattle, which were reared in the Islands, fed in mainland glens, then driven southwards to be fattened on lowland pastures and eaten in Edinburgh and London.

Rising population took a greater toll on land in moorland regions than elsewhere. On the Lizard there are many small crofts, often on islands of loess soil amid the otherwise uncultivable moors, dated probably to the sixteenth century. Similar expansions are known in South Wales and the Pennines. Pressure was greater still in the Scottish Highlands and Islands, where a multiplying and fiercely home-loving population wrested a miserable living from a shrinking area of mineral soil. Famine was not uncommon, although the introduction of the potato postponed disaster. Even the Atlantic rock of North Rona had a population of 30, who came to a ghastly end in 1685 when shipwrecked rats ate up their stores.

Industries had a local effect on moorland through the siting of mines and mining villages. Peat was a possible, but seldom an important, industrial fuel. Many miners had little farms, which in west Cornwall resulted in a remarkable industrial landscape. The moors, here of granite and not particularly infertile, were almost entirely eaten away by hundreds of cottage enclaves. Little is now left of the mining, but the cottages remain with innumerable lanes, small fields and little woods on the remaining scraps of common.

*Glen Muick Forest in operation. It is wrong to regard the hart as a specifically woodland animal. He is a beast of tundra and of the great glaciations – a kind of deputy mammoth. Red deer in moorland eat heather, cotton-grass, lichens, and other plants. They need shelter in the winter, but can travel in search of it, and are content with such meagre cover as old heather or tall bracken.*

*For thirty years Scottish Highlanders have complained that there are too many deer, but nobody knows how to keep the numbers down. (LC/NHPA, near Balmoral, Deeside, October 1990)*

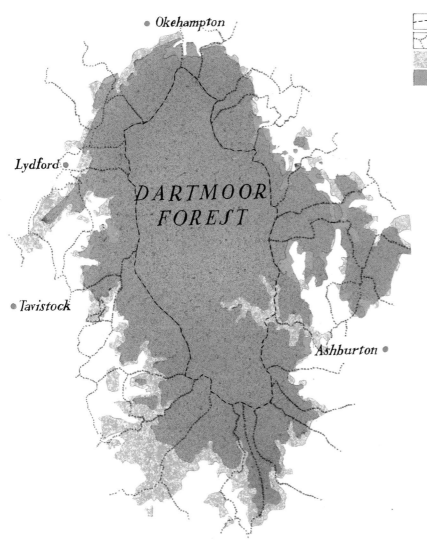

Okehampton

Lydford

DARTMOOR
FOREST

Tavistock

Ashburton

Boundary of legal Forest
Parish boundary
Approximate limit of moor
Land over 1,000ft

0    4    8
Kilometres
0         5
Miles

**Dartmoor**
The operation of moorland is best known from Dartmoor. The central part of the moor was extra-territorial, common to all the inhabitants of Devon except the folk of Bideford and Totnes; it is surrounded by the commons of 31 adjacent parishes. Perhaps for that reason, the middle of Dartmoor is not recorded in Domesday. When Dartmoor was made a Forest, only this central area was included; the Forest boundary (as in Exmoor) excluded the outer parts of the moor and all the surrounding woods. Even so, Dartmoor Forest covered 50,000 acres, bigger than any wooded Forest. The whole medieval moor, more than twice the size of the Forest, was a little smaller than the moor today; in many places it was bordered by an upper tier of now derelict little farms.

The Agricultural Revolution brought some drastic changes. In Wales and Highland England, many moorland commons were privatized by Enclosure Acts. In contrast to heaths, enclosure was not always followed by destruction. Much was said about 'improving' moorland. The celebrated John Knight, with a persistence worthy of a better cause, contrived to establish farmsteads even in the heart of Exmoor. Some smaller moors, such as Mendip, were largely eliminated. On Dartmoor, despite its legal protection, the hard labour of convicts created improved grassland on the middle of the moor, and loopholes in the bylaws allowed adjoining farmers to encroach on its edges. Elsewhere, most moorland remained, even though subdivided by stone or turf walls; blanket-peat defeated agricultural technology.

The moorland scene of today was set by a change from predominantly cattle farming to sheep, partly because of the breeding of Cheviots and Blackfaces which succeeded on moorland. This change is notoriously associated with the Highland Clearances in Scotland between 1782 and 1854.

The story has often been told of how certain landowners, notably

*A prehistoric pine stump revealed in a peat-cutting. Connemara, Ireland. (DW/WI, June 1987)*

the first Duke of Sutherland, coveted the ancestral lands of their tenants for sheep ranches, took advantage of the lax tenurial law, and hired agents who evicted the inhabitants by violence, bloodshed and arson. This was an outrageous example of the single-minded pursuit of agricultural profit, which has caused endless lesser mischief before and since. As often happens, the profit was short-lived, for the power of sheep to live off blanket-bog was overrated. But let us not blame the Duke and his friends, wicked as they were, for emptying all the glens. There are thousands of deserted settlements in the Highlands, and probably not one in ten tells the melancholy story of eviction.

The Highlands were dangerously overpopulated, and continued to be so despite the evictions. The population of Sutherland was at its highest in the 1850s, when the Clearances ended; it has since fallen by nearly half, most rapidly in the 1910s. Skye tells a similar story. For half a century the Highlands had lived on the brink of famine. When potato blight arrived in 1845 famine became a reality, though not so catastrophic as in Ireland. Emigration was an opportunity as well as a refuge. Why wring a miserable living from the edge of a bog when there was good land to be had in Canada?

After 1850 red deer were revived as beasts of the chase. Although few of the deer Forests whose names now sprinkle the Scottish Highlands are recorded before 1800, they are not all bogus Highland antiquarianisms; there is a genuine link with medieval Scots tradition. Forests never declined in Scotland as they did in England; many new ones were declared in the fifteenth, sixteenth and seventeenth centuries. By the eighteenth century they had spread even to the northwest. The moorland deer Forests of the Highlands still continue a practice which dates, though not in the same places, from the reign of Alexander I. Grouse-gamekeeping, however, is a nineteenth-century development. Grouse are often kept with sheep but are usually separated from deer.

Burning of moorland has probably always been more common than of heath. Numbers of grazing animals could rarely have been constant, and when they fared badly for a few years the vegetation would accumulate to a point where burning, called 'swaling' or 'swiddening', was needed to improve the pasture. Such fires were already getting out of hand on Exmoor in the fourteenth century.

In 1607 a statute forbade 'raysinge of Fires in moorishe Grounds and mountanous Countries' in the north of England between May and September, on pain of a month's imprisonment. It was alleged that

there happeneth yerelie a greate distruccion of the Broode of Wildfoule and Mooregame, and by the Multitude of grosse Vapours and Cloudes arrising from those greate Fyers, the Aire is soe distempered and such unseasonable and unnaturall Stormes are ingendred ... by the violence of those Fires driven wth the Wynd, great Feildes of Corne growinge have been consumed ...

Until about 1800 moor-burning was probably casual and sporadic. It became a regular management practice with the rise of sheep and grouse, which prefer the young heather which it generates. Older growth is woody, less palatable, and less nutritious. (Cattle and deer are less choosy.)

It is almost universally asserted that bracken has increased. The extent of the increase is not easy to ascertain, except in those few places where there are early photographs or vegetation maps. In many areas the spread of bracken has not been on the moors themselves but on the uppermost tier of medieval fields around them, now disused. F. Fraser Darling, the great authority on the Scottish Highlands, blamed the change from cattle to sheep for encouraging bracken; sheep hardly eat it and they trample it less than cattle. Improper burning, which too often goes with sheep-grazing, is also said to promote bracken rather than heather. More important still may be the 'improvements' of the last 100 years. Bracken is a clonal plant which inexorably spreads with time up to a limit set by its not tolerating wet ground. Improved drainage allows it to spread further. Fire and sheep are blamed also for the apparent spread of the tough inedible grass *Nardus stricta*, which now occupies wide areas of less peaty moorland.

*Peat ('turf') being cut by hand in the ancient manner, Killarney. This domestic use of peat contrasts with the use of raised bogs as fuel for power-stations which has laid waste great areas of the Irish midlands (p. 202). (BG/NI, May 1989)*

*Tin-mining engine-house at Camborne, west Cornwall. Tin-smelting does not require high-quality fuel, but any fuel was hard to get in Cornwall. Peat and peat charcoal were among those used, although the steam-engines ran on imported coal. (FCHB/SH)*

Camster Cairns in the Flow Country, Caithness. The burial cairns show that even the northern wilderness had some inhabitants.(DW/NHPA, November 1991)

Juniper at the Heights of Fodderty, Easter Ross. Juniper is permanently destroyed by burning. It has declined less on moorland than in other habitats, but survivors are in protected places on rock outcrops or islands. (OR, July 1978)

## Moors As They Are Now

Moors, like heaths, display the effects of soil differences, the natural behaviour of plants, and the presence of artefacts. Many moors develop a hummock-and-hollow structure repeated every few yards. For example, the uncomfortable tussocks of the grass *Molinia caerulea* cause the walker to avoid places where it grows (Walk V, pp. 210-13). It is in the nature of this grass to grow in tussocks, but other patterns involve the soil as well as the plant. Peat accumulates or erodes in response to different kinds of plant cover. Tussocks and pans on level moorland give way on steep slopes to regular 'terracets' – about three feet wide, much narrower than cultivation terraces – produced by the treading of beasts.

Slight variations in drainage produce different vegetation. These may be due to differences of slope or to the presence of a loess layer in the soil. *Molinia* often grows in wetter-than-average places, heather in drier-than-average. Barrows, banks and hut-circles, being better drained than the rest of the moor, stand out as patches or ribbons of furze or bell-heather. Even if at first sight a moor looks like a 'dreary waste', as literary writers used to call it, air photographs (especially in infra-red false-colour) reveal a fascinating array of superimposed natural features and remains of human activities. Reminders that the climate allows tree growth are occasional rowans perched on big boulders, often miles from woodland, and aspens and birches on cliffs. These are in places where they escape from grazing and peat.

*Moorland near Tomintoul, Inverness, showing a pattern of sharp-edged areas of different years' growth since burning. The object of burning is to produce a pure crop of heather, full of soft young shoots, which sheep and grouse favour. The favoured age for burning is 10 to 12 years, about a third of the lifespan of the heather plant, at which age it easily regenerates. If left longer the fire is hotter and more destructive and re-vegetation is uncertain. (BG/NI)*

In many areas, notably the Pennines, peat is now forming only locally if at all. Changes in management, air pollution and climate are possible explanations; past hiatuses in peat growth – 'recurrence surfaces' – are well known to pollen analysts. Blanket-peat is often dissected by erosion gullies (hags), which seem now to be specially active. One cause of hags – but not the only one – is excessive use of footpaths.

Moorlands are thick with the remains of prehistoric settlements and of later periods, both industrial – mine shafts, engine houses – and agricultural. In the wilds of Ross and Cromarty there are ruins of farms and industries wherever an acre or so of mineral soil emerges from the vast blanket of peat, even as high as 1,000 feet. People could hardly have been driven to wring a living out of this environment by anything but extremest overpopulation.

Field systems are best looked for in aerial photographs, or where a recent fire has revealed faint boundary banks or stone rows. Ridge-and-furrow was often made on former moorland as an aid to drainage. Stripes looking like ridge-and-furrow from the air may be produced by digging off peat to get rid of it, or by the parallel tracks of undefined roads.

Peat-cutting may affect large areas if the peat is thin. Large-scale aerial photographs of almost anywhere on the Lizard moors reveal a faint striation of curving lines, much smaller in scale than ridge-and-furrow and rarely visible on the ground. These are thought to be the result of paring off blanket-peat for fuel. There are also some hundreds of 'hut-rectangles', surrounded by shallow trenches filled with *Molinia*. They appear to be hearths for making peat charcoal.

## Conservation

Until recently moorland was less threatened than other wildland. It is not lost, like heath and woodland, through default and ignorance. The public loves moors and mountains: I need only mention Loch Lomond,

*A flourishing moor of heather and crowberry. Mount Blorenge, Abergavenny, SE Wales. (TM, July 1993)*

the Pennine Way, the Peak, and the Brecon Beacons. For centuries life in dark Satanic cities has been made liveable by thoughts of escape to the freedom and beauty and solitude of the fells. Encroachments are determinedly, often successfully, opposed. National Parks are concerned with moorland perhaps to the neglect of other roughland. Natural changes are less of a problem in moorland than in heath or fen.

However, some people still regard moorland as expendable, and thinly-populated areas as somehow an affront to civilization. The 'wet desert' habit of thought persists; some say moorland should be growing broadleaved trees, as if Scotland ought to be a second Norway. (Trees can invade moorland, but unfortunately they grow most easily in rocky patches which already diversify the scenery and vegetation.)

Until recently, moorland was being converted to improved grassland on a scale sufficient to threaten small important areas such as the North York Moors. However, the uniquely varied moors of the Lizard have at long last been recognized as National Nature Reserves. It seems that the long nibbling-away of Exmoor has at last been terminated. (The Enclosure Act of 1815 ended the legal protection of Exmoor as a Forest and parcelled it among private owners, who were at liberty to cultivate the moor as soon as they had solved the practical difficulties.)

The other threat is afforestation. It has been successively argued that growing trees on a moorland is profitable, creates employment, saves foreign imports, creates new habitats that are 'better' than

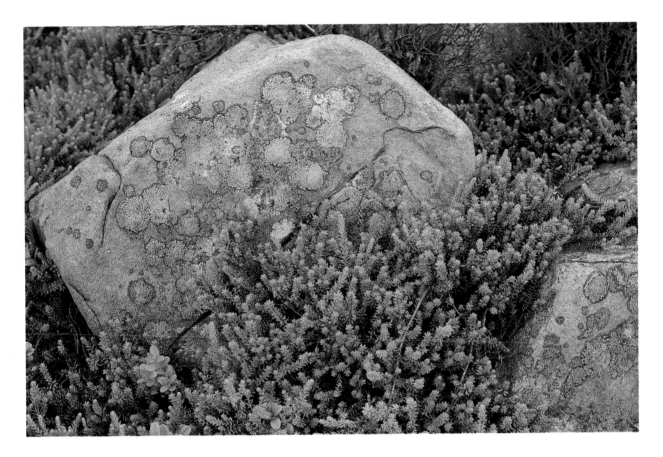

moorland, or saves other countries' wildwood by providing alternative timber. None of these claims has stood up for more than a decade or two, given the amount of land available and the trees that can be grown. Conservationists did not help by objecting most vehemently to 'blanket afforestation', as though a single plantation of 100 square miles did more damage than a hundred scattered plantations each of one square mile.

The case for afforestation nearly collapsed in ridicule over the Flow Country of Sutherland and Caithness. This marvellous peatland wilderness, the southernmost wholly natural tundra in Europe, was being forced by heroics of technology and at great public expense to grow trees: not fine tropical hardwoods, nor veneer-grade oak, but nearly useless lodgepole pine.

Moorland management is seldom ideal. There are complaints of too little grazing (as on the North York Moors and the Lizard) and too much (Dartmoor, Lake District, North Wales). Either may be responsible for a catastrophic decline of heather. There are too many deer in the Scottish Highlands. In overgrazed areas heather has almost become confined to cliffs.

Grouse-keeping flourishes, and the burning that goes with it; it is no longer so destructive of beasts and birds of prey. However, even well-organized burning is perhaps a second-best practice; it destroys animals and plants that are sensitive to fire and those that require old heather.

*Crowberry, a typical moorland plant. The various species of lichen (Rhizocarpon) on the boulders indicate that the rain is not particularly acid, despite the industrial history of this area. (TM, between Abergavenny and Blaenavon, SE Wales, July 1993)*

# PONDS, DELLS AND PITS

Nature created many kinds of holes in the ground. Over the centuries, some have been filled in by the growth of plants; others by people who prefer the land surface to be smooth. People have also made new holes for many different reasons. The result is a huge variety of *ponds* and *meres* (depressions with water in them most of the time), *dells* (natural dry holes) and *pits* (artificial dry holes). The Anglo-Saxons had at least seven words for different kinds.

Apart from the obvious drinking water and fish, ponds have been used for many industrial purposes. In the countryside, some were connected with textiles: retting flax and hemp, and beavering woad. Hemp-pits were used for steeping *Cannabis* in water to rot the soft tissues and leave the fibre. Beaver pits were used for fermenting woad to produce the dye. These messy and polluting processes needed to be kept away from drinking water, and were often done in isolated ponds which had originated in some quite unrelated way.

The history of ponds and pits can be difficult. The purpose for which a hole was last used may tell us nothing about its origin. For example, people sail on the Norfolk Broads, originally holes left by medieval peat-digging; a hemp-pit may have begun as a pingo, formed before the end of the last Ice Age by the uplifting of permafrost; almost any kind of pond can have been used as a fishpond.

*Abbotsbury Swannery, Dorset, with Chesil Beach behind. A swannery was originally concerned with fat swans as birds of the table. The pond in the foreground has arms at the corners which show it to be a duck decoy. The absence of a surrounding bank means that it is probably natural in origin, made out of a corner of the huge natural lagoon behind Chesil Beach (p. 186) (PS)*

**Questions to Ask of Depressions**
What happened to the contents of the hole? If a pond or pit was deliberately dug because it was wanted, the excavated material will usually be found close by as a bank or mound, unless attempts have been made to hide this by spreading it.

Did the hole result from digging some mineral? If so, what was the mineral? How did the digger know it was there? How did he take it away? Is there any track or ramp for access to the pit? Is there a bank or mound of discarded overburden or spoil?

Natural depressions, except pingos, do not have corresponding banks – there never were any contents – and their rounded contours contrast with the sharp edges of all but the oldest pits. Most natural depressions were formed in prehistory by processes that are very slow in historic terms, or have now ceased. They are older than any artificial earthwork. A pond which cuts through ridge-and-furrow is unlikely to be natural.

*Water being swallowed by a swallow-hole in Carboniferous limestone. Malham, Yorkshire. (BG/NI, June 1980)*

# SOME NATURAL HOLLOWS

## Kettleholes

These were formed in glacial times by the melting of blocks of ice embedded in debris left by retreating glaciers. Classic examples are the Cheshire and Shropshire meres. There is no reason why many smaller field-ponds in glacial deposits (from the last or an earlier glaciation) should not have been formed in a similar way.

## Swallow-holes and Sinkholes

Chalk and limestone are slowly dissolved even by ordinary rainwater, and especially by weak acids coming from vegetation and acid rocks. Dissolution is concentrated in particular places. Depressions can form by gradual solution, by the enlargement of fissures, or by caves collapsing. The result is a funnel-shaped or flat-bottomed hole from a few feet to a mile across, smooth or rugged according to the hardness of the rock. The bigger ones may have streams disappearing dramatically into their depths.

Swallows and sinks have to start in chalk or limestone, but this need not be visible on the surface. Cavities form just as easily – indeed they may be stimulated to form – where some other material lies on top of the limestone. The overlying rock tumbles into them. Probably the biggest flock of swallows in the British Isles, many thousands of them, is in the millstone grit mountains of South Wales. The grit has collapsed into cavities formed in limestone underneath it. Many of the ponds in East Anglia, although in boulder-clay or crag (a shelly sandstone), may result from sinkholes in the underlying chalk. Depressions called shakeholes arise in the alternating sandstones and limestones of northwest Yorkshire (p. 8; Walk IV, pp. 112-15).

## Landslips

When a slope of earth or soft rock gives way, it usually tilts and does not merely slide. The breakaway part comes to rest as a terrace, often crescent-shaped and sloping back into the hillside to form a dell. Landslip terraces persist for centuries and cannot usually be dated, except by the development of vegetation on the scarp at the back.

Landslips occur, often one after another, where a slope is unstable: usually clay alternates with other strata and is lubricated by springs. They are familiar on coastal cliffs, especially in Dorset and the Isle of Wight, and in motorway cuttings; but they can break out on long-established slopes even of only a few degrees. At the time of writing, a landslip had just eaten the best hotel in Scarborough (p. 187).

Landslip terraces have irregular, concave shapes which distinguish them from cultivation lynchets (p. 74). They are often found in woods.

## Pingos

The eastern margins of the Fens and the Breckland valleys swarm with ponds of a peculiar type. They are grouped close together, round or lobed in shape, and surrounded by banks which display extraordinary contrasts of vegetation. Good examples are to be seen at Foulden and Thomson Commons (Norfolk).

Well-preserved pingos have a convincingly artificial look, as though somebody had dug a pit and banked the earth around it. But they are certainly natural: there can be no arguing with the dwarf birch, purple saxifrage and other arctic plants from glacial times whose remains have been found. They were formed by ice action. Similar structures are now being formed in Arctic Canada; this is how the Eskimo word *pingo* comes to be used of East Anglia ponds.

Pingos occur in wet places where, if the surface were permanently frozen, water would be trapped beneath the permafrost layer under artesian pressure from surrounding hills. It is supposed that the permafrost was forced up by this pressure, perhaps over fissures in the underlying chalk, to form mounds of ice covered with frozen soil. The soil, melting in summer, would tend to slip off sideways. When the whole structure finally melted it would leave a pond with a bank round it.

### Lagoons

Where a river debouches on to a soft coast, its mouth is liable to be deflected by the movement of beach material, forming a bar or barrier beach. A small river may be completely blocked to form a lagoon. The people of Helston (Cornwall) used to have to dig through the barrier beach of the Loe Pool whenever it backed up to flood the lower part of the town, rendering to the lord of the manor a leathern purse containing three half-pence for permission to do so.

The best-known lagoons in Britain are the Fleet behind Chesil Beach (Dorset) (p. 169) and Slapton Ley (Devon).

### East Anglian Meres and Irish Turloughs

On East Wretham Heath in the Breckland (Norfolk Naturalists' Trust) is a curious group of ponds. Ringmere lies in a deep depression with a sandy floor. It can rise and fall by at least 15 feet; it can be full in a drought (as in 1724) and nearly dry in a wet summer (as in

*A pingo on Thomson Common, Norfolk: a natural Ice Age hollow, later used for various purposes including retting hemp. (PW/NI)*

**How Many Ponds Are There?**
One cannot define exactly what constitutes a pond. The earlier and better editions of the Ordnance Survey record wet ponds bigger than about 20 feet across. In 1880 there were about 800,000 of them in England and Wales (14 ponds to the square mile); including pits and dells the total would come to well over a million. At that time, the accumulation of natural and man-made depressions had reached its climax; there are unlikely to be so many now.

Ponds vary enormously in abundance. There are far more per square mile in East Anglia, Cheshire and south Lancashire than in the Pennines or Wales (except Anglesey). Ancient Countryside has more than twice as many ponds to the square mile as Planned Countryside. Some ancient woods contain more than a hundred ponds per square mile.

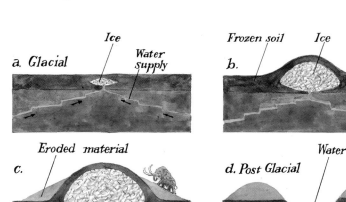

*A pingo: (a) in infancy in permafrost; (b) growing up; (c) fully developed, just before the general meltdown; (d) as it is now.*

1968). Langmere usually changes in step with Ringmere: when full it appears as a lake with an island, when low as a group of three ponds. A third, similarly fluctuating depression has been surrounded by two concentric ring-ditches for an unknown purpose. Between Langmere and Ringmere, and higher than either, is a patch of clay on which are two more ponds: one, called Fenmere, fills or dries up according to the weather; the other, nameless, is deep and never varies by more than a few inches. 'Hringmara heath', as the *Heimskringla Saga* tells us, ran red with blood in 1010 when St Olave smote the men of Ulfketel Snilling.

Langmere and Ringmere are examples of the Breckland meres, depressions in the chalk whose water levels are connected to a deep water table which gradually empties and recharges itself in accordance with variations in rainfall over a period of many months. Like other fluctuating ponds, these meres are rich in animal and plant life. They produce a surprising range of successive plant communities. Their edges get overgrown with trees, which are drowned and killed every few years. In most years, the meres swarm with little frogs and wildfowl. They were studied in detail by the Anglian Water Authority in order to protect their distinctive fluctuations against changes resulting from using the chalk for storing the public water supply.

Fluctuating meres are sometimes compared to the *turloughs* of western Ireland, flat-bottomed sinkholes in limestone which fill and empty more regularly than meres. Some of them are cultivated when dry. The short, regular flooding produces more permanent vegetation zones, including shrubs, than the slow, unpredictable changes of the Breckland meres. An outlying example in southwest Wales, attached to Carmel Woods, is famous because threatened by quarrying.

Deep round meres which do not fluctuate occur widely in East Anglia, often in groups. They are natural sinkholes in chalk, into which overlying clays and sands have collapsed. They have Anglo-Saxon names such as Livermere ('Sedge Mere') and medieval fishing rights.

Meres are known for convergences of parish boundaries. Six parishes meet at Ringmere. At Rymer Point, anciently also called Ringmere, between Thetford and Bury St Edmunds, nine parishes converge on a group of seven ponds and hollows. Doubtless the parishes concerned in Rymer and Ringmere all claimed access to water for their flocks, though the division is untidy; in neither place do the boundaries meet exactly at a point, nor do they share the waterholes equally.

Diss Mere sits, like the grandest of all village ponds, in the middle of the Norfolk town of Diss (which means 'mere'). Sylvia Peglar and John Birks have found in it one of the finest pollen records in Europe. In places it has been possible to count the layers of sediment deposited year by year in the mere. The sediment records, in turn, the coming of birch and pine after the last Ice Age, the growth of the wildwood, the sudden decline of elm (probably through disease), the grubbing-out of wildwood in the Bronze Age, cattle ranching in the Iron Age, the coming of rye, barley and *Cannabis*, and the growth of the medieval town.

## SOME ARTIFICIAL PONDS, LAKES AND PITS

The earliest known artificial excavations in Britain are Neolithic flint-mines. A few man-made ponds are known to be prehistoric: for instance, Point Pond, now in Great Ridge Wood west of Salisbury, which is older than the wood and older than the supposedly Bronze Age earthwork called Grim's Ditch.

### Pits, Quarries and Mines

The oldest mines are for flint; but coal, lead and other minerals have been won from mines, quarries and stream-beds at least since Roman times. Most of the visible coal deposits were in production by the late Middle Ages, sometimes by deep mining.

Primitive mines continued in use down the centuries. A *bell-pit* is a shaft sunk vertically down to the mineral-bearing rock. The coal or ore is won by undercutting the base of the shaft. When the miner dares undercut no further he sinks another shaft. Disused bell-pits leave funnel-shaped depressions, typically 20 feet across, surrounded by mounds of spoil.

A *drift* is produced by tunnelling into a mineral seam from an outcrop on a hillside. Drifts appear as rows of pits following the seam. Often there are remains of a track passing their mouths for carting away the mineral.

Clusters of bell-pits, usually undatable, are common in moorland and woodland in mining areas. Many of the sides of Welsh coal valleys are pockmarked with the rows of drifts of early miners attacking small seams. Other examples are 'lead-rakes', rows of pits in the Derbyshire lead country, and drifts for jet (a hard coal, treated as a gem) in northeast Yorkshire.

*Flashes* are shallow ponds produced by subsidence when disused mines collapse: for example, those above old coal-mines around Wigan. The flashes of Cheshire result from the collapse of caverns

*Two Breckland meres.*
Above left: *Langmere, moderately full. The water sometimes rises high enough to form a ring-shaped mere with the four old pines on a central island. It sometimes disappears completely. Note the young pines and birches which threaten to engulf the heath. (BS/Ardea, June 1985)*
Above: *Ringmere, moderately full. When the water rose higher, it submerged the sallows in the foreground; they responded by sprouting roots above ground into the water. (BG/NI, April 1986)*

### Marlpits

Many English soils are not formed by the weathering of the rocks, but come from thin surface layers of quite different material. Subsoil, dug up and added to the soil, often produces a mixture more fertile than either would be by itself. Marl means clayey chalk or chalky clay, dug up and applied to acid topsoils; but marling can include the use of any subsoil as fertilizer.

Marling may have Roman origins. The word 'loam-pit' occurs in Anglo-Saxon charters. By the thirteenth century, marling and disused marlpits are often documented. Many marlpits, however, were created by the renewed fashion for marling in the eighteenth and nineteenth centuries. There is a tradition among farmers of regarding any unexplained pond as a marlpit.

*A landscape of marlpits in Cheshire. To be genuine, a marlpit has to be geologically plausible: nobody digs for 'marl' where the bedrock is too hard or not different enough from the topsoil. It should be steep-sided, with a ramp for access by carts. Typical marlpits are in the middle of fields, one pit per field: pits in the corners of fields would double the labour of cartage. (BG/NI, June 1977)*

formed when rock salt was pumped out as brine.

Pits have been dug in all manner of places and for all kinds of materials. A favourite place was in the middle of the road: manorial courts fined people 'for Diging in the kinges hiewaye', and required the 'water-pits before men's gates' to be fenced to save men and beasts from falling in. Alongside roads, especially on common land, there are often small pits for gravel, chalk or stone to mend the road. In the *growan* pits of Cornwall, rotten granite and serpentine were dug for mortar in buildings, there being no source of lime.

Many stone quarries were for local use – sometimes very local, as with the little quarries in fields on the Derbyshire limestone, where the stone was raised with which to make the field-walls. This was not so everywhere. The limestones of Barnack (Northamptonshire) and Chilmark (Wiltshire) were transported far and wide in the Middle Ages; the tilestones of Collyweston (Northamptonshire) and Stonesfield (Oxford), and Cornish and Welsh slate, were also large commercial enterprises.

### Claypits

Clay is a raw material for earthworks as well as pottery. Great pits in the Fens provided the clay used as a thin core to seal banks and river walls made of permeable materials. Medieval archives record the use of clay for sealing dams or setting millposts.

As a building material, clay has been held to account for the profusion of ponds around clayland villages. How far this is true is difficult to tell. The daub between the timbers of even a large medieval house amounts to only about 40 cubic yards of clay: the contents of one good-sized pond would have made a whole village. But there have usually been uncounted generations of flimsy, short-lived earlier buildings.

There are also buildings with walls entirely of clay, which would have used more than those in which clay was merely an infill. Mud-brick in England is remarkably late; as John McCann has shown, it was invented in 1791 by John Austin of Shelford, Cambridgeshire. Cob (rammed earth) and other forms of solid earthen construction go back much earlier, although surviving earth houses can seldom be dated earlier than 1600. However, areas such as Devon, with a tradition of building whole houses out of mud, are not particularly prolific in ponds. Much would depend on how long a house lasted and whether the clay was recycled.

### Brick-pits

Bricks can be made from many kinds of mud or clay. 'Brickearth' consists of accumulations of wind-blown dust (loess) from glacial times. Bricks seem normally to have been burnt near where the material was dug. There is usually said to have been no brick-making in England between the Romans and the thirteenth century.

Brick-pits are of many kinds. Sometimes they are deep rectangular holes reaching a favourite stratum of clay. At Woolpit (Suffolk), with a long-established industry making several kinds of brick, there is a wide

*Neolithic flint-mines at Grime's Graves, in the Norfolk Breckland. Good-quality flint, called floorstone, has to be mined from deep in the chalk. The miners, around 2,700BC, sank 600 shafts up to forty feet deep to reach the floorstone, which they extracted with an efficiency which would do credit to modern mining. It was used for flint implements. Flint continued into medieval and modern times for architectural flintwork and for gun-flints. (EH, 1985)*

*A gravel-pit in Hatfield Forest. Gravel today seems ubiquitous and is profligately used, but in horse-and-cart times even a small deposit could be valuable. This little gravel-pit was the subject of two centuries of legal battles between the lord of the manor, the owner of the soil, and the commoners who claimed that it spoilt the grazing. It is now almost the only dry acidic grassland in inland Essex. (TM, April 1993)*

area of irregular holes and hills. Brickworks using loess scraped it up from wide, shallow excavations which may now be difficult to detect. The site of a works often becomes a 'Kiln Grove', a wood full of rejected bricks and tile-sherds.

## Coprolite-pits

Coprolites – 'dung-stones' – are lumps of phosphatic rock, so called by savants who thought them the dung of dinosaurs. In the 1860s and 1870s fortunes were made in a 'coprolite rush' for the phosphate in chalk and gault clay between Soham (Cambridgeshire) and Royston. Most of it was extracted from strip-workings which have left nothing but soil- and crop-marks. There are occasional deep water-filled pits with mounds, as on Quy Fen. On Coldham's Common, Cambridge, an avaricious Corporation cashed in on coprolite by a method which has left what looks deceptively like ridge-and-furrow.

## Broads

The Broads, well-loved, over-used and rapidly shrinking lakes in east Norfolk and northeast Suffolk, are not the remains of natural estuaries as was once thought. They are holes left by a huge industry of peat-digging. It is a remarkable illustration of the weakness of folk-memory and legend that this should have been totally forgotten in 300 years. The holes are not small: Fritton Lake was 2 miles long, 200 yards wide, and 15 feet deep.

None of the Broads has an Anglo-Saxon or Viking name. Proof that they are artificial came from a study of their sediments by Joyce Lambert and J.N. Jennings. Each Broad was originally a vast pit, with almost vertical sides penetrating through the surface layers into 'brushwood peat' laid down by fen wildwood in prehistory. The pits were subdivided by straight, narrow, vertical-sided, wall-like baulks of the same peat as the surroundings. The baulk tops were used as footpaths by the workmen; remains of gravel surfacing have been found. Since they were formed, the Broads have been partly filled in with mud and newer peat, which do not correspond to the older peat of the baulks and the surroundings.

Peat-digging probably began in the eleventh century. By the thirteenth century east Norfolk and east Suffolk were the most populous and most urbanized parts of the British Isles, and had very little woodland. They burnt peat on a vast scale, and were quite capable of consuming the 12 million 'turves' a year needed to produce the Broads. (The monks of Norwich Cathedral used at least 400,000 turves a year for cooking alone.)

Peat-digging on this scale would be impossible now because the workings would fill with water. In the Middle Ages sea-level was lower relative to the land, and the rivers were less tidal. The industry was ended by rising sea-level (especially after a cataclysmic surge in December 1287). Norwich turned to wood or coal brought from a distance, and the Broads were replaced by fens and waters. By the seventeenth century it no longer occurred to anyone that they were not natural.

## Moats

Castle moats have lesser counterparts around ordinary houses and gardens. In England there are more than 5,000 moats, more than anywhere else in Europe. Usually they are on their own or in pairs, but occasionally there are whole villages of moats. East Hatley (Cambridgeshire) has at least 12 moats in all, and there are eight in the deserted village of Bottisham Park (Cambridgeshire). There are about 750 moats in Ireland.

Moats are of various shapes and sizes, enclosing from four acres to one-eighth of an acre. The material from the ditch may form a bank on the outside or the inside, or may be spread out to raise the level of the interior. Rarely are there any ruins of a house. Houses in moats were wooden: either they still stand, or they have rotted away leaving at best a scatter of roof tiles. Moats had timber bridges (occasionally still preserved in the mud), or else gaps were left for access. Many have only three sides, and sometimes were never meant to be a complete circuit. Moats are often deliberately fed with water: the Bottisham Park moats have a stream directed to supply each in turn.

Moats used to be thought to go back to a rude antiquity of wolves and bears and clearings in wildwood. In fact, they date from long after wildwood had disappeared, and are not characteristic of regions such as the High Weald, Chilterns and Forest of Dean, where wildwood might have lingered longest.

*The moat of Kentwell Hall in Long Melford, Suffolk. This very grand moat belongs to a Tudor revival of the fashion for moats. It was dug to surround a magnificent mid-sixteenth-century mansion. The previous Kentwell Hall was elsewhere and had no moat. (Note the ancient park trees.)*

*Most moats go with middle-class houses. They represent an immense investment of labour. What were they for? Most of them, especially the three-sided ones, are not well designed for either defence or drainage. Their main function, as Christopher Taylor persuasively argues, was as status symbols in a very status-ridden age. They symbolize the status of the common yeoman, who did not aspire to battlements or his own gallows or park, but whose house was his castle.*

*Moats are most abundant in areas like Suffolk and Essex, where traditions of village communities and open-field agriculture were weak, and there were many small freeholders or weakly-bound tenants with independence to be asserted.*

*Moats are also ornamental, pleasure-giving and useful for sewage and fish. They were adapted or even created as garden features. (SBP, October 1993)*

Moats are poorly documented. The earliest reference is apparently thirteenth century. Numerous excavations show that moated houses were a definite fashion running from 1150 to 1330. There was a revival in Elizabethan times.

A special type of moat does go with woodland. The 'moat-in-a-wood' is frequent all over eastern England; for example, the small double moat in Eversden Wood, Cambridgeshire. Such moats often cut straight through the woodbank, but may be separated by an outer enclosure, as with the two moats in Gawdy Hall Wood (Redenhall, Norfolk). A few moats are humble enough to have been the homes of woodwards: there is a tiny one in Bonny Wood (Barking, Suffolk). Others suggest that moat-makers deliberately chose to live next to woods, perhaps for shelter or concealment.

Moats are still a mystery and a warning against trying to write history from documents alone. Most belonged to the middle class who kept few records: we should hardly know of their existence had the moats themselves not survived. Readers should look for unknown moats in groves and woods. Where a medieval house still stands in a moat, they should consider whether it is the original. In a deserted moat they should look for pottery excavated by moles and badgers. The vegetation of moats is too often ignored by archaeologists. Pollards and ancient trees may be a living link with the folk who lived in the moat; so are stinging-nettles (p. 54), which

### Fishponds

Medieval fishponds at Lyddington, Leicester. Fishponds belonged to a way of life now vanished from Britain. Their wooden sluices have rotted away, leaving earthworks in pasture.

The simplest fishpond was merely a dam or a flat-bottomed excavation with a bypass to divert flood water around the pond. Others had compartments for different species or ages of fish. The most elaborate had leats for controlling the water in the compartments independently. J.M. Steane has described many fine examples in Northamptonshire. Others can be seen at Denny and Anglesey Abbeys, Cambridgeshire; those at Anglesey have many compartments, apparently improvised out of two pre-existing moats.

Fishponds attracted thieves, and were usually attached to a house where an eye could have been kept upon them. The best-preserved are those of abbeys or others where the house has disappeared. Those attached to country houses which are still inhabited have at best been adapted into garden ponds and at worst drowned under a lake *á la* Capability Brown. (SBP, September 1991)

may tell us for how long the moat was inhabited and where people put their rubbish.

### Fishponds

The Middle Ages were a golden age of fish. With no polluting fertilizers, almost all ponds were fishponds. In thirteenth-century Hindolveston (Norfolk) a pond was made in the manor yard, 171 young pike were brought to put in it, and a net for eels was purchased. Stolen trout from the lord's pond pervade manorial court rolls. The archaeologist may be less interested in pike eating each other in field and woodland ponds than in ponds specially made or adapted for fish-farming.

Fish-farming goes back to remote antiquity; it was fully developed by the twelfth century. In La Dombes (France) there is a landscape of thousands of medieval and later fishponds still in use. In Britain, the most elaborate fishponds were royal and monastic, but nobility and gentry had them also. Kings were fond of pike and bream, especially for feasts that fell in Lent, and had many fishponds attached to palaces and royal manors; carpenters were often ordered to work on them.

Fish-farming declined after the dissolution of the monasteries. It was still taken seriously in the seventeenth century, although the little that Izaak Walton, the fishing writer, knew of fishponds came from France. Damage to fishponds and embezzlement of fish appeared in legal disputes; leases sometimes enumerated carp, perch and tench along

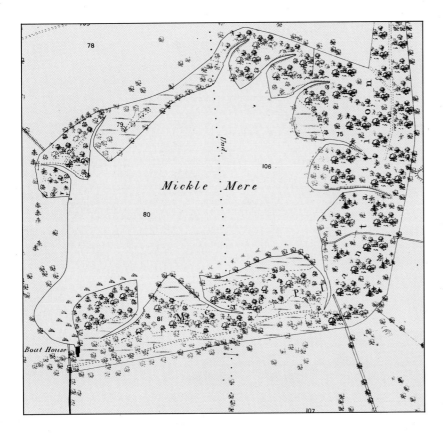

Above: *A pipe of a duck decoy in use at Abbotsbury Swannery, Dorset. (PS)*

Left: *Mickle Mere, a non-fluctuating Breckland mere. This natural lake was converted in the 1830s into a duck decoy with ten curving pipes. (BL/Ordnance Survey, 1882)*

| 0 | | 400 yards |
| 0 | | 400 metres |

with deer and other livestock. Fish-farming died out in England (before its recent reintroduction) in the early eighteenth century.

## Decoys

A decoy is a device for catching wild ducks *en masse* by making use of their companionable habits. A lake is provided with arms called pipes, each about 80 yards long, curved in shape and tapering from their mouths to a point. There should be at least four pipes for use in different directions of wind. (Fritton Lake, the largest of the Broads, was made in the eighteenth century into a giant decoy with at least 23 pipes.) In use they are roofed over with netting on hoops and surrounded by screens of reeds with peep-holes for observation. A flock of wild ducks alights on the lake and is decoyed into the mouth of one of the pipes: they will follow either tame ducks trained for the purpose or a trained dog dressed up as a fox. Once they are safely inside the pipe the decoy-man waves a red spotted handkerchief behind them. In panic they crowd into the little end of the pipe, where he wrings their necks and puts them on the London train for Leadenhall Market.

Decoys (and their name) are alleged to come from Holland. By the seventeenth century they were established in English practice and metaphor. In their heyday, there were more than a hundred decoys which slew half a million a year out of the then infinite number of ducks. The last decoy still worked may be that at Abbotsbury, Dorset, where ducks are caught to be ringed rather than wrung.

*The armed pond in Hayley Wood (Walk I, pp. 98-101). Ponds with arms, like decoys but much smaller, were once common in the east Midlands. Associated with hedged fields, they probably had some agricultural function such as watering cattle. There are possible armed ponds on a sixteenth-century map of Haveringland (Norfolk). In Aversley Wood (Huntingdonshire) there still exists one dug into earlier ridge-and-furrow, now under ancient secondary woodland.*

*This is a rare survivor, one of the few armed ponds in ancient woodland. In its present form it is artificial, with four arms, steep sides and a constructed bottom of glacial boulders. There is no mound corresponding. (TM, June 1993).*

## Dams

The Romans built many dams elsewhere in the Empire – some still function – but the earliest earthen dams in Britain derive from the water-mill technology of the Anglo-Saxons.

In the Middle Ages there were many dams for fishponds or to drive mills. They are recorded in connection with maintenance or prosecution for wilful damage. The five dams which still hold water in Sutton Coldfield Park, Birmingham, were made in about 1420, probably for fulling-mills used to pre-shrink cloth; they later drove a sword-mill, a button-mill, and other industries. Better known are the many hammer ponds for driving trip-hammers in the Sussex Weald and other iron-working areas. Ancient dams are quite common, especially in woods, even where there is no obvious industrial purpose.

A characteristic eighteenth-century dam is that creating the inevitable sinuous 'sheet of water' in landscape parks. This was not just ornamental: it produced ice, stored for the summer in an ice-house, a heavily insulated brick vault often buried in a mound. An ice-house implies that there should be a pond close by, even though the dam may have been breached long ago.

## Craters

A crater is a hole in the ground made by violence, most often by shells and bombs. In northeast France, World War I covered the countryside in craters upon craters for mile after mile, erasing all trace of the previous landscape except for elms. Much of the land has never been cultivated since and is now woodland.

In Britain a few craters remain from World War II and possibly World War I. Occasional bombs and sticks of bombs landed by chance on woods and fens, often remote from military targets, where their craters escaped notice and were never filled in.

A crater is a conical hole, typically a few yards across, surrounded by a bank of displaced earth. Craters can usually be distinguished from bell-pits and pingos by their perfectly circular shape and steep fresh contours. The age of trees growing in the pit or on the bank is a useful diagnostic: it is most unlikely that any craters in Britain date from before 1915.

## Ponds and Dells in Woods

Some depressions in woods are there by chance, or because woodland has grown up on land spoilt by quarrying or mining. A few are related to woodland as such. There is a large remainder for which human activity is not a sufficient explanation.

*Sawpits* were made to saw a log lengthwise with a two-man saw: one man stood on the log and the other in a pit beneath it. The practice appeared in the fourteenth century – previously one end of the log had been propped on a trestle – and continued into living memory. Sawpits could be dug in woods; sometimes they were permanent and give rise to place-names. I have yet to see a convincing sawpit, but would expect to find the weathered remains of a pit originally of the size and shape of a churchyard grave.

Charcoal was first made by setting fire to wood buried in a pit. Charking in pits went on from Anglo-Saxon times (or earlier) into the sixteenth century. Later, the practice was to set fire to a stack of wood covered with earth. On sloping ground it was necessary first to make a level platform. Such *charcoal-hearths* are to be seen in woods all over Europe: they are circular, about 20 feet across, scooped into the hillside. Under the leaf-litter they are thickly strewn with charcoal fragments.

Besides these obvious artificial excavations, ancient woods have natural ponds and dells, sometimes more of them than the same area of non-woodland. These depressions sink directly into the flat ground, with no trace of a corresponding mound or track by which earth might have been carried away. They are usually rounded in shape; sometimes they are mysteriously arranged in pairs (one long pond and one round)

### Dewponds

These are chalkland ponds, located (unlike meres) on high and seemingly arid hilltops. They are wonderful and have caused extravagant speculation.

A.J. Pugsley showed that dewponds are careful constructions, though set in natural dells. A dewpond is a hollow, lined with puddled clay, filled by rainfall and runoff from the surrounding slopes with some assistance from mist. It requires skilled attention to detail in choosing the site to make the most of the rainfall and reduce evaporation.

There is no evidence that the ponds, or the word, are older than the nineteenth century. They were not made in prehistory by a lost process which caused them to be filled by dew. There were still professional makers of dewponds in 1939.

*A charcoal-burning platform near Muker in Swaledale. As T. Gledhill has shown, these platforms indicate a greater extent of woodland than there is now. (TM, February 1994)*

or chains. They cut deeply into the subsoil and may have zones of vegetation on their sides and water in the bottom. Often they have ancient coppice stools within them.

Ancient woods, outside mining areas, have escaped most of the processes by which ponds and pits have been made or effaced. They indicate that the natural land surface was not smooth but full of holes. Possible explanations include kettle-holes and sinkholes; there may have been other pond-forming processes not yet identified.

These holes, being obstacles to cultivation, were doubtless more common on sites that were to be left as ancient woodland; but it would be surprising if they were confined to such places. Probably many field and village ponds, especially those in clusters, are of the same natural origin; but it is difficult to prove this of any particular pond.

## Conservation

Some people appreciate the beauty, the aquatic plants and animals, and the historic meaning of ponds and moats. Others have a similar affection for pits and dells. Even the humble sandpit or chalk-pit stands for wildness among endless houses or fields. Where else do children living far from the coast first see cliffs, fossils, sand-martins, or woody lianes? How else can geologists see, in the solid, materials otherwise accessible only as samples from boreholes?

Little is known of how fast depressions are disappearing or new ones are being created. Ponds and pits disappear through the English habit of putting rubbish in holes. They are hated by tidy-minded people and those who 'reclaim' industrial wasteland. Ponds also disappear from natural causes: they are filled with silt, or dead leaves. When the water gets shallower than about two feet, reeds and bulrushes root in the bottom and their remains quickly fill the pond. It is difficult to generalize as to how long this takes. Comparison of early maps indicates that many ordinary field ponds last only a century or so. The deeper basins of the Norfolk Broads, where plant growth was rapid, lasted on average about 600 years. But many Anglo-Saxon ponds are still there after a thousand years, and some pingos still have water in them after at least 14,000 years.

Ponds are threatened by human activity. They are polluted by the fertilizers and weedkillers which get into almost all farmland drainage water. The mania for land drainage has often dried up ponds at a distance. Some unknown curse has banished frogs and toads to remote places and suburban gardens. Ponds are rarely wanted for drinking or other traditional uses and are neglected. Neglect usually includes allowing trees to grow and shade out the aquatic plants. Too much tree growth also threatens dells and pits.

Ponds and pits, more than other habitats, justify the complacent argument that the loss or spoiling of existing sites does not matter if they are replaced by new ones. Aquatic plants and animals move from place to place more quickly than terrestrial, as can be seen in any newly-abandoned gravel pit. But no new excavation can recreate the meaning of an ancient pit or the primaeval landform of a dell. In practice the best depressions – those that are nature reserves or Sites of Special Scientific Interest (SSSIs) – are usually long-established. There is no practical way to recreate the habitats of specialized creatures, such as the rare mosses on weathered cliffs in Cambridgeshire chalk-pits, or the curious lichens of Mendip lead-mines. The most threatened plants are those that specialize in the alternation of wet and dry. Examples are the buttercup *Ranunculus ophioglossifolius*, a star turn of the Gloucestershire Trust for Nature Conservation, which grows in two otherwise ordinary ponds; *Lythrum hyssopifolia*, a rare plant of pingos; and the rare violet *Viola persicifolia* in turloughs.

With hundreds of thousands of ponds in existence, there is usually more to be said for conserving them than for making new ones. Conservation schemes for ponds can be overdone. People automatically include tree planting, forgetting that ponds all too easily acquire their own trees. They automatically dig out sediments; this is proper for ponds that have been periodically cleaned out, but in others (especially in woods) the mud contains part of the meaning of the pond, and to remove it is to destroy an unread document. The burgesses of Diss are to be congratulated on their good sense in not de-silting the Mere.

It is time for a similar interest to be taken in pits and dells, on whose conservation very little has been done, although much study has been given to hastening the growth of vegetation on newly-abandoned pits.

# MARSHES, FENS, RIVERS AND THE SEA

Wetlands illustrate how historians are lured into error by the written word. Fens have had a bad press from upland writers who despised a way of life that was not their own. Fenmen were depicted impressionistically as a race apart, fiercely independent, ague-ridden, web-footed, who lived precariously on birds and fish. From this impoverished indolence they were 'rescued' against their own unprogressive wishes by the Dutch engineering skills of Sir Cornelius Vermuyden and the capital of the fourth Earl of Bedford. These great men 'drained the Fens' in the seventeenth century, made them into 'rich farmland' and exalted their inhabitants into industrious moneymakers like the rest of us.

This story is endlessly repeated. But how is it to be reconciled with the glorious Fenland churches of Walsoken, Whittlesey and March? Or with the great abbeys of Ely, Peterborough, Ramsey, Thorney and Crowland? Or with the making of King's Lynn, Wisbech and Boston, with their magnificent medieval buildings? Or, in other fen districts, with Lydd church or Glastonbury or Selby abbeys? The real heyday of fenland was in the twelfth and thirteenth centuries, when fenmen, remote from political upheavals, enjoyed civilized prosperity. Vermuyden was a clever propagandist and should not be taken at his word.

The history of wetland is very largely the history of its destruction. About a quarter of the British Isles has been some kind of wetland.

Right: *The North Norfolk coast, very low-lying and bordered by a shallow, stormy sea. Wave action builds up sand-bars and shingle ridges parallel to the coast. These may go on to develop into vegetated sand-dune ridges. (TM, Holme-next-the-Sea, August 1993)*

**Land and Sea Levels**

The key to the history of coasts and coastal wetlands lies in the relative levels of land and sea. London is now sinking at about a foot a century (faster than Venice). Rising sea-level affects the erosion of cliffs and the behaviour of dunes and salt-marshes; it also backs up many miles inland into low-lying fenland. For the time being its obvious consequences have been averted by heightening river-walls and building barrages, but similar movements up or down have affected wetlands throughout human history.

Before the Neolithic period, when much of the world's water was locked up in enlarged ice-caps in the Arctic and Antarctic, sea-levels were lower than they are now. Since then they have fluctuated twice. In the Bronze Age and Anglo-Saxon period the sea was higher (relative to the land) than it is now, drowning the coastal wetlands. In the Iron Age to Roman period, and again in the Middle Ages, relative sea-level was lower than today.

Natural vegetation, from alders to primroses, is adapted to differing kinds, degrees and seasons of waterlogging. Although we have never developed a complete fenland economy as in China, in the Middle Ages men tried to exploit the distinctive character of fens and to use them in ways complementary to the upland. However, nearly all sown crops originated in semi-arid lands and will not withstand the slightest inundation. Farmers (and latterly taxpayers) have gone to great trouble and expense to override the natural characteristics of fenland and to reduce it, like the upland, to that imitation of a Turkish steppe in which wheat and barley are at home.

**Kinds of Wetlands**

Coastal wetlands arise where a low-lying coast is fringed by dunes, salt-marshes or cliffs of clay or sand. At high tide the sea covers the salt-marshes; it also causes low-lying rivers to back up and overflow their surroundings with fresh water. For example, the Norfolk Broads experience a freshwater tide as far inland as Norwich.

Inland wetlands are created by some combination of rainfall, springs and obstructed rivers. They may be just marshes or wet woods with a mineral soil; but where plant remains are kept continually wet they tend, instead of rotting, to accumulate to form peat. Areas of peat have formed in the inland parts of the great low-lying coastal fens: the Fens proper between Ely and Lincoln, the Norfolk Broads, the Yorkshire and Lancashire Fens, and the Somerset Levels. In

*Chesil Beach, Dorset. On soft coasts, small rivers are diverted at their mouths by shingle spits or sandy hooks, or blocked altogether by barrier beaches, as here, to form lagoons. Such features include the wonderful shingle ridges of Spurn Point (east Yorkshire) and Dungeness. The greatest curiosity of all, Orford Beach (Suffolk), is 10 miles long and at its neck is less than 100 yards wide; it reached approximately its present shape at least 450 years ago. (SAP, May 1984)*

# COASTAL EROSION

Erosion is often thought to be a serious matter: coastal authorities used to spend much more public money on defences against cliff erosion than the value of the farmland which would otherwise be lost in the lifetime of the works. The biggest losses have been in east Yorkshire, where a strip about 35 miles long and 2/3 mile wide has gone in 900 years. In Norfolk, the sea has eaten the medieval churches of Happisburgh and Eccles.

Since the Middle Ages people have tried to prevent erosion and accretion – the latter in order to keep harbours from being silted or masked by shingle-spits. To defend one place usually involves sacrificing another. This was soon appreciated, indeed used as a weapon to the perdition of a rival port, as the slow-motion warfare between Great Yarmouth and Lowestoft, or Southwold and Dunwich, illustrates.

The map shows the retreat of the Suffolk coast. The parishes of Dunwich and Easton Bavents have been reduced to slivers; the church of Easton and all but one of those in the town of Dunwich had fallen over the cliffs by 1700. Southwold protected itself.

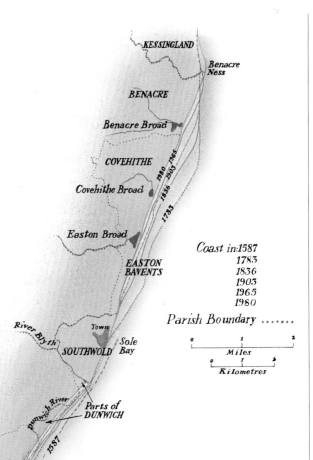

Coast in 1587
1783
1836
1903
1965
1980

Parish Boundary .......

A coastal slump devouring a Scarborough hotel. (TD/FSP, June 1993)

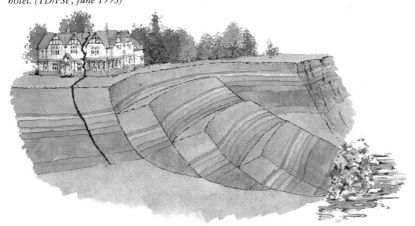

Erosion is betrayed by roads that now run into the sea, and by incongruous place-names. 'Sole Bay' has turned into the cape on which Southwold town now stands; 'Benacre Ness' has moved into the parish of Covehithe; 'Minsmere Haven' is a straight piece of beach. The three 'Broads' are not excavations like the Norfolk Broads but lagoons; they have migrated inland as the coast has retreated.

At present, accretion in eastern England is diminished because of rising sea-levels and the reckless building of sea-defences which cut off the supply of new material. Undefended coasts are probably being eroded faster than in previous centuries.

*A landslip. When a slope of earth or soft rock gives way, it usually tilts back into the hillside instead of merely sliding. This often happens (for example, in motorway cuttings) where clay alternates with other strata and is lubricated by springs. Inland landslips appear as a series of crescent-shaped terraces: there are fine examples in the Ironbridge Gorge, Shropshire. Where the sea attacks the tail of a landslip and washes away the debris, slumping can go on for ever; localities include the coasts of Dorset, the Isle of Wight, Norfolk and Yorkshire.*

*The Ouse Washes, Cambridgeshire, seen when full. Floods may come from surges of the sea – when storms pile the water against the coast – or from inland, from spates on the rivers, especially if a surge keeps the tidal sluices closed. To guard against this danger, lands called* washes *are set aside to be flooded when necessary. The Ouse Washes were constructed in the seventeenth century. This flood reservoir preserves a sample of fenland in its medieval state, and acts as an internationally famous reserve for wetland birds. (DW/WI, February 1989)*

high-rainfall areas peat can form even on a slope, giving rise to *blanket-bogs* (p. 154) which merge into moorland. In circumstances not well understood, peat can accumulate on level ground to produce a *raised bog* – a great dome of sphagnum moss. Ireland is (or was) famous for its raised bogs, but they also occur over much of Britain.

## Erosion and Accretion

Coast erosion happens when the sea is high enough to reach the bases of cliffs, and either to attack them directly or to wash away the debris of landslips and thus expose them to further collapse from within. Some of the material from the cliffs is transported by wave action or currents along the coast and is added to beaches, shingle ridges or salt-marshes elsewhere. Accretion and erosion have evened out 'soft' coasts into straight lines or very gentle curves, as in northeast Norfolk or east Yorkshire. Since Anglo-Saxon times, accretion has added some tens of thousands of acres to the area of Britain, especially in the salt-marshes of Essex and the Wash. These are less than has been gained through falling sea-levels, but are often in places where they have important effects: for instance, the medieval Welsh port of Harlech has been completely filled in.

## How Fens and Marshes Work

The Fens and most other large coastal wetlands consist of a salt-marsh fringe, a seaward *silt fen* or marsh, and a landward *peat fen*. The silt is usually slightly higher than the others, and in a natural state would rarely be flooded. The silt and peat fens are interspersed with islands of upland, and formerly with permanent meres or lakes. Salt-marshes are dissected by branching, meandering creeks which fill at high tide and empty at low. These are usually preserved as meandering dykes if the salt-marsh is made into farmland (air photograph, p. 224).

Fens have rivers, often big ones like the Great Ouse, flowing into them from the upland. Fen rivers, in their natural state, had broad channels meandering through peat and silt. The channels were lined with silt deposited by the rivers; they had natural embankments of silt, called *levées,* which confined the rivers during all but exceptional floods. Modern courses of fenland rivers are narrower and have artificial banks, often with sluices which allow the river to discharge at low tide but keep the sea out at high tide.

Artificial embanking does not prevent floods but makes them rare and catastrophic. Flood risks get worse with time, for two reasons. A fenland river deposits silt in its bed and rises above the surrounding land. Eventually it may become unstable, breach a levée, and make off across country in a new course. Strips of silt, called *roddons,* are left by the beds and levées of extinct rivers, and are a permanent record of all the fen rivers and canals that there have ever been. Their snaking shapes are familiar in air photographs.

When peatland is drained and cultivated, the peat wastes and shrinks. The land surface is lowered and drainage becomes more difficult. In the Fens, houses, bridges and railways subside and lean, and many rivers are now perched 14 feet or more above the farmland.

All native trees are very sensitive to salt in the soil, but many species tolerate some freshwater flooding. Fens quickly turn into woodland when not continuously wet. Most of Wicken Fen has thus become a wood in the last 60 years. Many fens were wooded in prehistory, but seldom in the last 1,000 years; most if not all fen woods are modern. Why this should be so is not clear, but it is an argument against the notion that fenland before Vermuyden was under-used.

## Fens in Prehistory

Coastal fens are the creation of rising sea-level. Before the Neolithic period they were covered with wildwood. Some of the 'submerged forests' of western coasts are the stumps of such trees, killed by rising sea-levels. The 'bog oaks' of the southern Fens include huge logs – 80 feet to the first branch is not uncommon – which represent the last generation of trees to grow on the mineral soil: they were killed by rising water-levels, crashed down in storms, and were entombed in the newly-forming peat. They include pine and yew as well as oak, but the lime, hazel and alder which (as the pollen record shows) accompanied them have not been preserved.

Civilization came to fenland at about the same time as the sea began to encroach on it. Fens were some of the earliest land to be used, although we do not know exactly how. In the Somerset Levels people lived on islands and peninsulas, and built wooden trackways. Trackways, preserved by the ever-growing peat, begin in the Neolithic period (about 4,000BC) and go on to the Iron Age or later. They are constructed in many different ways, sometimes of wattle hurdles, but also in ingenious ways which would never occur to the modern

### Reeds and Sedge

Much fenland was grassland of some kind. Medieval records mention useful plants such as *juncus, scirpus* and *star,* which translators carelessly render 'rush', 'flag' and so on, but which probably had definite meanings. *Arundo* 'reed' and *carex* 'sedge' are both still used for thatching and formerly also for fuel.

Reed is the giant grass *Phragmites australis.* For many centuries the reed thatcher has been a different profession from the straw thatcher. Reed continues to be cut annually in shallow water and was sometimes transported many miles from fenland. Sedge is properly *Cladium mariscus,* a much less common plant. Sedge makes even better thatch than reed, but is less used because it is so bloody to handle. As the *Runic Poem* put it more than a thousand years ago:

> Sedge hath its home   oftest in fen
> groweth in water   woundeth grimly,
> blood draweth   from any man
> that maketh any   grasp at it.

*Peat fens along the River Ant in the Norfolk Broads. At the top is Barton Broad, in which there are still traces of the baulks that subdivided the great peat excavation which formed the Broad in the thirteenth century. Crome's Broad, to the right, is another major medieval peat excavation. The other pools and lakes result from lesser excavations, not necessarily medieval. The white crosses are pumping windmills, relics of nineteenth-century attempts at drainage. Although very wet, the area is becoming overgrown with trees. (APL, November 1992)*

carpenter (pp. 35, 118). Similar trackways and artificial islands existed in the Fens, although less evidence has survived modern drainage. The Bronze Age artificial island at Flag Fen near Peterborough is the biggest known wooden structure that there has ever been in Britain.

Prehistoric fenland was probably a complexity of pools, reedbeds, grassland, bog-myrtle thickets and woods, full of wonderful birds and fishes, like the Great Okefenokee Swamp in Georgia today. Stumps of alders and birches, like those of modern secondary fen woodland, have been found in and around the Somerset trackways. In the Fens, some of the peat dried out enough for oak, pine and yew to grow.

### The First Draining of the Fens

Falling sea-level at the end of the Iron Age coincided with the coming of the Romans, who had the most elaborate fen-engineering technology that Europe has ever seen. For the first time, by nature and art, fen surfaces were made habitable. The story is best known in the Fens proper, where the siltlands were fully cultivated; farmsteads were at least as thick on the ground as they are now. The peat Fens were inhabited mainly on islands, levées and roddons.

The pattern of farms, fields and lanes was more haphazard than usual in a Roman colony. But it was assisted, and perhaps made possible, by great engineering works. The Car Dyke, the biggest artificial watercourse that the Fens have ever had, skirted their western edge for nearly 90 miles between Lincoln and Cambridge. Its main function was as a cut-off channel, intercepting lesser rivers and avoiding the burden of maintaining their courses across the fen. A main road ran through the middle of the Fens, connecting the Midlands to a port at Caister-by-Yarmouth.

The Fens were probably an overflow for population from a rather crowded upland. As in the Middle Ages, livestock may have been important, and the peat fens were used for summer and autumn grazing. There is a similar, though less fully understood, story from the Somerset Levels, and the inland fen of Otmoor (Oxfordshire).

Salt was made in coastal marshes. It began in the Iron Age and has left mounds of pottery and burnt earth ('Red Hills'). Their location suggests that silt fens produced fuel (reeds or sedge) for evaporation.

After about 200 years the Roman settlements fell into decline through rising sea-levels, the self-destructive tendency that plagues all fen drainage works, or a disintegrating society that could not keep up the engineering. The farms were deserted, though their fields remained visible until our own time. Some of the canals still function, such as Reach and Wicken Lodes (Cambridgeshire) and the Car Dyke along Potterhanworth Wood, Lincolnshire.

## The Second Draining of the Fens

In the darkest of the Dark Ages fenland was not wholly abandoned. The first fenman we know as a person, St Guthlac, went to live in 699 at Crowland in an old sarcophagus which treasure-hunters had dug up out of a barrow.

Re-settling the Fens began soon after. Place-names such as Skirbeck show that Vikings were involved. By Domesday there were 50 villages set out in an arc round the Wash from Skegness to King's Lynn. They lay on the highest belt of the silt Fen, least exposed to flooding, but they might not have been habitable without the protection of two great banks, the seabank in front and the fenbank in the rear. The banks are first heard of in post-Conquest documents, but were then already long-established. The inner Fens were thinly populated on islands. But even the peat fen itself was just as much parcelled into ownerships as was the upland. Natural lakes – Trundle Mere, Draymere, Whittlesey Mere – were valued as fisheries; and there were named rivers, dykes, weirs and bridges, as well as a few woods such as Alderlound and Apinholt. Already there are many refernces to drainage works such as the canal called 'King Cnut's Delf' (after which King's Delph in Whittlesey is named).

By the end of the Anglo-Saxon period civilization had come to most parts of the Fens, but was still rather thinly spread. Substantial engineering works had somehow been organized. To construct a seabank and a fenbank, each 50 miles long, is not something which even in the twentieth century is done every year.

The other great fenlands tell a similar story. Settlers were encouraged at first by falling sea-levels. Domesday records that this process was about half-finished in siltlands but still very incomplete in peatlands. Estates in Romney Marsh are recorded as far back as AD700, and by AD1,000 there was a town, New Romney. The Somerset Levels have charters mentioning artificial watercourses.

### The First Recorded Fenman

Guthlac, a hermit, went to live on an island in the Huntingdonshire Fens in the place which later became Crowland Abbey. This account was written about 50 years later.

> There is ... a most terrible fen of immense size, which begins at the banks of the river Gronta [now the Cam] not far from the little fort which is called Gronte [Cambridge]; now in fens, now in flashes, sometimes in black oozes swirling with mist, but also with many islands and groves ... up to the sea ...
>
> When [Guthlac] was questioning the nearest inhabitants ... a certain ... Tatwine declared that he knew another island ... many had tried to live there but had rejected it because of the unknown monster of the desert and the divers kinds of terrors ... It is called Crugland, an island sited in the middle of the fen ... no settler had been able to dwell there before ... because of the fantastic demons living there. Here Guthlac, the man of God ... began to dwell alone among the shady groves of the solitude ... He loved the remoteness of the place which God had given him ...
>
> There was in the said island a barrow ... which greedy visitors to the solitude had dug and excavated in order to find treasure there; in the side of this there appeared to be a kind of tank; in which Guthlac ... began to live, building a shanty over it.

Here, as in the Fens, habitation was mainly towards the sea; the great peat-bogs inland, in which King Alfred campaigned, were inhabited only on islands. By 1086 the Yorkshire marshes were nearly as densely settled as the rest of the county.

Salt-marsh, particularly in Essex and Kent, was highly valued in Anglo-Saxon times as pasture for sheep. Salt-marsh pastures were often at a distance from the places to which they belonged. Canvey Island (Essex) consists of 18 detached parts of ten upland parishes, situated up to seven miles away.

After the Norman Conquest, settlements in the Fens expanded seaward into salt-marsh and fenward into peatland. New banks were advanced and innings were made. The sea-banks culminated in the thirteenth century with the making, or re-making, of the 'Roman Bank', a mighty earthwork more than 60 miles long, with timber sluices at intervals, running all round the Wash and its inlets. This bank, the greatest of all fen engineering works, stood for 500 years and protected more than a million acres of land.

These works were organized between the Fenland abbeys, the Bishop of Ely, private landowners, and parishes (which had funds for the purpose). Conan Ellison of Holbeach may have been one of the chief engineers in the twelfth century, but he was not a propagandist like Vermuyden, and posterity has forgotten him. The maintenance of the works was at first organized locally by 'the custom of the marsh'. As sea-level rose it became more centralized, first through regional Courts of Sewers, later by the intervention of the Crown.

Medieval settlement has left an organized landscape of regular straight strips up to four miles long, differing from the less regular quadrilaterals of the Third Draining. Some of the strips can be no later than the twelfth century, as they contain Early English churches such as Elm and Parson Drove. Pre-Conquest farmland and the later seaward intakes are both very irregular, with ditches that preserve the meanders of salt-marsh creeks.

By the fourteenth century the Fens were much the most prosperous part of rural England, as we can still see from the splendid architecture. Where did this wealth come from? Fenmen were well placed to sell cash crops which could be taken away by barge. Fish and wild birds were important but were hardly wealth. There was some conventional agriculture. But their riches lay chiefly in grass. Fenmen had flocks and herds of their own, producing meat, butter, wool and livestock for sale; they sold hay and hired grazing to upland farmers; they sold reeds and sedge for thatching, and peat, reeds and sedge for fuel; they boiled and sold salt.

The inland Fens were less fully developed, but here too there were medieval drainage works and the remains of Roman works. Arable land covered the islands and some of the margins of the peat. Here, too, there are magnificent churches. Most unusually, men were working with the distinctive landscape of the Fens, using it to complement the upland, instead of against it. Many Fenland products grew on undrained or partly-drained land. Having the Fens at hand

*Eels are delicious fish which swarm mysteriously out of the far Atlantic. In the Middle Ages they were a speciality of the Fens. In Domesday Book, estates in the Cambridgeshire Fens were supposed to render over 100,000 eels annually to the Abbot of Ely (the place-name means 'eel-island') and other landlords. Eels still come up to Ely and Cambridge but are now a despised, proletarian dish. In these pictures baby eels are leaving the River Wye to make another ancient delicacy, elver-pie.*
*(Top photograph: IGM/OSF*
*Bottom photograph: RJ/OSF, June 1987)*

enabled Cambridge and similar places to dispense with pasture, meadow and woodland.

The Somerset Levels, also, complemented the upland; upland parishes had rights of pasture in them from many miles away. But arable was increasing, both on the siltlands and around islands in the peat. Rivers were diverted into straight courses, apparently for transport as well as flood-control. Much of this was organized by Glastonbury and Muchelney Abbeys. On the Essex coast, Foulness Island – a polder made entirely out of marshland – was enwalled, and a sixth of it ploughed, before 1420. In Romney Marsh, sea and river walls were built and canals dug. Up and down the country, innumerable sea-banks were built and rivers straightened.

Fens have always been vulnerable to the occasional big flood, but in the time of their general prosperity the loss of a year's crop now and then seems not to have been much missed. The 'super-surge' of 15 December 1287, which affected east Norfolk and Romney Marsh especially, was the first sign of the rising sea-levels which made the fenman's lot more and more difficult. Through the fourteenth century and beyond, there are many records of surges and breaches.

The defence of the marshes was largely successful. In contrast to the Netherlands, there were no big losses of enwalled land, and a few gains. Ploughland was even extended in fen and marsh when it was in retreat in the Midlands.

There was one great drawback to fenland. Malaria made life sickly and short. It is hard to believe that it was present in the medieval heyday, but by the sixteenth century it was prevalent in most of the coastal marshes. Possibly the encroachment of the sea favoured the brackish-water mosquito which may have been the chief carrier. Malaria was a notorious hazard of the Essex and Kent marshes, and died out (nobody knows why) only in the twentieth century.

## The Third Draining of the Fens

The medieval fen way of life survived the dissolution of the monasteries. In the sixteenth century the Fens were still wealthy. The incentive to change from 1600 onwards was not local dissatisfaction but the hopes of outside landowners, especially the Crown (as confiscator of monkish lands) and the Earl of Bedford, to make easy money out of arable crops and improved grassland in the peat fens.

The story of the draining of the 'Bedford Level', the peat portion of the Fens, is well known. On the advice of Vermuyden an elaborate system of drains and river-diversions was dug. These included the Old and New Bedford Rivers (1637 and 1651), probably the greatest artificial watercourses since Roman times. The scheme was unpopular: it infringed rights of property and took away common-rights which could not adequately be compensated; it bestowed people's lands on the 'adventurers' who had put up the capital; it made the inhabitants responsible for maintaining works which they had not asked for; it damaged the natural ecology and reduced the birds and fish. It was among the less scrupulous activities of Charles I and Cromwell.

*The Somerset Levels during an ordinary flood. Technologists have never quite succeeded in forcing the Levels into a dry-land way of life, as they have the Fens. (SBP, February 1988).*

*Peat wastage demonstrated by the Holme Fen Post. An iron column, 22 feet long, was buried upright in the peat of Holme Fen (Huntingdonshire) when it was drained, apparently for the first time, in 1848. The peat shrank 6 feet in the first twelve years. By 1890, 10 feet of the Post was exposed. Drainage was then abandoned, though the site continued to be affected by drainage of adjacent fens. In the century since then, less than three feet more shrinkage has occurred. (BG/NI, July 1986)*

*Sea-buckthorn on the dunes at Holme-next-the-Sea, Norfolk. Many plants are adapted to living in loose sand, but this is one of the few bushes to do so. It has separate sexes like ourselves; this is a female. (TM, August 1993)*

Vermuyden's scheme failed to allow for the shrinkage of the peat. Water which should have drained into the rivers by gravity had soon to be pumped by windmills. An ingeniously ramshackle system of drains at different levels had to be constructed and adapted. The thinner peats disappeared, and with them the best soils whose cultivation was the original object of the scheme. The lowering of land-level has so far been coped with by introducing steam, then diesel and now electric pumps.

Such a story is all too familiar in the twentieth century, especially in the Third World. An ill-researched scheme, imposed by greedy outsiders, runs into violent local opposition and then into unforeseen practical difficulties. These are overcome partly by modifying the original objectives and partly by new inventions. The result is a precarious victory for technology, made possible by vigilance, expensive repairs and an ever-increasing input of energy.

This was repeated on large fens and small all over Britain. Sometimes the drainers were defeated by Nature (as with the Yorkshire bogs) or by the local inhabitants (as, for a time, with the Somerset Levels). Successes tended to be remembered and perpetuated, while failures were forgotten. The Enclosure Act movement was very hostile to wetlands. Agricultural writers treated the existence of even small fens as an affront to civilization.

At times of prosperity almost every little corner of the Fens, and even the meres, has been drained. The destruction of Whittlesey Mere in 1851 was tragic and unreasonable, for Holme Fen nearby was abandoned not long after. Where the Third Draining was not wholly successful, something of the medieval landscape lingered on to within living memory, as by the River Lark near Mildenhall, which had beautiful meadows and commons up to World War I.

Despite rising sea-levels, further salt-marshes were enwalled. In the Wash, the coastline was advanced by about three miles between 1620 and 1770, and has been set forward by another mile since then. In Essex, Canvey Island was enwalled by Dutch 'adventurers' in the 1620s. The Traeth Mawr at Portmadoc, the most beautiful estuary in Wales, was destroyed in the 1800s by William Maddocks, a poetaster devoted to water-sprites.

With the general rise in sea-level, it has often become difficult to hold even the ancient innings. At Dagenham (Essex) a surge on 29 October 1707 made a 14-foot breach in the medieval sea-bank. Eighteenth-century technology took thirteen years to repair it. Many small innings have been lost; for instance, after the 1953 surge Bridgemarsh Island (Essex) was sacrificed in order to use the clay of its walls to repair breaches elsewhere. This will not be the last instance.

## Fens and Marshes As They Are Now

Best preserved are the salt-marshes. Innings from the land and rising sea-level have squeezed them to a fraction of their former extent, but they are still beautiful, have many kinds of vegetation, and are internationally important for their birds. Archaeological features include the Red Hills of salt evaporation, ruined or unfinished sea-walls, the ridge-and-furrow of brief attempts at cultivation, and the 'farmers' teeth' or lines of stakes, projecting from the mud, marking successive retreats of sea-defences.

Of fens, marshes and bogs, only small examples survive complete; even in Ireland an intact large bog is a rarity. Surviving fragments of large wetlands are usually degraded in some way: it is rarely possible to preserve a sample and to drain the rest.

About ten pieces of the Fens survive, mostly against the upland or in side-basins where they are partly protected from general drainage. A wonderful survival of the prehistoric Fens is Dersingham-Wolferton Fen, like a miniature Okefenokee Swamp, north of King's Lynn, fed by springs of acid water. It has great areas of sphagnum, with bogland plants such as bog-asphodel, cranberry and sundew. It is a relic of the raised bogs which once lay along the Fen-upland edge.

The best relic of the medieval silt Fens is the Ouse Washes between the Old and New Bedford Rivers. In summer they are dry and are grazed by cattle; in winter they are under water. The Washes are an internationally important reserve for migrating birds. The most prominent archaeological feature is the great roddon of the prehistoric River Cam at Welney, lined with Romano-British settlement earthworks.

In the Norfolk Broads the grazing marshes on the silt, though reduced, are still an impressive landscape; the meandering ditches – relics of saltmarsh creeks – were famous for plant life. The inland peat-

*Fen violet*, Viola persicifolia. *In 1982 it reappeared at Wicken Fen after a gap of 66 years. It comes after peat-digging and disturbance, and apparently can wait as buried seed, like a coppice-plant. (JH/NHPA, March 1989)*

*The fen ragwort* Senecio paludosus, *which until the nineteenth century occurred in Wicken Fen and other Cambridgeshire fens and ditches. It became extinct for no known reason – Wicken Fen still exists, and there have always been ditches. In 1972 it reappeared after a gap of 115 years. Another fen ragwort, S. palustris, also mysteriously became extinct, but has yet to reappear. (BG/NI, July 1992)*

*On the Helford River, Cornwall, one of the very few places where ancient woodland meets the sea. The boughs of the oaks dip into salt water at high tide. (This does not hurt the tree, as long as its roots are not submerged.) Oaks gradually topple into the creeks and are entombed in the mud. (TM, July 1993)*

fen, once grazed and cut for hay, is now largely woodland of alder, sallow and even oak. In the Somerset Levels there are grasslands on both the silt and the small area of remaining peat.

A diminished number of inland fens and bogs are either intact or have reverted from attempts at drainage. Redgrave and Lopham Fens lie on the Norfolk-Suffolk border, in that curious place where the rivers Waveney and Little Ouse flow east and west from the same source. The old peat-diggings here take the form of deep crater-like pits with paths winding between them. These pits are the only home of *Dolomedes plantarius*, the largest British spider. The Suffolk Trust for Nature Conservation here struggles against drying-out, tree growth and water pollution – the three enemies of fen conservation almost everywhere.

Fenland, even where reduced to arable, preserves some remains of its history. There are industrial monuments, such as the great steam-engine at Stretham (near Ely) and the pumping windmills of the east Norfolk marshes. Old sea-walls are often left behind inland. Arable fens are a palimpsest of soil-marks: roddons, irregular Roman fields, more regular later fields, and the big pale tracts of shell-marl that mark the sites of meres remain as a testament to wetlands and human intervention in them.

### Rivers As They Are Now

The natural habit of most gentle rivers and streams is to meander. Fiercer rivers may form multiple, braided courses like those of the

*An ox-bow lake, being a cut-off meander of the River Glass near Inverness. The parish boundary follows the ox-bow. (LC/NHPA, May 1992)*

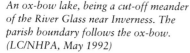

Swale (p. 115). Meanders and braids may change of themselves, but generally they disappear because people dislike them and cut them off. Sometimes this has a purpose, in that shorter watercourses in fenland delay the problem of silting. Cutting of meanders began in antiquity; as a result natural watercourses are now quite uncommon, except for very small ones and those, such as the River Tees, whose meanders were made by a greater river in geological antiquity and are too deep to be tidied away. Even if filled in, a former sinuous watercourse may be kept on record in the shape of a parish boundary which still follows the meanders.

The most familiar earthworks that go with rivers are mill-leats, canals which run parallel to a river but at a less gradient so as to gain a difference in height which drives a watermill. The technology goes back to Anglo-Saxon times. Leats often survive the disuse of the mill. In Cambridge city, the river itself has been made into a mill-leat, diverted by massive embankments to follow the edge of a natural gravel terrace.

### Wicken Fen

Wicken Fen, Cambridgeshire, has been a nature reserve of the National Trust for nearly a century. It survived because of complicated landownership: it was divided into strips like a dole-meadow. It is full of ridge-and-furrow made by nineteenth-century and earlier peat-digging. The Fen now stands about eight feet above its drained and shrunken surroundings. It is now much too dry, and water has to be pumped in. The peat shows some tendency to turn into a raised bog on drying: the surface of some of the ridges is strongly acid, with *Sphagnum*. After 1920 it was allowed to become woodland, with great detriment to its plants and insects. In the last 20 years the Trust has worked hard on grubbing out trees and in restoring the management of reed and sedge.

*The rear end of a watermill: the tail-race that returns the water to the river after it has done its job. Duddington Mill, Northamptonshire. (TM)*

198

# CONSERVATION

### 'THE YEARS THAT THE LOCUST HATH EATEN'

It is difficult to be up-to-date with conservation. The original of this book, written in 1984-85, contained a depressing review of changes since 1945. For thirty years the normal landscape dynamics of human adaptation and natural alteration had been replaced by simple destruction. The commonest cause was destruction by modern agriculture; the second, destruction by modern forestry. Urban development came a long way behind; roads, quarrying and so on were only locally important.

The previous worst year had been 1851, when Hainault Forest and Whittlesey Mere were destroyed. The grubbing up of the Forest triggered off the modern conservation movement; the draining of the Mere – the biggest lake in England outside the Lake District – produced hardly a cheep of protest. After 1950, similar tragedies were repeated every year for thirty years more. This was done mainly by farmers and foresters; there was a mania for making every inch of the country appear to be growing something saleable.

Writers of those days, such as Nan Fairbrother, wrote as if agricultural expansion would last for ever. It was futile for conservationists to oppose the destruction of hedges and roughland, which were only the product of agricultural customs of the recent past. The best to be hoped for was to identify and rescue a few areas as designated nature reserves, and to plead for some sort of cosmetics to mask the destruction of the countryside at large. There was a pathetic hope that worthwhile 'new lives, new landscapes' would somehow

Right: *The ruin of an ancient wood. An oakwood on the North Downs has been destroyed and replaced by a beech plantation, which in turn has been neglected and may never fulfil its intended destiny. Only the woodbank remains to show that it was once a wood. Fortunately such treatment does not always work. (TM, August 1993)*

emerge. Writers, despite not believing in the stability of the past, somehow expected a stable future.

Even bodies like the Countryside Commission and the National Trust accepted the Locust Years as the inexorable working of Destiny, rather than a storm to be weathered until it passed over. In the name of 'sound agricultural and forestry practice', the Trust improved grasslands and replanted woods even in places, like Hatfield Forest, given to them specially in order to escape such practices. My late friend Colin Ranson, of the Nature Conservancy, was one of the few conservationists who refused to accept the defeatist position.

However, times have changed. Ranson was right. Most of the crude destruction has come to an end – or, rather, the kinds of destruction that were once widespread tend now to be limited to single instances, publicly, and often successfully, opposed. This is illustrated by Oxleas Wood (Greenwich, London). In 1993, conservationists succeeded in getting a proposed main road rejected on the grounds that it would divide this ancient wood. In 1963, whole woods like Oxleas were being entirely destroyed at the rate of almost one a month, for slight reasons, with no questions asked.

Even in an ideal world, few conservationists could hope for the preservation of every minor site. Quite apart from conflicts with other human activities, the knowledge is simply not available to do this. A reasonable objective is a return to normal dynamics, whereby a few minor sites are lost over the years because of inevitable natural changes, or because this is the only way to create something of permanent value. What now seems inexcusable about the Locust Years (and 1851) is that so much of the depredation was in pursuit of dying causes: it merely added to the set-aside farmland and windblown plantations of the 1990s.

## The Position in 1994

Woodland has fared well. Ancient woodland is valued in its own right, not as vacant land which ought to be doing something. The depressing and unscientific task of trying to identify the 'best' woods for conservation - a Choosing of the Slain - has been replaced by a listing of all ancient woods.

Woods have played an active part in their own revival. Many an ancient wood, once felled, poisoned, replanted, and written off by conservationists, will not be lost for ever. The original trees recover and gradually overtake the planted ones, helped by neglect and drought. The great storm of 1987 plucked out the planted trees from many ancient woods, leaving the better-rooted original trees. Linwood Wood (Lincolnshire) is surely the most evocative of historic limewoods – from the shrunken Domesday Book village of Linwood, named after the wood, to the coat-of-arms on the funeral brass of John Lyndewode. It received the once usual Forestry Commission treatment: a visitor reported that 'the air was acrid with herbicides'. But times have changed. In 1993, Forest Enterprise foresters showed me something I thought never to see again: the huge ancient lime stools,

*The arms of John Lyndewode (1421), a chevron between three lime-leaves proper, in St Cornelius's Church, Linwood. (Pointed out by E.J. Gibbons, The Flora of Lincolnshire.)*

curiously scarred by poison, but now healthy and towering above the drought-bitten Norway spruce.

Not that the fashion for planting trees in ancient woods is quite dead. Some people still think it harmless, even laudable, if only the trees are broadleaved. But most owners realize the nonsense of planting trees where there are trees already.

Much ancient woodland is now in conservationist hands. Enlarged scale transforms management. No longer is coppicing a matter of volunteers cutting the odd half-acre. It becomes possible to employ woodmen, to acquire suitable small-scale machinery, and to organize the marketing of produce. Coppicing has been expanding for twenty years, and its future looks brighter than at any previous time this century.

Or so it would but for the increase of deer, a development of the twentieth century around the globe from Canada to Japan. There are more deer in England than there have been for a thousand years. The first question to ask in managing an ancient wood is: Are there deer? Happy is the wood that has none. The arts of living with deer need to be revived.

Wood-pasture is another success story, following a long period of neglect. The lead has been set by the City of London Corporation at Burnham Beeches and Epping Forest, and the National Trust at Hatfield Forest. At Burnham Beeches the last junipers have been rescued from shade, re-pollarding experiments continued, pigs re-introduced, and even new pollards started.

*The effects of deer in Hayley Wood are shown in the two photographs (above and below). Here is an unfenced area, showing a gap under the trees and weak ground vegetation. The deer have eaten the bottom out of the wood. (TM, June 1993)*

*An area in Hayley Wood from which deer are excluded, showing plenty of low cover and normal ground vegetation. (TM, June 1993)*

Left: *Individualistic trees. Elms are among the trees which make Swaledale distinctive. These, near Keld, have been hard hit by Elm Disease but may yet recover. (TM, February 1994)*

## Land Drainage

Land drainage brings out the worst in people. Jeremy Purseglove's enlightening book, *Taming the Flood*, tells a horrid story of greed, corruption, indifference to consequences, and the kind of hard-headed stupidity that wrecked Whittlesey Mere. The locusts were busy well into the 1980s. There was a series of classic disputes between conservationists, an out-of-date Ministry of Agriculture, and unreformed Internal Drainage Boards. Sites included the Somerset Levels, Amberley Wildbrooks (Sussex), the Derwent Ings (east Yorkshire) and Halvergate Marshes (Norfolk). Conservationists won their first big case at Amberley in 1978. In later cases they have usually prevailed, but only after much damage has been done, as at Halvergate. The last victory for the destroyers was on the River Blackwater in Northern Ireland in 1986, eating up miles of wonderful wetlands for the sake of farmland needed for five years.

The people of the Irish Republic, who for decades had been recklessly eating up their bogs to fire power-stations, were persuaded by the Dutch (who had already frittered away their bogs) to set up the National Peatland Conservation Council, now one of the most influential conservation bodies in Ireland. It is time to persuade the English.

Heath and old grassland were conservation disasters of the Locust Years, except where protected by the military. Most of those that still survive are recognized, and often owned, by conservation bodies. With little left to destroy, problems of management have come to the fore. Many heaths and grasslands are small, awkwardly-shaped, and difficult to fence – factors that together have seemed an insuperable obstacle to resuming the grazing of animals. Countryside Stewardship grants have solved this problem in some areas.

In churchyards, the Locust Years were expressed as a fashion for 're-ordering'. The delicate, wayward complexity of God's Acre was too often reduced to an acre of plastic-like grass with an incongruous church in the middle. But times have changed. One still sometimes sees a patch of coarse tussocky grass labelled 'Set Aside for Wildlife' and never mown at all, but real understanding is spreading. Meadow saxifrage may yet grow on my grave.

Moorland, the least affected by the Locust Years, is now probably the most threatened habitat. It is still encroached upon by forestry and farming, often for trifling reasons (as in the great wilderness of the far north). Much of the remaining moorland has lost its identity; heather and *Sphagnum* are replaced by grass and bracken.

Wetlands are prized by a nation of birdwatchers. The biggest change in Norfolk bird life this century has been the huge increase in aquatic birds. Most of the larger wetlands are recognized and well cared for. The great cranberry bog at Dersingham (Norfolk) is in a better state than for thirty years, after the labours of English Nature in persecuting encroaching trees and rhododendrons.

Rivers have suffered pollution and destructive management. The most polluted rivers have tended to get better, and the less polluted to get worse. During the Locust Years, drainage authorities mindlessly straightened and canalized watercourses and destroyed riverside trees. This is now less common, partly because even drainage boards find it difficult to get money, but also because they are at last realizing that it is counterproductive. Excessive drainage inevitably promotes flooding; 'flood control' suppresses small upstream floods but aggravates large downstream ones. (Even as I write, however, in the middle of Cambridge, costly tin piles are being banged into a riverbank that wants to turn into a shelving gravel bank.)

The coast has a mixed record. Another benefit of financial recession is that less money is thrown at the kind of coastal defences which destroy natural features and shift erosion elsewhere. For decades salt-marshes were squeezed between rising sea-level and encroaching invasions by the land. It is a welcome (if inevitable) change of policy not to try to protect all farmland forever. Proposals for damming estuaries went out of fashion before any actual dam was built. Developers still covet the coast, however, as witness proposals for Rainham Marshes (Essex) and a harebrained scheme to make Cardiff mudflats into a holiday resort.

*Industrial peat-digging in Ireland, which contrasts with the age-old, almost harmless digging of peat by people for their own use. (RHPL)*

## The Ordinary Countryside

These successes of conservation have been in recognizing, protecting, and discovering how to maintain, a large number of special areas. What of the ordinary landscape – fields, hedges, green lanes, and all the rest?

The extent of countryside decreases. Attempts to measure it founder on problems of definition. (Do airports count as 'urban' or 'grassland'?) New forms of urbanization are invented, such as golf-courses, which (I understand) no longer consist of a few artificial sand-dunes and a shed for the mower. How far this affects those features that give meaning to the landscape is hard to say. Southeast Essex demonstrates how ancient woods, and even hedges, can survive in urban surroundings at least as well as they would in farmland.

The general landscape is nibbled away by a myriad little acts of vandalism: digging out ditches, grading steep roadside banks, straightening watercourses. Graham Easy relates how certain local authorities destroy any giant black poplars that they can lay their hands on, on the off-chance that they might fall on someone's head. To treat the landscape as a garden devalues both gardens and the general countryside.

Destruction of hedges is far less common. I see fewer hedges grubbed out in one year now than I saw in one week in the 1960s. Recent claims to the contrary are based on the interpretation of air photographs – a difficult art – and seem to depend on a curiously narrow definition of a hedge. A hedge that has grown up into a row of trees is no longer counted as a hedge. Whether this change of state can or should be prevented is debatable, but it is not destruction. Hedges suffer from under- and over-management, but this is hardly an urgent conservation problem. A land in which every hedge had ideal management would be a dull land.

Hedgerow trees are faring better. Part of this, as often in the past, is a consequence of recession. The recovery of elms after Elm Disease is particularly encouraging.

Minor antiquities are better appreciated. English Heritage and Cambridgeshire County Council have contrived to rehabilitate an Iron Age fort in the Fens, half destroyed since 1964. There are still gaps in appreciation. I was amazed to discover that Welshbury near the Forest of Dean, one of the finest of hillforts *and* one of the finest of limewoods, is not a scheduled monument.

The landscape continues to be polluted by half a century's accumulation of chemical and mineral fertilizers. Nobody knows how to get rid of them, and they do not stay where they were applied. They contaminate watercourses and get about the country in dust and bird-droppings. The result is an increase in dandelions, nettles, and coarse grasses, even in ancient woodland.

Much needs to be done to sustain small farmers at the limits of farming, especially in the Lake District and west Cornwall. These people did not indulge in the excesses of agri-business. They maintain ancient field-systems, moors, and fens which would otherwise turn into bracken or woodland. Their historic landscape survives, although not in full working order: cereals have dropped out, leaving the countryside to either cattle or sheep, whose existence is now precarious (for example, because of the continued presence of radioactive caesium in sheep-grazing land). If anyone deserves

*Individualistic trees. This pollard ('copt') hawthorn in Swaledale may have been a landmark before the wall was built. Are there not two places called Copthorne in Sussex? (TM, February 1994)*

European Community subsidies, it is these farmers, and their brethren in other countries.

A surprisingly well-preserved county is Essex, in which the County Council has been active in conservation for sixty years. A recent initiative is the designation of Historic Landscapes where the ancient fabric of the countryside – hedges, roads, hamlets – is still reasonably complete. One such is Writtle Forest, that little-known sister of Hatfield Forest. This could well be copied elsewhere. As in the early days of listed historic buildings, the mere act of scheduling historic features protects them against ignorant destruction, even if no grants or legal obligations are involved.

### Education

The state of ecological education seems to be deplorable. Ecology is the most complex subject taught in schools – far more complex than physics or history – and has become fashionable without there being time, or often knowledge, to teach it properly. The subject is divided between biology and geography. Textbooks are rotten with factoids, unverified statistics, academic generalities, and political correctness. Examples are often drawn not from our own countries (where data might be checked and experiments performed) but from other people's impressions of far-away lands. There is a lack of training in how to recognize what is or is not abnormal – that skill which, above all others, the next generation of citizens will need.

Times have changed in higher education. In my own university, teaching and research in ecology have actually declined in the 1990s. My colleagues (with a few honourable exceptions) no longer take the interest in local ecology that they did all through the Locust Years. When reviewing the British Ecological Society's conservation research volume for 1989, I could not help drawing unfavourable comparisons with the 1970 volume.

Lack of education has not yet had all the evil consequences that one might expect – but there are some. Planting trees is thought of as the essence of conservation, rather than an admission that conservation has failed. The real essence of small-scale conservation – resisting the impulse to tidy up – is not widely appreciated. Where countryfolk have not been educated in what trees to plant, they choose fashionable species with urban associations: horse-chestnut, weeping willow, balsam poplar, Leyland cypress. These urbanize the landscape, but have the merit of being impermanent. Where conservationists give them good advice, people plant a depressingly inevitable mixture of oak, ash, maple and hornbeam, with the statutory cherry, lime and service, the same from Cornwall to Northumberland.

*Individualistic trees. Which is the most popular tree in Hatfield Forest? Answer, a long-dead, collapsed pollard oak. (TM, April 1993)*

### Conservation Agencies

The public conservation agencies – now English Heritage, English Nature, and their Scottish and Welsh counterparts – have suffered from the inconsistency of their government masters, but are faring better than they did. English Nature has survived the deluge of

*Individualistic trees. These yews, about 120 years old, were half overturned by the great storm of October 1987. There seems to be no biological reason why they should not still be telling the story of that storm in 2987. (TM, August 1993)*

bureaucratic paperwork that threatened to bog down its predecessor after the Wildlife and Countryside Act, 1981.

The Forestry Commission was denounced in my previous books for what it did to Linwood and to hundreds of other historic woods. But times have changed. Operations like Linwood were not worth while even on their own terms. A new generation of foresters has grown up with better things to do with their lives than to grow millions of identical trees. The objectives of the Commission's successors, Forest Enterprise and Forest Authority, have widened, and many of their ancient woods are being rehabilitated. At Chalkney Wood (Earl's Colne, Essex), the visitor can compare the rival management of the two owners: rehabilitation by Forest Enterprise and continued coppicing by Essex County Council. The breach between woodmanship and forestry is now, at last, nearly healed.

Voluntary conservation bodies, such as the Royal Society for the Protection of Birds and the county wildlife trusts, go from strength to strength. The Woodland Trust must by now own the second largest area of ancient woodland in the kingdom. I was once doubtful about the wisdom of expansion, but conservation bodies are acquiring skills to manage sites as well as the money to buy them.

What of the National Trust? The Trust's first purpose, a century ago, was to acquire and manage land such as Wicken Fen. It then became involved with historic buildings, in which it has a worldwide reputation for scholarly attention to the details of conservation. For a long time that attention to detail was strangely lacking in relation to the conservation of landscapes. The Trust insisted on the correct kind of nails in historic furniture, but summarily destroyed ancient grassland in the name of improvement. But times have changed. The Trust now has a Conservation Division staffed by some of the country's best practical ecologists. Hatfield Forest, which the Trust owned for half a century without realizing that it was as historic a property as any great house, now has a management plan specifying every pollard tree.

For once it is private owners who are often backward – especially those who are inexperienced in managing estates. At the time of writing, the possible privatization of military and Forestry Commission lands is a cause for concern. At best it would force conservation bodies to acquire large areas of land unnecessarily.

### Conservation and the Meaning of Landscape

Writers in the 1960s and 1970s seldom argued in detail for what it was they wanted from landscape. That it should look beautiful or natural or interesting, or be a pleasant place to live in, are unexceptionable but vague ideals, and are notoriously subject to fashion. We happen to hate straight lines today, but straight lines have been loved in the past and doubtless will be again. I do not undervalue aesthetics, but (like economics) they are too brittle to be the basis of conservation by themselves.

Developers plead to be allowed to destroy a habitat on promising to create a replica or equivalent elsewhere. ('Eurotunnel Moves Ancient Wood', as a conservation journal put it.) This is a dubious argument. Attempts to move natural vegetation often fail; the new site may be unsuitable, especially if it is fertilizer-sodden farmland. In at least two cases so far, the site proposed for the substitute is itself of value; the proposal would destroy two sites instead of one. No developer can promise to remain in existence for the 200 years or so needed to complete the project and to know whether it has worked. A reconstruction, however well organized, can incorporate only those features that were known about at the time it was begun. It is a pastiche – the equivalent of throwing away a painting by Constable and substituting a painting by Tom Keating in the style of Constable.

Plants and animals have a meaning apart from their mere existence. Hayley Wood is not the same as the collection of Hayley Wood plants in Cambridge Botanic Garden. Tree-planters suppose that a planted tree has the same value as a wild tree. There are several reasons why this should not be so. Oaks from commercial sources have been selected according to mid-twentieth-century ideas of timber quality; individuality has, as far as possible, been bred out of them. They will lack the odd shapes and twiggy trunks and rugged bark that give oak its beauty and meaning and most of its value as a habitat. A Euro-oak is not a substitute for a Welsh oak in Wales or a Slovak oak in

Slovakia. With rare trees like lime and service, their meaning lies in being absent from 99 per cent of the countryside. To include them in the Standard Broadleaf Mixture destroys the mystery and delight of lime and service.

This book has dealt with some of the meanings of landscape. There are many others, as readers of Richard Mabey's books know well. Landscapes are associated with historical events, battles, and personages. John Clare was the poet of landscape destruction; he bitterly denounced the destruction of the medieval landscape of the Soke of Peterborough in the 1810s (p. 94). Who does not feel a special twinge of disgust that Clare's favourite wood escaped that destruction only to be casually swept away in the 1960s? Who does not feel a secret thrill that the limes of Linwood, with all their associations, withstood the unreformed Forestry Commission's attack?

Conservation should encompass all these meanings. It is many things, from the conservation of the Amazon rainforest to the conservation of manuscripts in the Fitzwilliam Museum. In the countryside, different kinds of conservationist need to collaborate. Biological and archaeological conservationists should not meet only when a public inquiry forces them together.

## The Future

The last few years have seen a dramatic change in favour of conservation. Will this continue? Reduced pressure on land comes from the success of plant breeders in enabling farmers to grow 2½ bushels of wheat where but one grew before. The release of the land on which the extra 1½ bushels used to grow dwarfs any increased pressure from other directions. It seems set to last: indeed, as soon as eastern Europe gets organized, the change will spread there. In Russia and Ukraine, Stalin shot the plantbreeders; but one day, with their excellent land, these countries will become the suppliers of the wheat-eating world.

Other generalities are not so predictable. Conservation has become over-dependent on money. Conservationists, like most people in the last 25 years, imagine that money is God, and will solve all problems. Those who know the history of the landscape are sceptical. Mammon is a good slave but a bad master – and a most unreliable deity, liable to withdraw his favour suddenly, and capable of active malevolence. Too much money has done more damage than too little. 'The recession came just in time to save Barchester', as an archaeologist with Barsetshire County Council remarked to me.

Governments have become increasingly involved in conservation. This might seem a good thing until, once in a while, a whimsical and radical government arises which sets about undoing the work of its predecessors. Governments, like money, are too shortlived to be a trustworthy support for a permanent activity like conservation.

Conservation has become directed by professional conservationists. This has disadvantages as well as advantages. It increases the dependence on money, and the damage ensuing when the money runs out. Professional conservationists tend to stay only a few years and then to be promoted elsewhere.

Fashions in land-use extend into conservation; even people whose business is to uphold continuity are not immune from them. This did not matter too much when people learnt from their fathers how to manage estates. It is much worse in an age of professionals, who take their knowledge away with them when they get a better job. How do we ensure that the wisdom and folly of one generation are remembered by the next?

The answer was once thought to be management plans, to be read and acted upon by successive managers of a site. Alas, management plans have been bureaucratized: too often written to a prescribed form, platitudinous, full of conservationists' claptrap, bulky without being informative, and as readable as an income-tax form. Their fate will be to remain unread, forgotten, and not acted upon.

Conservationists, like foresters, are tempted to the sin of triumphalism. They record successes but forget about failures. Failures are treated as something to be lived down, rather than as experiments with a definite outcome from which future generations may learn. People thus repeat their grandfathers' mistakes. Disasters of the 1960s, such as the replanting of ancient woods, had already happened on a smaller scale in the 1860s. Will they happen again in the 2060s? 'Those who cannot remember the past are condemned to repeat it.'

*Individualistic trees. This improbably vast pollard beech stands on Mount Blorenge, near Abergavenny, close to the highest limit at which trees will grow. The cloud beneath it conceals the breakneck depths of the Punchbowl: a jungle into which avalanches plunge in winter. (TM, July 1993)*

# WALK V:
## *Lizard Peninsula, Cornwall*

Grid Reference: SW 726 211

Tremayne Woods belong to the National Trust.
Goonhilly Downs are a National Nature Reserve.
Walking boots needed. The manuscript of the Traboe
Perambulation is reproduced on p. 12.

The Lizard Peninsula is in two parts. The north is old-
fashioned farmland with deep lanes, little fields and
hamlets. The south is on serpentine and other curious
rocks, with wide soggy moors and rare plants.

At the Dry Tree, five parishes converge on a
Bronze Age barrow on the Goonhilly Downs. In the
*Trefwurabo* (Traboe) Perambulation of 977 this
was *Cruc drænoc*, Hawthorny Barrow. It was
approached from the south, past 'Raven's Nest
Rocks' and 'Two Rocks on the Ridge', by a 'way',
predecessor of the main road. The convergence is
distorted by a croft at the Dry Tree (probably
seventeenth-century) and partly hidden by the
telecommunication station.

The perambulation crosses the moor (avoid the
tussocky Tall Heath in wet places), past a barrow
later called 'Green Borough', to *carrecwynn*, White
Outcrop. Here it enters farmland. It passes to
*pollicerr*, now Polkerth farm; thence by rather
complicated ditches and a road to *poll hæscen*, Pool
of the Hassock[-sedges]; thence 'down by the
brook' to *ryt cendeurion*, Ford at the Junction of
Two Rivers, now Tregidden Mill.

The Traboe Perambulation now goes on its way.
Anyone wanting to see an Anglo-Saxon *herepað*
should go a mile to the east, where there is one
mentioned in the *Lesmanaoc* perambulation of 967.

The little perambulation of *Trefdewig*, now
Trethewey, in 977 is followed by the road (then a
'way') and the public footpath past Barrimaylor
(then *pennhal meglar*). Another point was *lyncenin*,
Pool of the Ramsons, where (as D.E. Coombe tells
me) that plant still grows.

The walk goes by many lanes, close to the big
hillfort-like structures of Gear (The Fort) and
Caervallack (Vallum-y Fort), down through a ravine
of recent woodland and dripping banks, to an
ancient oakwood on the shores of the Helford River.

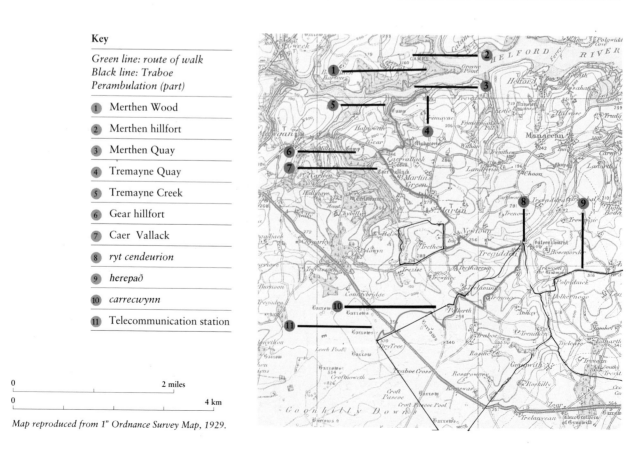

**Key**

*Green line: route of walk*
*Black line: Traboe*
*Perambulation (part)*

1. Merthen Wood
2. Merthen hillfort
3. Merthen Quay
4. Tremayne Quay
5. Tremayne Creek
6. Gear hillfort
7. Caer Vallack
8. *ryt cendeurion*
9. *herepað*
10. *carrecwynn*
11. Telecommunication station

0         2 miles
0         4 km

*Map reproduced from 1" Ordnance Survey Map, 1929.*

**Dry Tree Croft**
pre-1700, but too young to have a Cornish name.

**Green Borough**

**World War II mounds**
with poles on them
to prevent gliders from
landing

**Key**

*White line: route of walk*

*Dotted line: Traboe
Perambulation (part)*

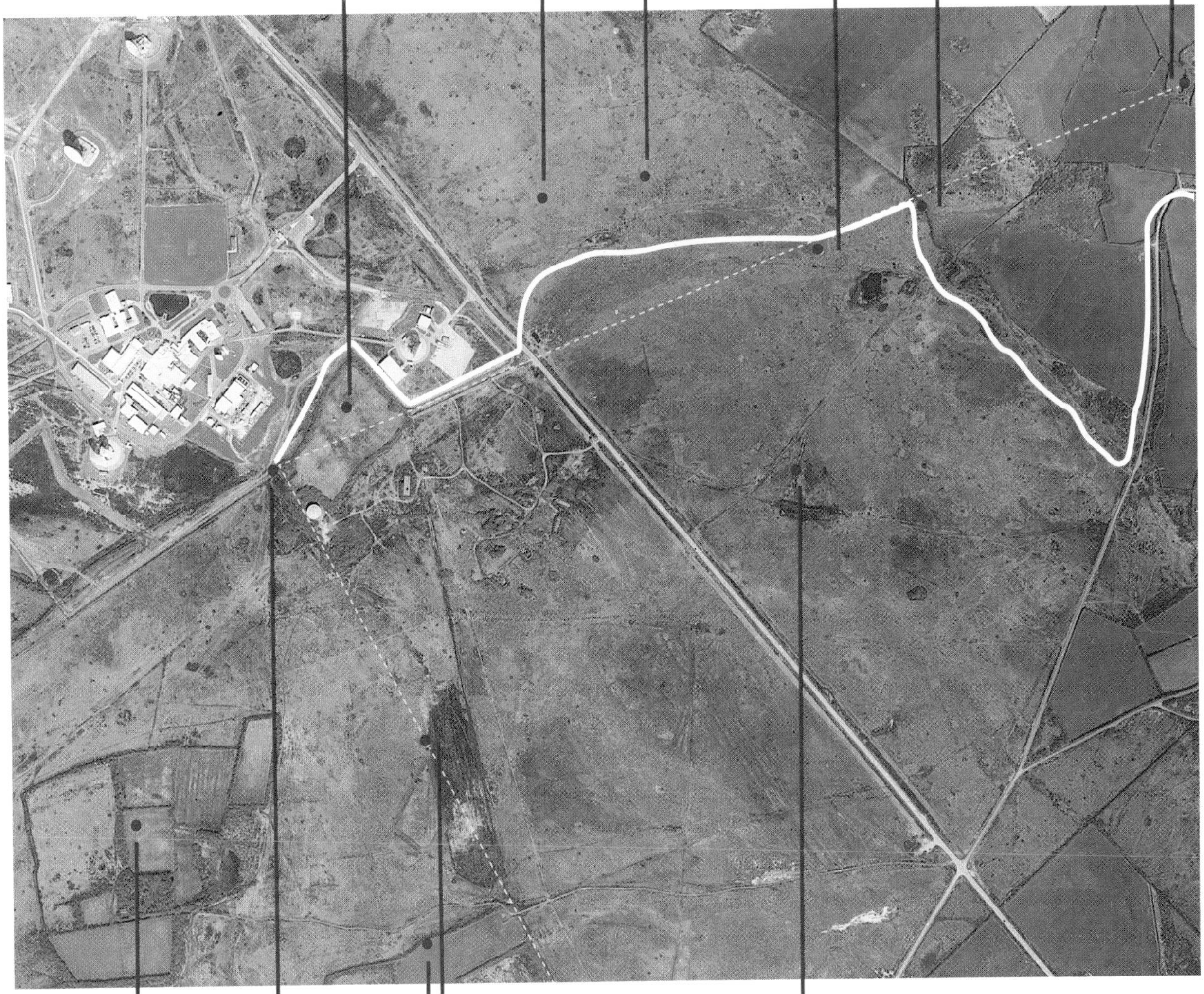

**Short Heath**
Heather and other
species of heath,
in less wet places.

*Carrecwynn,*
White Outcrop

Polkerth

**Croftnoweth,
New Croft.**
Old enough
to have a
Cornish name.

**Dry Tree,**
*Cruc drænoc*

'Way of *Cruc drænoc*'

**Tall Heath**
Tussocky with *Molinia, Schoenus* and
Cornish heath, in wet places.

| 0 | 500m |
|---|------|
| 0 | 500 yards |

*Air photograph: Geonex (© Cornwall County
Council), April 1988*

**Croft Pascoe**

Above: *A dripping cliff on the way down to Tremayne Creek. Some of the rare Lizard mosses and liverworts, like the large pellucid* Hookeria lucens, *live in spots which are contiually wet and never see the sun.*

Right: *Merthen Wood seen across the Helford River. This is one of the finest coppiced oakwoods of the Celtic world, recorded back to the 13th century, known in Cornish as* Coesenys *and* Cosabnack. *It has seen the tin industry come and go, leaving charcoal-hearths scattered through the wood. A narrow sunken horsepath, walled on either side, leads down to the granite-built quay, the port of Constantine. Tremayne Great Wood, publicly accessible on this side, is similar; there has been some re-coppicing by the National Trust.*

*Tremayne Quay. The Helford River is one of the few places where ancient woodland meets the sea. On the north side there are service-trees scattered on the edge of the cliff.*

*A Cornish stile, made of bars of serpentine rock. This one is on the footpath which follows the Trethewey Perambulation.*

*All photographs: TM, July 1993*

Above: *Tregidden Mill, the 'ford at the junction of two rivers' on the Traboe Peram-bulation. A thousand years later it is still a ford, with a clapper-bridge for pedestrians.*

Left: *The Dry Tree at the middle of the Lizard, where five parishes converge, with relics of the Bronze and the Space Ages. The exact convergence was probably meant to be a barrow. The standing stone, made of gabbro, was brought from a distance. It was evidently not a landmark at the time of the Traboe Perambulation; it was re-erected about a century ago. The name Dry Tree, which goes back at least to the 17th century, suggests a gibbet as well.*

*The 'white outcrop' of the Traboe Perambulation. It is of serpentine, and has mostly been quarried away. The name presumably comes from the white Ochrolechia lichen.*

*Cornish Heath, Erica vagans, one of the commonest plants on the Lizard moors, and one of the rarest anywhere else in Britain.*

# WALK VI:
## *Abergavenny to Blaenavon, SE Wales*

Grid Reference: SO 292 139

Walking boots and compass needed. The moorland section should not be attempted in low cloud.

The South Wales valleys are full of antiquities from the Bronze Age to the Age of Industry. Despite their industrial reputation, the rural landscape is predominantly medieval. Cwm Tillery, in the next valley to the west, has the highest known natural wood in England and Wales.

Abergavenny town began around the castle of the de Braoses. The way begins over the medieval long bridge; then by lanes (with a few old pollards) through Llanfoist; then steeply up to the Monmouth and Brecon Canal.

The path turns into the track-bed of an inclined plane belonging to the early days of railways. It tunnels under the canal, then up through Coed-y-Person, a fine example of a South Wales

beechwood, whose ancient stools adorn these pages. At the top, where the winding-house would have stood, the railway, now the path, turns aside to follow the contours, leading through the moor-wall on to Mount Blorenge.

Blorenge – for a short time it was a Forest – is surrounded by little farms. On this high, north-facing slope the farms of the upper tier have proved untenable. The highest farmstead, Cwm Craf, has long vanished, its fields overrun by bracken and its hedges grown into great trees. Bracken flourishes on these well-drained slopes and has occupied the moor as well. The view over Abergavenny rises to the Sugarloaf Mountain, its lower slopes dotted with the scattered farmsteads of Ancient Countryside. The hollow to the right of the peak contains Abergavenny Great Park with its oakwoods.

We pass the Punchbowl, an amazing wood-pasture which somewhat recalls the high-altitude beechwoods of Italy and Slovenia, and emerge on to the moorland plateau. This was the common pasture of various manors; a seventeenth-century cast-iron post, probably an early product of

## Key

*Green line: route of walk*

1. Abergavenny Bridge
2. Coed-y-Person
3. Mount Blorenge
4. Punchbowl
5. Carn-y-Defaid
6. Site of Capel-Newydd
7. Blaenavon Beeches

*Map reproduced from 1"*
*Ordnance Survey Map, 1929.*

0        2 miles

0        2 km

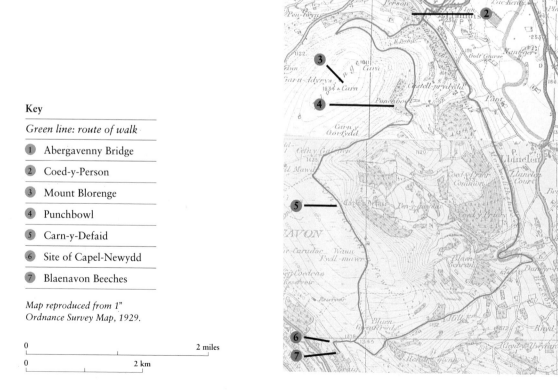

Cwm Craf deserted farm

Inclined plane through Coed-y-Person

**Key**

*White line: route of walk*

0                  500 m

0                  ½ m

from Abergavenny

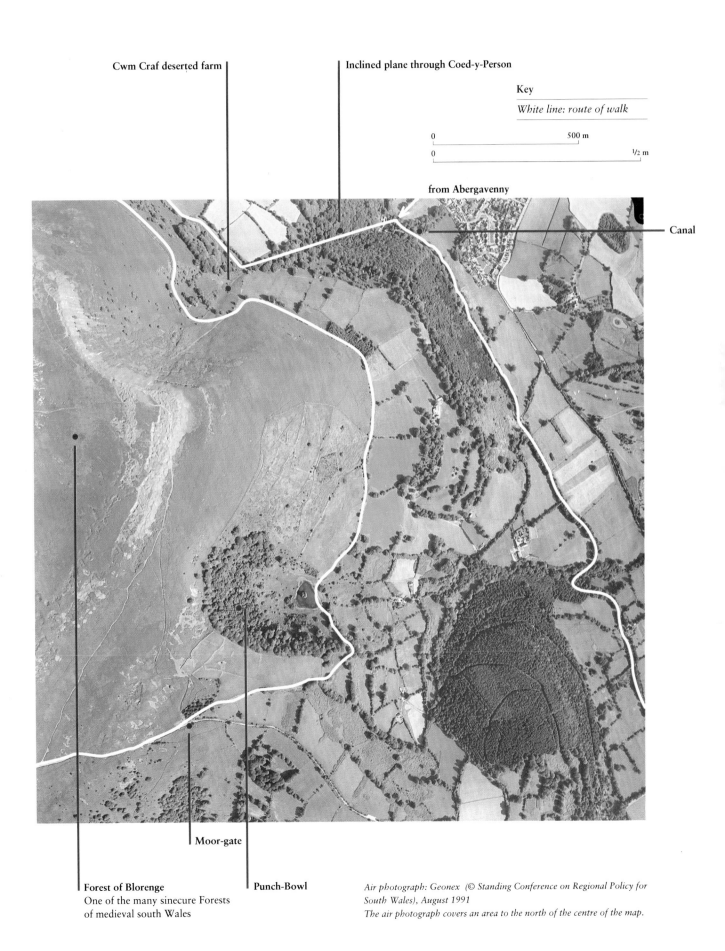

Canal

Moor-gate

**Forest of Blorenge**
One of the many sinecure Forests
of medieval south Wales

**Punch-Bowl**

*Air photograph: Geonex (© Standing Conference on Regional Policy for
South Wales), August 1991*
*The air photograph covers an area to the north of the centre of the map.*

*Stone blocks of the inclined plane, with remains of iron spikes in them to hold the rails. This was one of the earliest railways, apparently earlier than the canal which passed over it and earlier than the use of sleepers. The gradient of the inclined plane is about 25°, and trucks would have been lowered by ropes. At the top they would have been hauled by horses round Mount Blorenge from a furnace on the other side.*

*All photographs: TM, July 1993*

Blaenavon ironworks, marks the boundary of Llanellen. The moors seem not to be regularly burnt; they grow up to tall thick heather and crowberry which burn in fierce, unscheduled fires.

The huge cairn Carn-y-Defaid is a reminder that these, like most moors, have a prehistoric origin. Faint banks crossing the moor could represent prehistoric fields or pastures.

Due south of Carn-y-Defaid, in a nook of the writhing lodgepole pine plantations, an iron cross marks the site of the ancient isolated *Capel Newydd*, 'New Chapel'.

A stile and path through the pines leads to Blaenavon Beeches, part of Blaenavon Community Wood. This is an example of that combination of ancient woodland and more recent industrial ruins so typical of South Wales. Beech takes all the forms that it is capable of: pollards, coppice stools and the gnarled shapes of long-neglected beech hedges. A great wall separates the beeches from the moor; but the wall is ruinous, and (as in most Welsh woods) sheep get in. Forest Enterprise has done some experiments on re-pollarding, re-coppicing, and fencing. The plantations are mainly on former farmland.

The way back is by the road over the moor and through the lanes. This is very evocative of Ancient Countryside: a tangle of steep holloways, overhung by the gnarled roots of immense beeches far above, hedged with hazel and lime and walled with pennywort and ferns, past hidden farmsteads and pollards in fields, ending in a breakneck descent to the canal.

*The medieval long bridge of Abergavenny, which still carries a main road over the River Usk. As in most early bridges, the arches are of different shapes.*

*Monmouth and Brecon Canal, part-way up Mount Blorenge, built in the 1790s and still in use. It is a real mountain canal; its maintenance, on these unstable slopes, is nearly as remarkable an achievement as its building.*

*Ancient beech stools in Coed-y-Person. Beech as a native is a lowland, south-eastern tree, but there is a remarkable outlier in the Forest of Dean and the southeastern Welsh mountains. Coed-y-Person ('Parson's Wood') is otherwise a normal coppice-wood, bisected by the canal. Other trees include native lime, which can be seen from the towpath to the north. Beech prospers even at high altitudes and on north-facing slopes; it sets good seed, though at long intervals of years.*

*Beeches forming the boundary between the Cwm Craf grove and the moorland above. Formerly both wood and moor were intensively used and carefully separated. These great gnarled trees have grown up out of a beech hedge. In other places woods have encroached on moorland despite the browsing.*

*The Punchbowl, a remarkable glacial hollow in Mount Blorenge. Here is one of the highest native woods in Britain (up to 1,440 feet), one of the steepest not on a cliff (slope more than 45°) and one of the few affected by avalanches. The trees are immense beech pollards of surrealist shape (p. 209). It belongs to the Woodland Trust.*

'How green was my valley': Cwm Afon below Blaenavon.
Blaenavon, more fortunate than most industrial towns, lasted
through two industries, iron and then coal. In its heyday it may
have been austere, smoky, dirty and dangerous; but magnificent
countryside was never more than a short walk away. The
surroundings have recovered from industrialization with
remarkable speed. This valley with scattered farms, surviving
from before the industrial period, once contained several parallel
railways. It has not suffered the loss of woodland that happened
in other Welsh coalfield valleys early this century.

*Left: Moorland, with Carn-y-Defaid in the distance. The cairn is probably a huge chamber tomb, a great monument meant to be seen from a distance. It shows that the moors were already treeless in the Bronze Age, although they had probably been wooded earlier. There are several lesser tombs. The moor is remarkably stony – almost pure scree in places – with very little peat. Crowberry is an unusual species of heath characteristic of these moors. There was a severe fire about 1980, after which mosses became abundant; crowberry seems to have been encouraged. Note the beautiful lichens on the stones.*

*A pollard in Blaenavon Beeches. The Forestry Commission (contrary to its former practice elsewhere) seems to have scrupulously preserved most of the remaining native woodland in the South Welsh valleys, although planting trees around the original ones. Here Forest Enterprise has resumed coppicing and pollarding.*

*Blaenavon Beeches. Another remarkable high-altitude beechwood, with pollards and coppice stools. A century ago it was swarming with tramways converging on an inclined plane. Some of the many quarries were for limestone to make lime in the limekiln shown here. All this industry has vanished, leaving the wood almost undisturbed except for the quarries.*

# WALK VII:
## *North Downs between Guildford and Dorking, Surrey*

Grid reference: TQ 044 492

In part: Newlands Corner Country Park (Surrey County Council); North Downs Way.
The main Guildford to Dorking road bears many dangerously fast drivers.

Surrey is a land of geological contrasts. The great chalk ridge of the North Downs is covered by clay-with-flints and loess (wind-blown dust), both of which produce acid soils. Chalk is exposed only on the steep south-facing slope. Below this is a narrow valley of Upper Greensand and Gault Clay. To the south rise the high hills of Lower Greensand, with the clay of the Low Weald beyond.

The great change in Surrey is the increase in woodland. Two centuries ago settlement and farming were mainly along the fertile Upper Greensand and Gault. The North Downs plateau was heath with scattered pollard yews and beeches; the chalk scarp was downland. Great heathy commons covered the Lower Greensand hills. The heaths had probably been made out of wood-pasture in the Middle Ages or earlier. Ancient woodland was confined to the Weald and a few isolated woods elsewhere. From the villages, holloways, worn by centuries of boot and hoof, ran up to the heathland.

During the nineteenth century the commons fell into disuse and grew up to great woods. Some of them were privatized and replaced by plantations, especially of beech; more recently, ancient woods have been turned into plantations too. Surrey as a whole was about 20 per cent heath and 4 per cent woodland in 1790; it is now about 3 per cent heath and 16 per cent woodland and plantation.

On the plateau, formerly Albury Downs, the new woods are natural and are of oak, ash and yew; Turkey oak, introduced from the Mediterranean, turned out to be very invasive. On the chalk scarp the change was later, and there is still some downland left. There are various stages of a classic succession from chalk grassland via hawthorn and whitebeam to yew-wood. The entire chalkland flora is lost, and not much of a woodland flora replaces it.

## Key

*Green line: route of walk*

1. Holloway
2. Plantation
3. King's Wood
4. Pollard Oak
5. Pill-box
6. Dry valley with beeches

*Map reproduced from 1" Ordnance Survey Map, 1929.*

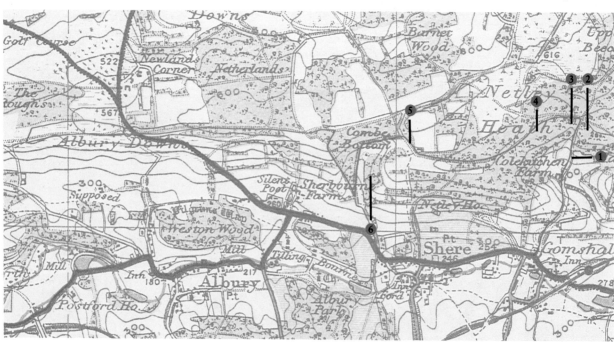

0     1 mile

0     1 km

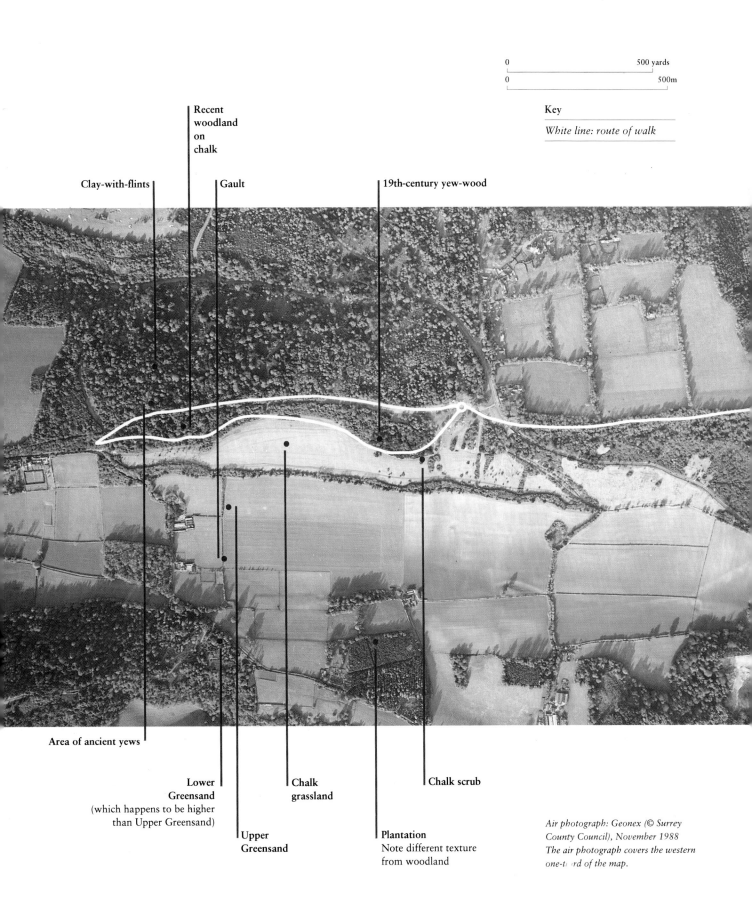

0            500 yards

0            500m

Key

*White line: route of walk*

Recent woodland on chalk

Clay-with-flints

Gault

19th-century yew-wood

Area of ancient yews

Lower Greensand
(which happens to be higher than Upper Greensand)

Chalk grassland

Chalk scrub

Upper Greensand

Plantation
Note different texture from woodland

*Air photograph: Geonex (© Surrey County Council), November 1988
The air photograph covers the western one-third of the map.*

Above: *Woodland in the making: 'scrub' about to turn into 'young woodland'. A clump of ash, whitebeam, buckthorn, wayfaring-tree and hawthorn has sprung up on chalk grassland when there was not enough browsing to prevent it. In the middle, protected from browsing, is one yew tree, palatable to animals (though poisonous).*

*All photographs: TM, August 1993*

Right: *Chalk grassland which has become dominated by strong-growing grasses and knapweed, probably through not being grazed enough.*

*The interior of a yew-wood. The inner yews and whitebeams sprang up c.1817, when there was an agricultural depression after the Napoleonic Wars. The younger yews date from the next depression in the 1870s. They are lopsided because of competition from trees already there.*

*A view from the North Downs, across the inhabited clay vale with its ancient settlements and hedges, to the hills of Upper Greensand. These were traditionally heath – the name Blackheath implies heather – and are now woodland or plantation.*

*An ancient pollard yew, one of the original trees, parents of all the other yews here. It is much older than the woodland trees around it. The 'big-bellied' shape is distinctive. For most of its life it stood out on open downland. Yew wood-pastures seem to have been a feature of the downs. Why anyone should want to pollard yew is a mystery.*

*A 'pill-box' of the Second World War, guarding an ancient holloway. These miniature forts were carefully located in a series of lines of defence around London. C.S. Forester wrote a fictional climax to the war in which Hitler's invading troops were defeated not far from here.*

*Beeches in Coombe Bottom, a chalkland dry valley. The oldest beeches are wood-pasture pollards on the clay-with-flints plateau, a few of which survive. Beech later spread to, or was planted on, the chalk slopes, where it has often not prospered. Many died in the 1976 drought and others have yellow foliage. Ash and yew fare better on chalk.*

*Coppiced oak with holly in a surviving fragment of King's Wood, an ancient wood – otherwise replanted – on the plateau. Oak as underwood, though common in Cornwall and Wales, is rare in SE England. It is characteristic, with holly, of ancient woods on very acid, infertile soils – here loess over clay-with-flints.*

# WALK VIII:
## *Holme-next-the-Sea, Norfolk*

Grid Reference: TL 699 434

Property of Norfolk Naturalists' Trust and Thornham Parish Wildfowlers' Association, whose directions must be followed.
The fords at the mouths of creeks are passable only at low tide. The main A149 road is dangerously fast and crowded.

North Norfolk is a classic example of a low-lying soft coast of shingle ridges ('scalps'), salt-marshes, dunes and sandy hooks, little affected by sea 'defences' or cord-grass encroachment (p. 27). It is relatively unstable and can change dramatically through storms. This corner of Norfolk has changed little since Faden's map of 1797 (the Ordnance Survey of 1824 is very different, but probably wrong). However, salt-marshes have been lost through enwalling on the land side, and the foreshore (though still very wide) has shrunk through rising relative sea-level. Dramatic natural changes are likely before long.

Wave action builds up a series of sand-bars and shingle-ridges parallel to the shore (p. 184). Some of these come to be high enough for plants such as marram-grass to grow and trap blowing sand building up dunes. (The high dunes on Scolt Head Island can be seen in the distance to the east.) Behind the dunes and at mouths of little rivers mud accumulates to form salt-marshes. Each of these has its highly specialized plant, bird, and invertebrate life. Saltmarshes have various zones depending on how often they are covered by the tide, ranging from samphire at the bottom to the various sea-lavenders near the top; creeks are fringed with the grey foliage of sea-purslane.

Dunes tend to become more stable with time. On some of the dunes here, at least 200 years old, marram has given way to rabbit-grazed chalk grassland (the sand being made largely of fragments of shell). Sea-buckthorn, a big shrub which copes with being gradually buried in sand, forms colourful thorny thickets. Dunes slowly roll inland. They can be destabilized by rabbits or by people making paths, creating blowouts from which the stablilization process begins again.

## Key

*Green line: route of walk*

① Peddar's Way

② Broad Water

*Map reproduced from 1" Ordnance Survey Map, 1929.*

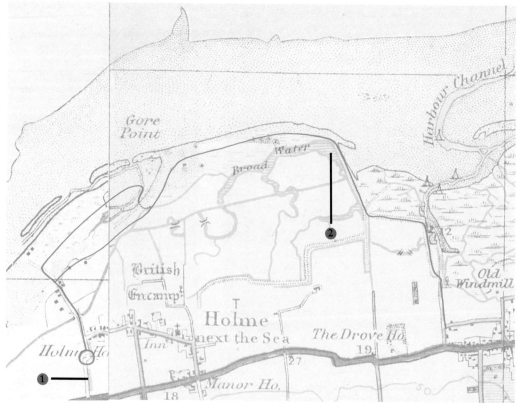

**Shingle ridge**
A nesting site for terns, which must not be disturbed

**Pines**
The dune ridge is double; the outer ridge is the highest part of the dunes and is getting perilously narrow.
Pines were planted at an unknown date on the inner ridge and spread seaward in the 1950s to 1970s. They are pruned to strange shapes by salt-laden winds

**Samphire saltmarsh**
Samphire, *Salicornia*, is an edible plant growing on low-lying saltmarsh mud

**Old meandering river**
cut off by a 19th-century marsh-wall

**Dune ridge**
Old, stable dunes grown with marram grass and thickets of sea-buckthorn and elder

**Polder**
This roughly square area was separately embanked in or before the 18th century.
The Ordnance Survey of *c*.1920 regards it (probably wrongly) as a 'British Encampment'

**Early marsh-wall**

**Peddar's Way**
This Roman road ran for 41 miles in three dead-straight lengths; here it became crooked on meeting a pre-existing field system

**Ghosts of saltmarsh creeks**

**Iron Age planned landscape**
The strong rectangular pattern in and around Holme village is due to an ancient field layout

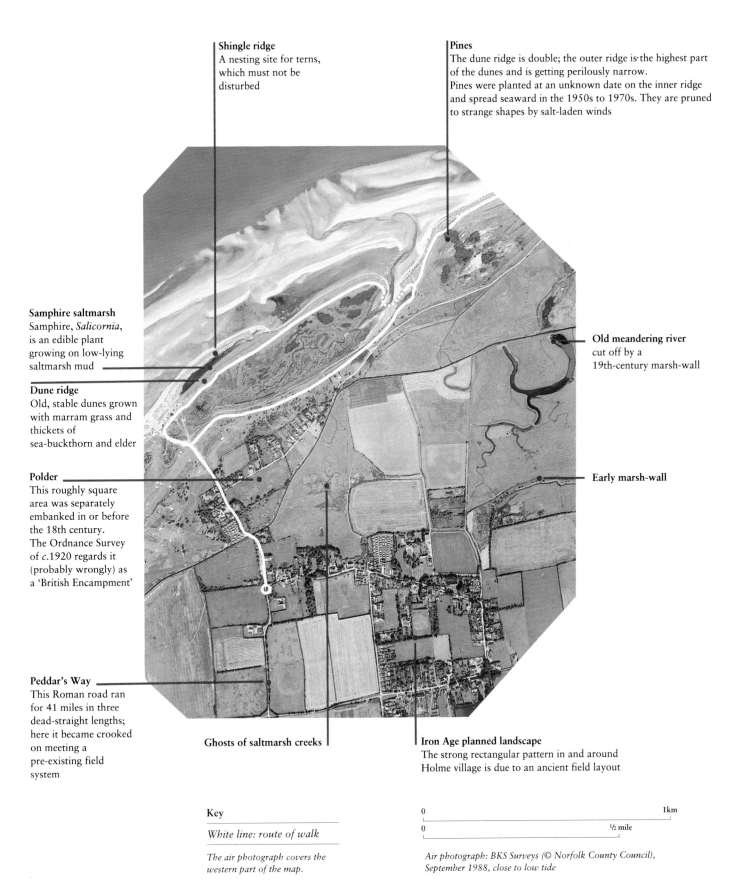

**Key**

*White line: route of walk*

*The air photograph covers the western part of the map.*

0 — 1km
0 — ½ mile

*Air photograph: BKS Surveys (© Norfolk County Council), September 1988, close to low tide*

This part of Norfolk has a great variety of building materials: carrstone (brown sandstone), ironstone conglomerate (darker brown), white chalk, pink chalk (to be seen in the parti-coloured cliffs of Hunstanton), flint, millstone grit brought by glaciers from the north (grey), limestone fetched in the Middle Ages from Barnack in Northamptonshire (not shown here), brick.

*All photographs: TM, August 1993*

Occasionally a great storm makes a permanent breach.

Salt-marshes used to be valuable grazing land. From the Middle Ages onwards, the inland parts have been enwalled with earthen banks, either to use them as arable or to prevent them from being lost to rising sea-level. Many successive walls can be seen here. Towards Thornham Harbour (east of the air photograph, p. 225), the forlorn walls of unfinished intakes run out into the saltmarsh. The sea is slowly winning this battle, and some nineteenth-century intakes have reverted to brackish marsh (itself an important habitat).

Faden's map shows a 'Mussel Scalp' and 'Crab Scalps'. A 'Wreck House', roughly where the present Visitor Centre is, was a reminder that this was an exceedingly dangerous coast for shipping. The nearby breach in the dunes probably did not then exist.

Most of west Norfolk was woodless, indeed largely treeless, for over a thousand years. The Iron Age is very prominent: the Snettisham Treasure, one of the great hoards of Europe, was buried six miles away. Here is the mysterious end of Peddar's Way, a Roman road from nowhere to nowhere (p. 121). Holme village and the fields to the south conform to a regular field pattern probably earlier than Peddar's Way. Northwest Norfolk was later a stronghold of a local variant of open-field agriculture; the open-field furlongs, the village closes, and the modern Enclosure-Act fields all perpetuated the pre-existing planned layout.

*The north end of Peddar's Way.*

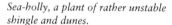

*Sea-holly, a plant of rather unstable shingle and dunes.*

Above: *One of the less common sea-lavenders.*

Left: *A sea-lavender marsh.*

Below: *Broad Water, the end of a small river from the upland, cut off and made into a lagoon by nineteenth-century enwalling.*

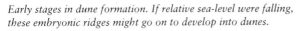

*Early stages in dune formation. If relative sea-level were falling, these embryonic ridges might go on to develop into dunes.*

# BIBLIOGRAPHY

These are selected works of general interest. For detailed references and citations the reader is referred to my original *The History of the Countryside* (Dent 1986) from which most of the text of this book has been abridged.

**Aberg, F.A.** (1978) *Medieval moated sites* Council for British Archaeology Research Report 17.

**Atheden, M.** (1992) *Upland Britain: a natural history* Manchester University Press.

**Aston, M.** (ed)(1988) *Aspects of the medieval landscape of Somerset* Somerset County Council.

**Baker, A.R.H.** and **Butlin, R.A.** (eds)(1973) *Studies of field systems in the British Isles* Cambridge.

**Beresford, M.** (1957, 2nd ed 1971) *History on the ground* Methuen, London.

**Body, R.** (1982) *Agriculture: the triumph and the shame* Temple Smith, London.

**Bowen, H.C.** and **Fowler, P.J.** (eds)(1978) *Early land allotment* British Archaeological Reports, British Series 48.

**Buckley, G.P.** (ed) (1992) *Ecology and management of coppice woodlands* Chapman & Hall, London.

**Chadwick, L.** (1982) *In search of heathland* Dennis Dobson, London.

**Crawford, O.G.S.** (1953) *Archaeology in the field* Dent, London.

**Darby, H.C.** (1971) *The Domesday geography of Eastern England* Cambridge. (Parallel volumes for other regions.)

**Darby, H.C.** (ed)(1973) *A new historical geography of England* Cambridge.

**Dimbleby, G.W.** (1962) *The development of British heathlands and their soils* Oxford.

**Duffey, E.** (ed)(1974) *Grassland ecology and wildlife management* Institute of Terrestrial Ecology, London.

**Dymond, D.** and **Martin, E.** (eds)(1988) *An historical atlas of Suffolk* Suffolk County Council.

**Ekwall, E.** (1960) *The concise Oxford dictionary of English place-names* Oxford.

**Fitzrandolph, H.E.** and **Hay, M.D.** (1926) *The rural industries of England and Wales. I. Timber and underwood industries and some village workshops* Oxford.

**Gilbert, J.M.** (1979) *Hunting and hunting reserves in medieval Scotland* John Donald, Edinburgh.

**Gimingham, C.H.** (1972) *Ecology of heathlands* Chapman & Hall, London.

**Godwin, H.** (1975) *History of the British flora* 2nd ed Cambridge.

**Godwin, H.** (1978) *Fenland: its ancient past and uncertain future* Cambridge.

**Hawksworth, D.L.** (ed)(1974) *The changing flora and fauna of Britain* Academic Press, London.

**Hooke, D.** (1981) *Anglo-Saxon landscapes in the west Midlands: the charter evidence* British Archaeological Reports, British Series.

**Hoskins, W.G.** (1955) *The making of the English landscape* Hodder & Stoughton, London.

**Hoskins, W.G.** (1959) *Local history in England* Longmans, London.

**Hoskins, W.G.** (1967) *Fieldwork in local history* Faber, London.

**Lambert, J.M., Jennings, J.N., Smith, C.T., Green, C.** and **Hutchinson, J.N.** (1960) *The making of the of the Broads: a reconsideration of their origin in the light of new evidence* Royal Geographical Society, London.

**Lever, C.** (1977) *The naturalized animals of the British Isles* Hutchinson, London.

**Linnard, W.** (1982) *Welsh woods and forests: history and utilization* Cardiff.

Mabey, R. (1980) *The common ground: a place for nature in Britain's future?* Hutchinson, London.

Margary, I.D. (1973) *Roman roads in Britain* 3rd ed Baker, London.

Milne, G. (ed)(1992) *Timber building techniques in London c. 900-1400* London & Middlesex Archaeological Society.

Peterken, G.F. (1993) *Woodland conservation and management* 2nd ed Chapman & Hall, London.

Pollard, E., Hooper M.D. and Moore, N.W. (1974) *Hedges* Collins, London.

Prince, H.C. (1964) 'The origin of pits and depressions in Norfolk' *Geography* **49** 15-32.

Pugsley, A.J. (1939) *Dewponds in fact and fable* Country Life, London.

Purseglove, J. (1988) *Taming the flood* Oxford.

Rackham, O. (1975) *Hayley Wood: its history and ecology* Cambs & Isle of Ely Naturalists' Trust, Cambridge.

Rackham, O. (1990) *Trees and woodland in the British landscape* 2nd ed Dent, London.

Rackham, O. (1978) 'Archaeology and land-use history' *Epping Forest – the natural aspect?* ed D. Corke *Essex Naturalist* N.S.2 16-57.

Rackham, O. (1980) *Ancient woodland: its history, vegetation and uses in England* Edward Arnold, London.

Rackham, O. (1989) *The Last Forest: the story of Hatfield Forest* Dent, London.

Rackham, O. and Moody, J.A. (1994) *The making of the Cretan landscape* Manchester University Press.

Ratcliffe, D.A. (1977) *A nature conservation review* Cambridge.

Richens, R.H. (1983) *Elm* Cambridge.

Rodwell, J.S. (1991) *British plant communities: woodlands and scrub* Cambridge.

Rowley, T. (ed)(1981) *The evolution of marshland landscapes* Department of External Studies, Oxford.

St. Joseph, J.K.S. (ed)(1977) *The uses of air photography* 2nd ed Baker, London.

Sheail, J. (1971) *Rabbits and their history* Newton Abbot.

Shoard, M. (1980) *The theft of the countryside* Bath.

Smith, A.H. (1956) *English place-name elements* Cambridge.

Spratt, D. and Harrison, B.J.D. (eds) (1989) *The North York Moors* David & Charles, Newton Abbot.

Steers, J.A. (1969) *The sea coast* 2nd ed Collins, London.

Tansley, A.G. (1939) *The British Islands and their vegetation* Cambridge.

Taylor, C. (1974) *Fieldwork in medieval archaeology* Batsford, London.

Taylor, C. (1975) *Fields in the English landscape* Dent, London.

Taylor, C. (1979) *Roads and tracks of Britain* Dent, London.

Timperley, H.W. and Brill, E. (1965) *Ancient trackways of Wessex* Dent, London.

West, R.G. (1977) *Pleistocene geology and biology* 2nd ed Longmans, London.

Williamson, T. (1993) *The origin of Norfolk* Manchester University Press.

# ACKNOWLEDGEMENTS

Topographical history is an interest given me by my father, the late Mr G.H. Rackham. I was fortunate enough to be instructed in the Cambridge ecological tradition of Dr A.S. Watt and his successors. Among these, I am specially grateful to Dr D.E. Coombe for introducing me to historical ecology and to the workings of woods and heaths, and for a quarter of a century of visits to wonderful places – notably to the Lizard Peninsula which has been a resort of Cambridge botanists for 300 years.

Material for the original version of this book was gathered during research supported by the Nature Conservancy Council and Natural Environment Research Council. I am indebted for much help and encouragement to colleagues in Cambridge University Botany School and Corpus Christi College, Cambridge. Almost everything in this book has come into my mind through some friend or invitation or visit or reading, and I cannot hope to acknowledge them all except in a general way.

Among individual Cambridge botanists my thanks are due to Dr H.J.B. Birks, Dr and Mrs G.C. Evans, Professor C.D. Pigott, Dr J. Rishbeth, Mr P.D. Sell, Dr S.M. Walters, Professor R.G. West, and the late Mr W.H. Palmer. Among historians I must mention Mr D.P. Dymond and Mrs C.P. Hall. Those who have helped me in other parts of England include Dr Margaret Atherden, Mr J. Bingley, Mr S. Bott, Mr B. Cave, Mrs V. Chesher, Dr A. Fleming, Mr T. Gledhill, Mr and Mrs J. Hart, Mrs K. Hayward, Mrs H. Heygate, Dr and the late Mrs J. Litchfield, Dr C. Lovatt, Mr A. Sims, Professor and Mrs P.M. Warren, and Lady Willoughby de Eresby. In Wales I have been helped by Professor W. Linnard and by Dr P.F. Williams and his colleagues; in Scotland by Mr R. Callander, Dr J.H. Dickson, Mrs A. McBurney and the late Professor C.B. McBurney, Dr J.H. Dickson, and Dr M.D. Swaine; and in Ireland by Dr R. Bradshaw, Dr D.L. Kelly and Mr J. Hunter. In Europe I am grateful to Dr J. Bintliff, Mr A.T. Grove, Dr D. Moreno, Miss J.A. Moody, Professor A.M. Snodgrass, Madame and the late Monsieur F. Vuillermet, and Professor P.M. Warren. For American parallels I acknowledge the kindness and the hospitality of Dr Kathy Biddick, Dr Susan P. Bratton, Dr R. Brewer, Dr D. Houston, Miss J.A. Moody, Mr G. Stanford, and Dr P. White.

The work would have not been possible without the friendly cooperation of many landowners and keepers of archives and of the staff of the Map Room, Cambridge University Library. Specific acknowledgements for permission to reproduce are made on p. 240.

# INDEX & GLOSSARY

# PICTURE CREDITS